To —
    John Burn...
        Great-nephew
            Gerald Elliot
    from
        Mary Burnet.

D1645342

ESSAYS & ADDRESSES
BY JOHN BURNET

John Burnet

ESSAYS
AND ADDRESSES

By

JOHN BURNET

FELLOW OF THE BRITISH ACADEMY

With a Memoir by
Lord Charnwood

LONDON

CHATTO & WINDUS

MCMXXIX

PREFACE

THANKS are due to *The International Journal of Ethics*, the Classical Association of Scotland, the University of St. Andrews, the Council of the British Academy, the Editor of *A Book of Homage to Shakespeare*, the Delegates of the Clarendon Press, the Leeds and District Branch of the Classical Association, and the Editor of *Scientia* for their permission to reprint the various essays and addresses included in this volume.

Special thanks are due to Lord Charnwood and Mr. W. L. Lorimer : to the former for his Memoir and the interest he has taken in the making of this book ; to Mr. Lorimer for his valuable help and advice throughout. On his advice the essays and addresses have been left as they stand ; they are arranged in chronological order. Had they been collected during the author's lifetime, the collection would have been larger, and certain repetitions which inevitably appear in the present volume would have been removed.

M. B.

ST. ANDREWS,
July 1, 1929.

CONTENTS

MEMOIR
BY LORD CHARNWOOD

MEMOIR

Of John Burnet, for thirty-four years Professor of Greek in the University of St. Andrews, a great teacher and a great scholar, the lectures and essays, composed at intervals over a long time and now selected to form this volume, might stand alone as a fitting and characteristic memorial. I have been asked, however, to write by way of preface to them some account of their author and appreciation of his work. I am but ill qualified to do so. In his mature years distance prevented our meeting often, and my own studies in the subjects which he made his own had stopped short at the point at which his began to be profound. But I had been intimate with him in years of youth and of difficulty ; and, if what I can write can be forgiven for being a slight and peculiarly personal impression, it may be of some interest. For Burnet was the kind of man whom old acquaintances, encountering him after the lapse of years, would feel had in no way become a stranger. His days, as Wordsworth wished for himself, were ' bound each to each by natural piety ' ; and, as I read the most mature of the discourses in this volume, I wonder whether any of the multifarious interests and studies of his early days ever quite ran to waste, and wonder too whether the Professor, revered by pupils and trusted by grave colleagues, had ever quite brought within bounds any boyish oddity or perversity. I do not suppose that I should be either surprised or horrified if some mild unaccountable eccentricity or imprudence of the years in which I knew him so little could suddenly be disclosed to me. I am certain that I should not have to hear of any early loyalty betrayed or any generous ardour gone tepid.

3

John Burnet was born at Edinburgh on 9th December 1863. He was the son of Mr. John Burnet, an Advocate, and had a brother and three sisters younger than himself. Mr. Burnet, the father, was a man of manifest ability, formidable to a young acquaintance and perhaps what the Scots mean by 'dour,' but apparently fond of his family and not, I think, in any way an unkindly man. As a young man he distinguished himself at the Bar, was made Advocate Depute under the Conservative administration of 1874 to 1880, and was expected to achieve great success. But in middle life he fell strangely into a habit of drinking, which destroyed his prospects, scattered his earnings and rapidly killed him. This sad memory must be set down here, because for Jack, the son, this downfall of the father whom he admired, happening at the critical time of his own Oxford career on which his future seemed to depend, meant the sudden pressure of poverty, unexpected responsibilities for his family, and a keen sorrow constantly felt, of which hardly any of those around him knew. Something of that forcefulness which marked the father's features and bearing appeared in those of his more gently and genially and, on the whole, more securely gifted son.

Jack's mother, who had been Miss Kay, daughter of Dr. James Cleghorn Kay, R.N., was a very gentle lady, of whose later years many residents in St. Andrews must have pleasant memories—abounding in shrewdly humorous perception and in warmth of affectionate kindness. She added something to diminishing family resources by translating for a great publishing firm several, then notable, works of German New Testament scholarship. She was attached to that school of the established Church of Scotland which an Englishman might call Liberal, but which in its own tradition was, I think, called Moderate. A forgotten but charming

book, Dean Stanley's *Scottish Church*, describes well
what formed the background in the past of Jack's
religious upbringing. Patriotism, not theology, enabled him as a young man to work up tender emotions
even towards Supralapsarian Calvinism. Like many
other young Scotsmen, he came naturally to regard the
actual beliefs, on which professedly his Church was
founded, as matters of historical interest only, retaining
undiminished (perhaps not even with an interval of
serious disturbance) a simple piety which leavened very
powerfully the more or less definite philosophic creed
that thereafter contented him.

His boyhood was passed chiefly in Edinburgh ; but
there were country holidays at a farm in Aberdeenshire
and at a village in Gloucestershire, and later on the
family had a summer home near Gourock on the Clyde,
with a glorious outlook upon the Argyllshire Highlands
across the firth. He got his schooling at Edinburgh
High School under Dr. Donaldson, who was afterwards
his respected Principal at St. Andrews. But later he
spent a short time at a school near Geneva. A little
later still he paid a visit or two to Paris, which awoke
in him not only a love of the French theatre, but a
faculty which he never lost of entering readily into the
thoughts and ways of foreign peoples. Meanwhile, he
had in due course entered the University of Edinburgh.
There he delighted greatly in the teaching or the
personal peculiarities, as the case might be, of famous
instructors, among whom were Sellar, Tait, Masson,
Sir Alexander Grant, Blackie, and Henry Butcher. It
did him good service in his work long afterwards that
while his gifts as a scholar were beginning to ripen at
Edinburgh he also received a thorough grounding,
which most scholars at Oxford in his time lacked, in the
fundamental principles of physics as then understood.
In October 1883 he went up to Balliol as the senior

Scholar of his year. There in due course he took a
'First' in 'Mods' and then in 'Greats'; he won
besides the Taylorian Scholarship in French and came
second only to a learned Indian in the competition for
the Boden Sanskrit Scholarship—which out-of-the-way
achievements did not console the College authorities for
his falling short of their high expectations when he ran
for prizes more commonly sought by a brilliant classical
scholar. After taking his degree in 1887 he first served
as Assistant to Lewis Campbell, his accomplished and
lovable predecessor in the Greek Chair at St. Andrews.
There followed next a short experimental period as a
master at Harrow. Meanwhile he became a Fellow
of Merton. He went into residence at Merton for
some time to pursue his own studies quietly. After a
term spent as Interim Professor of Humanity (that is to
say Latin) at Edinburgh, he returned to St. Andrews in
1891 to fill the place of Campbell, who had gone abroad
for his health. Finally, on Campbell's death, he was
appointed permanently to his Chair in 1892.

In 1894 he married Miss Mary Farmer of Oxford.
He was now in his thirty-first year and well launched
on his life's work. But my concern is chiefly with his
days as an undergraduate at Balliol, and as a young
Fellow at Merton.

When he first came up to Balliol he appeared to his
contemporaries an older man, and indeed a more solemn
personage, than he really was. This was partly due to
the stores of knowledge, often on subjects of which
they were wholly ignorant, which he would unlade with
half-humorous dogmatism but quite without pedantry
or conceit, if he talked at all. But it was still more the
result of a moustache of more imposing growth than
theirs and of the stately corpulence to which his massive
frame inclined. For he was already a robust man of
the type from which one may expect the capacity to sup-

port great toil, bodily or mental, but not perhaps length
of days.   It was a somewhat unwieldy frame, unsuited
for athletics, to which, besides, nothing in his earlier
life had inclined him; but almost every movement, from
the quick walk with which he went to his work, to the
speed of his bold and well-formed handwriting, be-
tokened energy.   He could put forth much muscular
strength upon sufficient occasion, as, for example, at the
oars in a sudden squall upon the Firth of Clyde.   If
encouraged, he could enjoy sculling and rejoice in
swimming ; rivers and lakes fill a large space in the
background of my memory of him.   But he was one
of those strong men who, throughout their lives, find
the chief enjoyment of their strength in more sustained
labour at the work of their choice than is possible to
ordinary people.   Such men need not be dull dogs for
all that, and John Burnet's hardest work was often done
with high animal spirits and quick readiness to find
amusement ; but the relaxations to which he turned
most easily were of an intellectual kind—his love of
French comedy, and the little repertory which he possessed of French music-hall songs and German students'
songs, may serve as examples.

He was not at all one of those able young Scotsmen,
with whom Oxford and Cambridge are familiar, who
come to an English University obviously and inno-
cently resolved to assimilate, as much as possible, the
speech, vesture, manner, pursuits, prejudices, and
religion of the southern race among whom God has
appointed that they shall rise to some consequential
position.   Though there was never anything aggres-
sively Scottish in his accent, outlook, or temperament,
and though his later work shows plainly enough what
he derived from Oxford and its School of Literae
Humaniores, he was sturdily loyal to earlier objects of
his reverence, and forfeited nothing of what he had

derived from the influences of his native soil.   There
will be found later in this volume the tribute which his
mature judgment paid not only to English scholarship
but to the whole wide service to national life which the
English Universities and Public Schools between them
render ; that high tribute must be taken as an un-
biassed finding of one who, for better or worse, was
not upon the whole a typical Oxford man.

Industrious, portly, and ever so slightly awkward
or uncouth, he was an odd as well as an interesting
figure, and it might possibly have been expected that
his fellow-undergraduates would laugh at him.   Only
they did not.   For he was obviously a man of force as
well as a clever man, no less free from intellectual
snobbishness than from undue deference to any sort of
social pretension, and, whenever people met him, good
company.   In a sense he was a social being, not much
liking to be alone, and finding himself at his ease in
that sort of set gathering for more or less festive purposes at which most English youths are not good.   And
in an unselfconscious way he possessed already an
instinct for decorous and effective public appearance.
Perhaps that impressiveness of lucid utterance and
courteous dignity of official presence, which pupils of
his at St. Andrews found so becoming to him later, and
which his full and pleasant voice much enhanced, had
a ludicrous side when they were displayed, already full-
blown, to his own profane equals in a college debating
society ; but they went down all right.   When, not
long after he took his degree, this bookish youth from
a strange country took the chair at a political meeting
of agricultural labourers in the heart of Oxfordshire, he
did it with remarkable success.   Yet for all this, in
closer contact with men he was sensitive and proudly
shy to an extent which no one who met him casually
would have expected.   Under the most favourable

circumstances he would have been likely to have few habitual companions and very few intimate friends, either among his equals or among his elders ; probably he found greater ease in his dealings afterwards with younger men. He appreciated intensely the lectures, the tuition, and the personal qualities of the several memorable teachers under whom he came at Oxford, and whose names might be looked for here. But not one of these sympathetic older men ever penetrated his reserve in the days when, as a man of some standing in college, he seemed likely to know them well. From one only of his elders in Oxford did he derive that sort of spiritual support which a younger man receives when an older man whom he entirely respects makes himself entirely accessible to him without being obtrusively familiar. This was the great-hearted, genial musician John Farmer, afterwards his father-in-law, who, with curiously varied adventures and experiences behind him, came to Balliol in those days, bringing with him as a stranger to Oxford his happily incorrigible idiosyncrasies.

Circumstances did not, except at first, favour his happiness while at Oxford. It has already been said that he underwent during this time a great strain. It drove him unduly in upon himself ; without indeed abating his industry, it made concentrated purpose hard to him ; and it caused him to suffer behind the scenes deep gloom which was not wholly relieved for some years. It brought about also some passing but alarming symptoms of a malady which was to return nearly forty years later ; and during the next two years he would occasionally fall into a curious condition of unstrung nerves about some trifle which normally he would scarcely have noticed. No more need be said about the cause of his trouble, and no exaggerated picture shall here be drawn of tragic trials

and tragic humours.   But since from the course of his
later life—from the even tenor of his successful labour
upon the subjects of his choice in a situation congenial
to him and with most happy marriage behind it all—
Burnet might seem to have been an uncommonly fortunate man, it must be recorded that in his earlier days
he passed through a valley of dark shadows and had to
struggle hard for the mastery of himself.

Throughout these earlier years the range and variety
of his studies were remarkable.   Subjects that lay out
of his way were taken up, always with enthusiasm, and
some of them necessarily were dropped comparatively
soon; and he might have seemed to waste his time in
aimlessly acquiring unrelated slices of learning.   But
in the end all his knowledge—except perhaps heraldry,
which he at least professed once to have looked into—
became serviceable to the devoted teacher of Greek
whose supreme devotion was to Plato.   At first there
was perhaps a little waywardness in his suddenly plung-
ing into Sanskrit, then into German history, and then
perhaps into comparative philology, or Biblical criticism,
or Spanish, or jurisprudence.   Yet from the first there
was little that was really idle or superficial in these
apparent essays at omniscience.   He had the faculty of
seizing rapidly in any book or any branch of knowledge
the vital points which would be of lasting interest to
him, and of seizing those points accurately.   He soon
learnt, too, to test pretty severely the trustworthiness of
any learned book that at first captivated him.   His
childlike enjoyment in pouring out over some one else
the latest garnered fruits of his study helped him.   It
certainly helped such fellow-students as the friend who
shared his lodgings, and so got the results of his wide
reading at second-hand.   Such fellow-students learnt
how solid Burnet's work was apt to be.

Readers of this volume and of Burnet's other books

will find some fresh and arresting idea on almost every
page ; but the decisive, sweeping and sometimes summary way in which it is propounded may occasionally
make them cautious of accepting it.   Possibly the impression which he made on those who were associated
with him when his work was beginning may be of use to
such readers now.   He was always enthusiastic ; to the
end of his days everything new that he learnt must have
been an excitement and delight to him.   And he was
didactic, he loved teaching.   And he had a rhetorical
bent, a love of clear and strong phrase which, if it did
not define his meaning accurately, at any rate challenged
the opponents whom he wanted to challenge.   So he
was rather given to paradox, without being in the least
taken in by it himself.   He entered upon his researches
with great originality and great readiness to appreciate
work done by his predecessors (Lewis Campbell, for
example) which had been unfairly overlooked ; but he
carried out these researches with the greatest thorough-
ness.   When this had resulted in his proving up to the
hilt something which was in itself surprising to most
people, he was a little inclined to express his real
discovery in slightly exaggerated terms, which might
indeed draw more attention to what he said, but would
also make some hearers or readers less ready to accept
as fully as they ought what he really was concerned to
say.   A large part of this volume is occupied by his
exposition of views, as to what the greatest Greek philosophers accomplished and as to their relations to one
another, markedly different from any views which most
scholars had previously accepted.   An old and critical
friend of Burnet's (and his friends could hardly escape
being critical of his boldly pronounced opinions), finding himself now in no position to check Burnet's arguments very closely, would bet that there could be found
in them some manifest exaggerations, but would also

bet that the whole mass of those exaggerations put together is negligible in comparison with the substance underlying them, which is as sound as it is fresh.

These recollections of his early life would be grievously incomplete without one further word. Politics played no part in his career, but the spirit of his work as a scholar can be little appreciated by any one who does not perceive how closely his study of the literature and the speculative thought of past ages was linked with an intense interest in public causes which in altered shapes endure. And this interest was in no degree merely historical or merely theoretic ; it resulted from his student days onward in sustained and alert observation of the current events of his time. Few young men at Oxford were less committed to any cut-and-dried party formulas that had been impressed upon them (his own ineradicable Liberalism, in a broad sense of that term, signified perhaps revolt from the party allegiance of his father). Few also were less likely (for all that enthusiasm of temper which has been noticed already) to be swept along by temporary currents of political excitement. But he steadily watched public affairs with an uncommonly clear eye for the chief ascertainable facts that bore on each successive controversy, and a deep underlying sense that there is a cause of human advancement, a cause of the common man, and a cause of the heritage committed to the English and Scottish peoples ; and upon sufficient emergencies—as in 1886, when Gladstone brought to the front the great issue of Irish national claims—he would range himself at once with intense and unshakeable conviction upon the side which enlisted his love of righteousness.

From the time of Burnet's return to St. Andrews in 1891, for many years onwards, the events of his life which require to be chronicled are chiefly the produc-

tion of his books.   In 1892 he completed and published his *Early Greek Philosophy*, which at once established his reputation in foreign countries as well as in
England, and in particular won the approval of the
German scholar, Professor Diels, to whom he was most
indebted.   In 1897 he published a school book, *Greek
Rudiments*, in which may be traced some decided views
of his own about the teaching of Greek, and which
other teachers have valued highly.   This was followed
in 1900 by his edition of the *Ethics* of Aristotle.   From
that year till 1906 he was engaged in preparing for the
Oxford University Press a revised text of Plato.   In
1911 he brought out an edition with notes of the *Phaedo*
of Plato, and in the brief introduction to it expounded
for the first time the novel view which he had formed
for himself of Socrates and of the relation of Plato's
work to his.   In 1914 appeared his *Greek Philosophy*,
Part I., a complete expression of the results up till
then of his study of Greek Philosophers down to the
death of Plato.   Part II., which should have begun
with Aristotle, was never to be completed, for immediately after the publication of Part I. came the Great
War.   The War, however, called forth from him a
book of another kind, *Higher Education and the War*,
published in 1917.   As it was in large part a criticism
of higher education in Germany then, and as many
things have changed since, this very powerful book has
been allowed to go out of print, but a chapter of it
entitled ' Kultur ' is reprinted in this volume, and a
reader who wants to appreciate fully the spirit in
which Burnet regarded the scholastic tasks in which
he was engaged, might do well to turn first to that
chapter.   This volume contains also, in chronological
order, certain earlier short writings of his, and, with the
two exceptions about to be mentioned, all that he
completed for publication after the War.   It includes

the chapter on Greek Philosophy which he contributed
in 1921 to that remarkable collection of Essays, *The
Legacy of Greece*, a chapter which is the completest and
best, though not in all respects the final expression of
the main results of his researches.   It includes also the
Romanes Lecture, delivered in all but tragic circumstances, which must in a moment be related.   But it
does not include public lectures, of which there remain
ample notes, which sufficed him in delivering them but
would fail to do him justice if now printed.   Apart
from the papers here included, he completed after the
War two books : he published in 1924 an edition with
notes of the *Euthyphro*, *Apology*, and *Crito*; and *Platonism*, being the lectures on Plato which he delivered in
California in 1926, in the form in which with failing
strength he was endeavouring to reproduce them in the
last months and weeks of his life, has been published
earlier in the present year.   This tale, however, of his
labours at his desk would not be complete without
mention of the project of a Lexicon of Plato which he
inherited from Lewis Campbell.   He worked at it a
great deal from 1908 to 1919, but ultimately had to
abandon hope of putting it through single-handed.

   The great work as a scholar which these various
publications represent was, it must next be observed,
accomplished by a man who all the while unreservedly
recognised as his principal duty the labour, in itself
exacting, of a Professor upon whom, with one Assistant
under him, rested the whole teaching of the Greek
classes in his University.   Burnet developed quite
early a manner of lecturing—it would seem also a
manner of private teaching—which, like that of other
great University teachers of our time with whom he
might be compared, was peculiarly his own.   Being
so, it was not merely efficient for purposes of instruction ; it gave his students, as one of them has said, the

sense ' that his was a large personality, seeming to give all that he gave from an inexhaustible knowledge not only of books but of men and affairs '—' moving through life superbly '—moving through it also, as others of his students and as writers from abroad bear witness, with a large kindliness and courtesy and with very ready sympathy.

The inspiriting work of a teacher thus conscious of his high calling is generally linked in practice with work in the administration and government of educational institutions; and the branches of administration or of politics which are connected with education, possess a dreariness (together often with a capacity for producing petty irritation or even bitterness) surpassing by far the dreariness of any other branch of public affairs. The part which John Burnet played both in the internal politics of St. Andrews and in the educational politics of Scotland generally, cannot be conceived by his friends to have been either a placid or an unfruitful part. It involved, of course, some mortifications ; but it involved achievement also. He was a member of that Committee on classical education which the Government appointed during the War, and when a Board was appointed to conduct entrance examinations for all the Scottish Universities, he was made its Chairman. The present Principal of St. Andrews has told how ungrudgingly and thoroughly he shared in all the burdens of University business.

Andrew Lang, himself an Oxford scholar, has described in what must rank among the very best of his verses, ' Almae Matres,' the spell, stronger, he would have us believe, than that even of Oxford, which the little, ancient and hauntingly beautiful University on the north-east sea can cast upon the affections of its sons. It cast that spell upon its adopted son, John Burnet, of whom by the way it should be recorded that among the honours which came to him from foreign lands was the offer of the Chair of Greek at Harvard, and that it did not tempt him away. But St. Andrews, though the oldest of the Scottish Universities, remained—so at least the lecture upon its history in this volume would suggest—for a long while chiefly distinguished among them by its age. In recent years it has attained a new lustre and a distinctive importance of its own among the teaching institutions of Great Britain. John Burnet would have liked well to be remembered—and will be so—as a leader among the few to whom this is due, and of whom none can have conceived his aim more clearly, and none perhaps followed it with quite so much ardour as he.

In the midst of a career of so much ardour and so much toil there came upon him, as on us all, the strain of the War. Few classes of men were quicker to see the great issue involved in that struggle than the teachers of highest distinction in our Schools and Universities, and to no class of men was the toll which it took of the best youth of the country brought more poignantly home. Upon such men, too, as upon many unremembered servants in our public offices, there fell, as their own special form of service, the cheerful discharge of their ordinary duty in peace time coupled with that of others who were able to go to the Front. As was the case with many such men, the added labour of war time had at least a large share in bringing about the failure of Burnet's strength, though this did not make itself plainly apparent till a few years later. It made itself apparent then suddenly and in a tragic manner. He was chosen to give the Romanes Lecture at Oxford in 1923. It will be found below in this volume. It is a daring discourse on knowledge, entitled ' Ignorance,' and with its slight touch of whimsicality, and its touch, by no means slight, of a genius not so fully manifested elsewhere in his writing, is likely to arrest profounder attention than any other of these papers. But it was heard with difficulty by the great audience in the Sheldonian, and followed by his friends there with anxiety. For that morning he had been visited by a severe seizure of the kind that had threatened him in youth. The doctor who was called in told him, when the fit had passed, that he could only deliver the lecture at great danger to his life. Burnet replied that he had come to Oxford to give that lecture and was going to give it ; so he did.

From this time forward his health was a matter of grave concern ; and at least on one later occasion, when he had an important discourse to deliver, his wonted facility of public utterance forsook him. In 1925 he had been invited to deliver during the following year the Sather Lectures in the University of California. Again his doctor insisted that he would go there at great risk to his life. With a fine courage his wife decided that the discouragement and depression which must have resulted from his giving up the undertaking, were worse evils than the risk. So she and his daughter accepted for themselves the terrible anxiety of taking him out, with the result that his strength greatly revived for a time. His lectures when delivered were brilliantly successful, and his whole visit aroused deep gratitude among scholars in California. He decided, however, before returning to St. Andrews, to resign his Professorship and devote himself to writing. During the next year, 1927, the University which he had served conferred upon him the degree of LL.D., in a manner which made that honour, not in itself uncommon, peculiarly gratifying. On 26th May 1928, working almost to the last at the revision of his Californian lectures on Plato, he died, at the age of sixty-four.

The aims and achievements of the great Humanists,

B

who at the close of the Middle Ages set themselves to
recover the knowledge of Greek as the key to science,
were a theme upon which Burnet liked to dwell.   The
key was found and the door opened, and their work
might seem to have been accomplished once for all.
Yet for reasons which great Englishmen from Chatham
to Mr. Baldwin have felt deeply, 'the more humane
letters,' and Greek in particular, have not lost their
value as instruments in the training of men who in any
walk of national life may be called upon to play a leading
part.   And, strangely enough, the progress of the
sciences and of the modern philosophy which long
seemed to be divorced from them has in our day led
to a point at which true understanding of the Greek
pioneers of thought may be of peculiar service.   Of
John Burnet it can be said at the least that he worthily
carried on the tradition of the Humanists.

The more specific service which he rendered to learning can be indicated in a very few words.   In doing so,
it is needless to inquire precisely what he was the first
to discover and what he learnt from scholars to whom
others had not sufficiently listened ; those of his views
which have earned most attention happen to have been
peculiarly his own ; but robust independence and
generous appreciation of what others could teach him
were equally marked features of his mind.   First, then,
more completely than any previous historian, he set
the profoundest metaphysical and ethical thought of
Greece in its living context and in its due relation
alike to physics and to the political problems of the
time. Secondly, in his treatment of Socrates and of
Plato, while establishing the points that certain positive
doctrines are in substance to be attributed to Socrates,
and that a certain cleavage must be noted between
Plato's earlier or Socratic writing and his own distinctive teaching thereafter as the master of the Academy,

Burnet enabled us to see in the march of Greek philosophy not the successive rise and fall of cut-and-dried systems to which one philosopher or another was blindly committed, but a continuous process of inquiry in which one after another contributed his share, and those who had most to contribute continued to be the readiest to learn.

But whatever be the enduring legacy which Burnet has left to special scholars and to other thoughtful men, it may be illuminating to those who read his books to recognise them as in a sense a by-product of his working days.   Those days were before all consecrated to helping in the actual upbringing of young Scotsmen, to the end that they might thereafter worthily play their part in the life of a great country, and that a country whose patriotism is loyal to the larger cause of God and man. Men whom he thus served in their youth have borne witness, in terms of praise as ample as it is evidently sincere, to what he did for them.   An Oxford man who knew him not as a pupil but as his Assistant at St. Andrews, Mr. W. L. Lorimer, has analysed his influence as a teacher with such discernment that the last words which shall here be said of John Burnet shall be his.   Mr. Lorimer writes :—

' His pupils found in him one whose firmness of touch inspired confidence ; who was impressive without heaviness, and suggestive without vagueness ; whose union of profound knowledge with uncommon clarity of mind and lucidity of language enabled him to make the complicated simple and the chaotic orderly ; who breathed life (and manifestly enjoyed the doing of it) into the dry bones of morphology and metric and palæography ; whose dramatic perception was as keen as his linguistic sense and his philosophic understanding ; who could in a few concise sentences light up whole tracts of Hellenic thought and feeling ; above all, who continually filled them, they knew not well how, with a lively sense of the importance of all that they read and studied with him, and of the lasting worth of Greek literature, philosophy and civilisation. What was the secret of it ? Not certainly any acquired and applied technique of instruction. . . . There is no teachable way of great teaching. . . . It is not an affair of rules but of personality. And, if Burnet was able to influence the minds of his pupils as he did, it was because his teaching was not merely illuminated by the light of the intellect but quickened by the fires of the spirit. But, deep as was the influence which he exercised on his students through the quality of his lectures, it does not suffice to explain the enthusiastic affection which he inspired in them. What won their devotion was rather the total impression of his personality upon them—his buoyant optimism, his dignity and courtesy and modesty, and above all, his devotion, manifested in deeds not words, to them and their best interests. For at all times he gave them of his best without stint, whether in the way of instruction or advice. His counsel was often sought, and was ever found wise, helpful, sympathetic. Had he never published a line, Professor Burnet would have served his day and generation eminently well. But one cannot easily imagine him content to have the walls of his classroom for his horizon.'

ESSAYS & ADDRESSES
BY JOHN BURNET

LAW AND NATURE IN GREEK ETHICS

Reprinted from the INTERNATIONAL JOURNAL OF ETHICS,
April 1897

IN a well-known passage of the *Ethics*, Aristotle says
that ' things fair and things just are liable to such varia-
tion and fluctuation that they are believed to exist by
law only and not by nature.'[1] Although much has
been written, and well written, on this distinction, it
still seems possible to throw a little fresh light upon it.
It is easier now than it used to be to trace the thread of
historical continuity in Greek thought, and to understand what the doctrines of Greek philosophers really
meant to the men who taught them and heard them.
And we can do this by looking at our problem in the
twofold light of earlier speculation and contemporary
culture.

I. To understand what the Greeks of the fifth century
B.C. meant by φύσις—a word very inadequately rendered by ' nature '—we must cast a glance backwards
upon those cosmological inquiries which had just
reached their highest point in the Atomic Theory of
Leucippus and Democritus.   I have shown elsewhere[2]
that the cosmologists from the Milesian School onwards
had given the name φύσις to that primary substance
which they were all in search of.   It meant to them the
most real thing, that which must underlie the world
with all its manifold appearances and changes.   To
put the matter simply, science began with the child's

---

[1] *Eth. Nic. A*, 1094 *b*, 14, τὰ δὲ καλὰ καὶ τὰ δίκαια . . . πολλὴν ἔχει
διαφορὰν καὶ πλάνην, ὥστε δοκεῖν νόμῳ μόνον εἶναι, φύσει δὲ μή.
[2] *Early Greek Philosophy*, pp. 10 sqq. [3rd Ed. pp. 10 sqq.].   I still hold
firmly that we have no right to ascribe the term ἀρχή to the cosmologists.

question, 'What is the world made of ? '   The answers
that were given to this question covered the whole
range from the Water of Thales to the ' Seeds ' of
Anaxagoras or the Atoms of Leucippus.   But the question was always the same, and every answer to it was a
new account of the φύσις of things, or, as we should
say, of the element or elements to which things can be
reduced and of which they are composed.

This primary element was, of course, corporeal like
the world itself.   The time had not yet come when the
bond of the world could be sought in an ideal unity.
Even the Pythagorean ' numbers ' were spatial, and
space was not clearly distinguished from body before
the rise of the Atomic Theory.   Now the fact that
ultimate reality and the world of common experience
were both regarded as corporeal had serious consequences.   Both were of the same kind, and therefore
comparison was inevitable.   In proportion as the idea
of φύσις was more thoroughly worked out, it naturally
tended to become something more and more remote
from common experience, and thus to make that experience seem by comparison more and more unreal and
illusory.   The Water of Thales was, indeed, something
we know, and we could see without too much effort
how everything else might be solidified or vaporized
water.   But now Parmenides has shown once for all
that, if we are going to take the reality of φύσις seriously, we are bound to deny of it all motion, change,
and variety.   'It is,' and that means that it always
was and always will be,—or rather that time is a fiction,
—that It is absolutely continuous, homogeneous, and
motionless.   This makes the breach between the
world we seem to know and the world as it is for
thought complete.   The ' real ' of Parmenides is in
fact an extended and corporeal ' Thing in itself,' which
not only fails to explain the everyday world, but

banishes it to the realm of the unreal. The Atomic Theory sought, indeed, to make the 'real' yield an explanation of the world by multiplying the One of Parmenides into innumerable atoms, but this only served to bring out more clearly than ever the disparity between φύσις and our everyday experience.

II. This explains why the ethical problem, when once it was raised, took the form of a search for φύσις, for an underlying and permanent reality, in the vast mass of traditional morality embodied in the uses and observances which varied so strangely from city to city, to say nothing of the bewildering maze of 'barbarian' institutions. These presented a problem precisely analogous to the problem of the manifold world around us, with its endless diversity and its never-ceasing war of opposites. And so the question soon resolved itself into a search for the φύσις or underlying reality of all the complex social arrangements and institutions we know. Is there anything in human life that corresponds to the One of the Eleatics or to Atoms and the Void?

Now, just as cosmological speculation had been forced to deny the reality of the everyday world because it sought for ultimate reality in something corporeal, so the new ethical speculation was soon forced to deny the validity of ordinary morality, and for just the same reason, because the underlying principle it sought was of one kind with the facts it was meant to explain. If we look for ethical reality in some code of rules which are 'really' binding, instead of seeking it in that which gives binding force to the moral codes which already exist, we are bound to regard the latter as invalid and arbitrary. And further, just in proportion as we carry out the search logically, the poorer will be the content of our 'real' code of morals. For in truth, however much we may disguise the fact, such a code is reached by abstraction. Just as nothing was left by the Eleatics and the Atomists but extension and body, so nothing is left by the later ' sophists ' but brute force and the good pleasure of the individual. Morality, too, becomes an affair of Atoms and the Void.

III. The word which was used to denote the existing code of morality in any given state was νόμος, a word which originally meant ' use,' but covers also what we call ' law.' When the oracle of Apollo advised men to worship the gods, νόμῳ πόλεως, it is as if it had said ' after the use of Sarum.' Now we find that this word is used in a metaphorical sense by Democritus to express the unreal character of our everyday knowledge of the world, and nothing can show more clearly the close parallelism between the ethical and cosmological speculation of the time. In making his famous distinction between ' true-born ' and ' bastard ' knowledge,[1] Democritus used these words :—

' By use there is sweet and by use there is bitter ; by use there is hot, by use there is cold, by use there is colour. But in sooth there are Atoms and the Void.'[2]

Why should what we call the ' secondary qualities of matter ' be assigned to the province of Use ? The answer to this question will give us the key to the whole theory of Law and Nature.

It is evident that the great outburst of legislative activity which marked the preceding age had done not a little to foster moral scepticism. Just as the beginnings of applied natural science had brought men face to face with the problem of the world, so did practical legislation raise the problem of ethics. It had been possible to regard the customary laws of older times as something fundamental, or even divine. Their

[1] That this is the true meaning of the γνησίη and σκοτίη γνώμη was first pointed out by Natorp (*Archiv*, i., p. 355).

[2] Sext. *Math.* vii., 135, Νόμῳ γλυκὺ καὶ νόμῳ πικρόν, νόμῳ θερμόν, νόμῳ ψυχρόν, νόμῳ χροιή· ἐτεῇ δὲ ἄτομα καὶ κενόν.

authority was questioned just as little as the reality of the everyday world. The kings might give 'crooked dooms' (σκολιαὶ θέμιστες), but the existence of the 'dooms' themselves, and the fact that they came from Zeus, was not doubted for a moment. All the old 'taboos' and all the old rites were as real and unquestionable as the succession of seed-time and harvest or the rise of Ram, Bull, or Twins at the appointed season. Indeed, the regularity and constancy of human affairs was far more clearly apprehended than the even course of nature. Man lived in a charmed circle of law and custom, but the world around him still seemed lawless. So much was this so, indeed, that, when the regular course of natural phenomena began to be observed, no better word could be found for it than δίκη. Anaximander spoke of the encroachment of one element on another as 'injustice,' and, according to Heracleitus, it is the Erinyes, 'the avenging handmaids of Dike,' who keep the sun from 'overstepping' his measures.[1]

But a code of laws framed by a known lawgiver, a Zaleucus or a Charondas, a Lycurgus or a Solon, could not be accepted in this way as part of the everlasting order of things. It was clearly 'made,' and, therefore, from the point of view of φύσις, artificial and arbitrary. It seemed as if it might just as well have been made otherwise, or not made at all. A generation which had seen laws in the making could hardly help asking whether all morality had not been 'made' in the same way.

That this really was the point of view from which the ethical problem was regarded is shown by the use of the word θέσις in much the same sense as νόμος. This word may mean either the giving of laws or the adoption of laws so given,[2] and it thus contains the

---

[1] *Early Greek Philosophy*, pp. 51, 73, 147. [3rd Ed. pp. 51, 65, 144.]
[2] According as it is referred to the active, νόμους θεῖναι or the middle, νόμους θέσθαι.

germ, not only of the theory of an original legislator, but also of that known as the Social Contract.

The growing knowledge of the diversity of customs and institutions in the world, both Hellenic and barbarian, must have strengthened men's suspicion of the arbitrariness of all moral judgments. Herodotus is full of this feeling. The strongest proof he can give of the madness of King Cambyses is that he laughed at the rites and customs of other nations as if those of his own were a bit less artificial. ' If we were to set before all men a choice, and bid them pick out the best uses from all the uses there are, each people, after examining them all, would choose those of their own nation.' So ' it is not likely that any one but a madman would laugh at such things,' and Pindar is right in saying that ' use is king of all.'

IV. We find, then, a close parallelism between the cosmological and the ethical problem of the fifth century B.C. The world of everyday experience was seen to be unreal in comparison with the ultimate φύσις of things, however that might be explained, and the ordinary codes of morals were felt to be unreal in comparison with a similar abstract ideal of right. In both cases the error, or rather the inadequacy, of the views held came from the same source. The underlying reality of the world and that of conduct were sought *in pari materia*. The reality of the corporeal world was supposed to be a still more real body, and the reality of conduct was supposed to be a still more valid rule of life. Such is the real meaning and origin of an opposition which was natural and inevitable in the beginnings of philosophy, but which is surely an anachronism now. And yet it still lives on, and it is the same type of mind which would reduce the world to the interaction of vibrations and society to a compromise of ' natural rights.'

FORM AND MATTER IN CLASSICAL TEACHING

Read before the Classical Association of Scotland at St. Andrews,
March 12, 1904

THERE is far too much uneasiness just now among the friends of classical education. No doubt it is a good thing to ask ourselves from time to time where we stand; but it is, I think, a great mistake to take up a purely defensive attitude. In some of the pleas put forward on our behalf, there is a certain apologetic tone, a readiness to make concessions, which I fear can lead to no good. It is deplorable strategy that seeks to propitiate the enemy by yielding one point after another till there is nothing left worth fighting for. Our concessions will be accepted without thanks, and it will be found in the end that we have given up the key to our position. In particular, it will not do to shirk the advocacy of classical education as above all a training in form, and to defend it mainly on the ground of the interest and importance of its subject-matter. This seems to me like throwing away our case, and it is a plea for the formal side of classical teaching that I wish to lay before the association to-day.

There is no doubt that the tendency to put matter in the place of form is growing among us. Hardly any one dares to say a word for verse composition now, and the spectacle of what is happening in France and Germany should warn us that prose composition is not safe either. Everywhere we see that knowledge is being substituted for discipline, and breadth for accuracy, that the unique value of classical training is being sacrificed in a vain effort to assimilate its methods to those of other subjects, vaguely called scientific. One of the greatest living scholars, Professor von Wilamowitz-Moellendorff, says expressly : ' We do not learn Greek to form our minds by means of grammar and style. . . . We learn Greek exclusively to read Greek books.' [1] This is the point of view which I believe to be radically wrong, and which I wish to examine in this paper.

If we say that we teach Greek exclusively to enable our pupils to read Greek books, we at once lay ourselves open to some very damaging retorts. The most serious of these is the charge that, after four or five years of study, a boy is unable to read a Greek book for pleasure, as he can read a play of Shakespeare or even of Molière. I am sorry to say that the truth of this charge is often sorrowfully admitted by our defenders, whereas, if we look at classical teaching from the true point of view, it will be seen to be altogether beside the mark. Of course, if reading a book ' for pleasure ' means reading it carelessly, we are not concerned to defend ourselves. It is just one of the great virtues of a classical education that it makes it hard for us to read any good book ' for pleasure ' in that sense, whether it be written in Greek or in our own tongue. People think they are ' reading Shakespeare ' when they are really doing nothing of the sort. They are quite content to miss the meaning of half a dozen words to every page, to lose the point of three or four verses at a time from failure to catch an allusion, and to get the sense only in the most general way. Our pupils can read Virgil and Sophocles after that fashion too—only

[1] *Griechisches Lesebuch, Vorrede,* pp. III.-IV.—It is true that Wilamowitz admits the exceptional suitability of Greek for this formal training, but he holds that it is sufficiently provided by the study of Latin. This is to miss the point that the logical and juristic form of Latin is quite different from the psychological and aesthetic form of Greek. Latin alone is apt to prove a very one-sided instrument of training, as may be seen in France.

it makes them uncomfortable. I do not say it would
be a bad thing if we were to encourage more cursory
reading among our pupils ; it would, indeed, be a very
good thing. A book of Homer can be read in about an
hour, and it would be an excellent thing for a boy to go
right through the Iliad and Odyssey in a month or six
weeks, giving one or two hours a day to it. We can
teach that sort of facility quite easily if we choose, and
perhaps we ought to do so more than we do at present ;
but we must never forget that what we mean by *reading*
is quite another matter.

Our accusers also lose sight of the fact that many of
the books they expect our pupils to read ' for pleasure '
are extremely difficult, quite apart from the question of
language. We should not deny a Frenchman's knowledge of English because he found it hard to read
George Meredith in the train, and yet this is the sort of
test that is applied to us. It is ridiculous to expect us
to enable our pupils to read with ease things that a
Greek boy of their own age would have found puzzling.
Does any one imagine that young Greeks could read
Pindar and Aeschylus ' for pleasure ' ? Simonides
was notoriously easier, and yet we see from Plato's
Protagoras that the most cultivated men of the fifth
century B.C. might find considerable difficulty in making him out. All that can be expected of us is that we
should teach our boys to read a piece of Homer without
too many hard words in it, a straightforward bit of
Attic prose, and an ordinary passage of dramatic
dialogue. Once we have done that, we have put them
in almost as favourable a position for the study of Greek
literature as they are for that of their own, and in almost
as favourable a position as a Greek boy of their own
years would have been. What more can any one ask ?
All the rest will always require minute, prolonged
study, and above all, a growing experience of life.

But, it will be said, our pupils do not, as a matter of fact, read Greek and Latin books for themselves after their school and college course is over.   That is to some extent true, but it is once more quite beside the mark. To have read even a few books in a scholarly way is a permanent gain, even if the language in which they are written has been forgotten.   The content, the matter, may pass away, but the form abides.   At the very least, we can give our pupils a habit of lucidity which will stand them in good stead afterwards, whether it be the Westminster Confession or the Fiscal Bluebook that they have to deal with.   Nor is that the only gain. There is many an old gentleman alive to-day who owes to the old-fashioned scholarship of his youth a fine appreciation of English literature and a genuine love of good writing.   He may not be quite sure now whether the perfect participle of *obliviscor* is or is not a dactyl, but his boyish struggles with the *Gradus ad Parnassum* have given his mind a bent which it will never lose. He has acquired a lasting sense of literary form, and is not to be taken in by tinsel and glitter.   There is surely no need for us to be apologetic about a system which produces such a result as that.

It must also be remembered that in the great days of ' pure scholarship ' men did read the classics all their lives, and, if they do not do so now, that is mainly because they have not had the same formal training in their youth.   Here, too, it is the substitution of matter for form that is killing the study of the classics.   A man who has been taught the origin of the legend of Aeneas will not read Virgil in later life ; a man who has been taught to write hexameters will.

It is true, of course, that the subject-matter of ancient literature is of exceptional interest and importance ; but it is only one subject-matter among others, and it would be hard to convince an unbeliever that it deserves the predominance we claim for it. It has even been argued with some plausibility that it is by no means specially adapted to youthful minds. I am very sure that it is not on any such ground that most of us in our hearts believe in classical education. We make a far higher claim for it than that. We claim that it is the best training in form, and that all education is essentially a training in form. We believe that the classics can do for most people what mathematics admittedly does for some, and that these two disciplines stand quite alone as educational instruments. It is worth while, I think, for us to ask ourselves why the claims of mathematics are almost universally allowed, while ours are disputed. It cannot be due to the practical value of mathematics. To the great majority of ordinary people Latin is actually of more use in daily life than mathematics ever can be. It is rather, I believe, because the mathematical mind is not prone to conciliation and compromise, and so teachers of mathematics do not trouble to defend their subject on inadequate grounds. They do not tell the public that trigonometry is useful in landscape gardening ; they go on serenely with their teaching, never admitting a question of its value, and the public takes them very much at their own estimate, as it nearly always takes everybody. We have much to learn from our friends the mathematicians in this respect.

I hold, then, that classical education is essentially a formal discipline, and, if this is so, two practical conclusions follow at once. In the first place, we in the universities must rank pure scholarship higher than what is called ' research,' and, in the next place, composition, and especially verse composition, must be restored to its rightful place in our schools. These two positions require illustration and defence.

c

I

I have said, in the first place, that pure scholarship must be ranked above what is called 'research' in the universities. I shall be told that this is hopelessly reactionary. Well, I think the time has come for a little plain speaking on this subject, and I do not mean to shirk it.

In our department, however it may be in others, no research worthy of the name has ever been done except by men who simply could not help doing it, and none has ever been done but for its own sake. A man is led by some feeling of kinship for what is greater than himself to devote his life to the interpretation of a poet, philosopher, or historian, to the elucidation of the language itself on its purely linguistic side, or to that of the art or institutions of antiquity. Such a man will freely give himself up to the most arid and laborious investigations. No erasure in a manuscript, no half-read scholium, no fragmentary inscription will seem unworthy of his attention ; no grammatical nicety or stylistic peculiarity will be passed by as too trivial for his patient study. All these things will live in his hands ; for they are all transformed by his faith in something to which he can hardly give a name, but which, to him, is more real than anything else. He is investigating, let us say, the uses of the optative mood ; but he expects to find something more than optatives with and without ἄν. It is this search for the something more that makes the real scholar, and I do not see how it is to be 'promoted' or 'encouraged' by regulations and endowments. You might as well expect to promote lyric poetry by founding fellowships for the purpose. The spirit bloweth where it listeth, and no ordinances of any human commissioners can bind it.

I do not think that the man I have tried to describe

will talk very much about ' research,' at any rate in connexion with his own work.   When you are really building anything, you do not call the public in to admire the beautiful scaffolding.   On the other hand, he will be of a simple and generous nature, and will be ready to credit others with an ardour like his own.   He will not be conscious of the gulf that is fixed between his work and the grotesque parody of it that surrounds him, and he will fail to see that much of what passes for ' research ' is at best an excuse for idleness, and may even degenerate into imposture.

If you watch carefully the language of those who talk most about research, you will find that they use the word in a very peculiar way.   It is ' research ' to study the manuscripts of an author's text, but it is not ' research ' to interpret his meaning or to show the significance of the form in which he clothes it.   The aesthetic interpretation of a tragedy or the philosophical interpretation of a Platonic dialogue is not ' research ' ; the investigation of scholia and lexica is.   Again, it is ' research ' to argue about the name of a figure in the Parthenon pediment ; it is not 'research' to investigate its aesthetic significance.   It is ' research ' to count the average number of prepositions to the Teubner page in the text of the orators ; it is not ' research ' to study the rhetorical structure of the *De Corona*.   The more we consider the matter, the more we shall see that, in the minds of its loudest advocates, everything that is merely external and subsidiary is a fit object for ' research,' while the study of the things themselves is the province of the *littérateur* and the *dilettante*.

Now this is quite a new thing.   The great scholars of the past never talked about research at all, though they did an amount of it that casts our efforts wholly into the shade.   All their work was subordinated to one end, the enjoyment of the things themselves.

Nothing is more striking in the lives of these great men than the way in which they read and re-read the whole of ancient literature for the sheer joy of it. They did not dally with the handmaids like Penelope's suitors ; it was the image of Antiquity in its strength and beauty they really cared for, and the rest of their work was but the brightening of the glass through which we behold it, and the removal of excrescences from the surface of the image itself.

But nowadays learning has become a trade, and the trail of βαναυσία is over it all. There are posts to be won and reputations to be made with the least possible expenditure of time and trouble, and the easiest thing to do is to imitate a little piece of the great men's scaffolding. You need not trouble about the plan of the building ; indeed, there need not be a building at all, if only the scaffolding is sufficiently elaborate. Scholarship in the old-fashioned sense is a thing of slow growth ; it implies ripe knowledge and a trained judgment. ' Research,' on the other hand, is certainly laborious ; but, in its lower forms, it requires little knowledge and makes few calls upon the higher powers of the mind. That is why we hear most talk of it in the newer American and colonial universities, where there is not yet any great tradition of scholarship. It is the desire to get results without the processes which alone can give them value, that is at the bottom of the whole movement. I propose now to show you how the thing is done.

By common consent, the constitution of an author's text is the highest aim that a scholar can set before himself. It is also one of the most difficult things in the world. Most people, however, are quite ignorant of the difference between a real recension and the production of a readable text that will pass muster. So much has been done already, that the production of a respectable text is not really very difficult. Up to a certain point, a sort of rough common sense, a sort of ἄγροικος σοφία, will acquit itself tolerably well in a task of this kind. Of course you do not trouble to collate MSS. or to study the tradition of your author's text. You take for granted that a certain MS. is ' the best,' and you follow that as closely as you dare, on the plea that you believe in ' objective criticism.' You need not go beyond the critical apparatus of the latest German edition. Indeed, you need not go so far. To most people, textual criticism is a mystery altogether, and they will respect you if you reprint the Teubner text with a selection of readings from Bekker or Dindorf at the bottom of the page. The risk of detection is very slight indeed. Even good scholars seldom know much about the text of more than one or two authors, and a few judicious compliments in the preface will probably silence the two or three men who could expose you if they thought it worth while. Even if one of them does say anything, that can always be put down to professional jealousy and brazened out somehow.

This kind of thing is being done every day, and it is directly encouraged by loose talk about ' research.' But there are lower depths still. A man who knows little more than the Greek alphabet can count preposi-tions by the fireside. Of course it is dry work, but there are universities which will give you a doctor's degree for it, you will be accounted a truly scientific philologist, and you will be entitled to look down upon the man who can only write Latin prose or Greek iambics, though he may have a thousand times more knowledge and skill than you have. This is a pretty pass for classical scholarship to come to, but every one who has ever felt it his duty to read through what is facetiously called the ' literature ' of a subject knows that the picture I have drawn is not exaggerated.

It is to be observed also that the people who talk most about ' research ' are not those who have done any. It is a word which is most often on the lips of people who say they would do it if they were ' encouraged,' that is to say, practically, if they were paid for it in advance. It is this which has vulgarized the word and made it offensive to many people. We hear of the ' endowment of research,' ' research scholarships,' and the like, as if it was all a question of money. But true research can never be fostered in that way. I don't suppose that any of the greatest discoveries have ever been paid for at all, and I am sure that they have all been made by men who had no thought of being paid for them. Let a man get his living by performing some definite social service like teaching, and keep his research work free from contamination by the thought of promotion or gain.

And, after all, it is interpretation of what is already partially known that must always be the scholar's chief task. The research which neglects the known for the unknown destroys itself in the end. Even in natural science we see that this is so. Even there the process of discovery is subject to the law of diminishing returns, and the nearer a science approaches perfection, the less it is studied. Astronomy, the eldest of the sciences and the queen of them all, seems to have reached this stage, and others are fast approaching it. Far more will this be the case with our studies. If we leave out of account the possibilities of archaeological discovery and of new finds of papyri—and even these possibilities are limited—it is safe to say that the results of future research are not likely to approach in value what is already contained in our school books. If we content ourselves with these lessening returns, we may be sure the common sense of mankind will regard our pursuits with contempt, or at best, with an amused tolerance.

It will certainly come to the conclusion that they have no educational value. This association stands for the faith that a classical training is the best, though not the only, kind of education, and we betray that faith if we insist on reducing our studies to the level of a specialist's profession.

For the supremacy of classical education is based upon the fact that it is concerned with the interpretation of the highest products of the human mind, products of which the significance is in truth inexhaustible. There is no law of diminishing returns here ; for we can never feel that we have understood Sophocles or Plato or Virgil enough, and each step forward in our appreciation is of more significance than the last. And this work of interpretation is always having to be done afresh. It cannot be stored or transmitted in books, and the best of it is, strictly speaking, incommunicable. Each fresh soul has to understand the masterpieces for itself as if no one had ever understood them before, and the most our teaching can do is to give our pupils the key by which they can unlock for themselves the great treasure-house of mankind. Not all of them will make full use of their privilege ; but there will always be some, and even those who do not enter behind the veil will feel, if only their teacher is one worthy of the name, that it is good for them to be there.

II

I have said also that, in our school teaching, form should rank above matter, and I have interpreted that to mean that we ought to pay more attention than we do to composition. Of course I include under the head of composition the practice of translation, which is at once the best way of teaching composition in our own language, and the best way of bringing out the real characteristics of Greek and Latin. It is only by means of these formal disciplines that we can give our pupils that mastery of the languages on which all scholarship worthy of the name must be based. In particular, I would urge that more attention should be given to verse composition in the early stages of instruction. By this I do not mean that we should endeavour to train skilled writers of Greek and Latin verses. The power to produce these is a natural gift which may be trusted to look after itself. But I do very decidedly mean that elementary verse composition is almost the most valuable educational instrument in existence. It is really much easier than prose composition for a young boy. It is possible to be absolutely correct in the making of simple verses in a way that is barely possible in prose. The strict limitations of the form exclude many chances of error, and the language of Greek and Latin poetry has been so moulded by the hexameter and the iambic that the right and inevitable thing soon suggests itself. This is in itself a tremendous advantage ; for every teacher knows that there is nothing more encouraging to a boy than to feel that he has done something which is really right, and that sense of achievement comes quicker in easy verse composition than anywhere else. This used to be better understood in Scotland than it is now. I remember very well that, when I was eleven years old, we used to do elegiacs in the High School of Edinburgh. We did not carry them very far, I know, but it is all I remember of what I was taught then. The geography of Asia, the dates of the kings of England, and all the so-called ' useful knowledge ' has disappeared from my mind completely, but I can remember some of the first Latin verses I ever made, and I feel that training, elementary as it was, to be a real part of me now.[1] Boys

---

[1] I wish to put on record that this was in 1874. Surely what was done then can be done now.

have no matter of experience that is worth expressing, but even a baby of a few weeks rejoices in rhythmical form.   It is a natural instinct and one that the educator should get hold of at all costs.   I may be wrong, but I hold very strongly that the growing neglect of form in classical teaching is depriving it of most of its value, and I think that, unless we go back boldly to the traditions of earlier days, we shall find that our subject has become merely one branch of study among others. The Greeks seem to have derived great educational advantages from learning in boyhood to tune a lyre. We have no lyres now, and piano-tuning is rather too complicated to be introduced into our schools.   The writing of verses is the nearest thing we can get to what the Greeks called μουσική.

Now, I know it will be said that there is no time to teach these things in our schools, and I wish to examine that plea very carefully.   I am well aware that, to the practical schoolmaster, the problem that presents itself in teaching Greek is how to get a boy up to the standard of the Higher Grade, or, it may be, the Honours Leaving Certificate in three, or at most four, years, and I should be very sorry indeed to suggest any addition to the burden which schoolmasters already have to bear in doing this.   I am not at all sure, however, that the method I am advocating would not prove the least burdensome in the end, and I think I can show how.

In the first place, you have all, I doubt not, read with satisfaction the latest deliverance of the Scotch Education Department on the subject of the papers to be set in Greek and Latin.   ' My lords ' are now of opinion that it is desirable, ' while restricting the questions or exercises to a moderate standard, to be severe in exacting a certain amount of correct answering as a minimum.'   That is certainly the only sound method of examination, and, if the Department's examiners act, as

I have no doubt they will, on the principles now laid down, the burden of which schoolmasters complain will be sensibly lightened, and it will be just those schools which pay most attention to form and accuracy that will be most successful.

In the second place, there will be abundant room for the training in form if a great deal of the matter is cast aside. Much of it is mere traditional deadweight. There are still many schools in Scotland where precious time is wasted over the late Alexandrian paradigm of τύπτω. What is the good of teaching boys the future τύψω when it does not appear in literature till the fifth century A.D., or the perfect τέτυφα which exists nowhere at all outside of grammars? Why should we teach that the vocative of αἰδώς is αἰδοῖ, when no such word ever existed or could exist? And what is the use of learning half the irregular verbs that boys get up? I have inspected a class that could tell me that the perfect of βλαστάνω was βεβλάστηκα or ἐβλάστηκα. I confess that I was not aware of the fact myself, though I found when I got home that it was so. But what does it matter? The chances are that none of the boys who knew it would ever meet either one form or the other in the whole course of their lives, and, if they did, it would not be hard to deal with. The Education Department and the Joint Board are not responsible for this. They never ask questions of that sort, I am happy to say, and I fancy that a practical schoolmaster who would make a table of what is actually asked for by these bodies would find that he could save hours in his grammar teaching. That sort of thing is what I mean by matter. The only excuse for it would be that it was necessary. It is mostly unnecessary even for examination purposes, it has no educational value, it is mere lumber, and it stands in the way of better things.

In the third place, verse composition is actually the

easiest and best way of fixing in the memory such
grammatical information as is necessary. It is not easy
to forget a Latin perfect infinitive that has once fallen
neatly into its place in the second half of a pentameter,
and the quantities come of themselves. Again, a boy
who does Greek iambics soon learns the convenience
of being able to say στυγεῖν or μισεῖν, θνητός or
βροτός, and when he finds that he has not the same
liberty in prose, he is well on the track of the most important fact about Greek literature, and ultimately all
literature. Our present system, on the other hand,
directly discourages the treatment of ancient literature
as literature.

And this leads in practice to very serious consequences. It is, I believe, a fact that the young men
and women of the present day read less good literature,
and especially less good poetry, than was the case even
twenty-five years ago. Those of us who were in our
first youth then perhaps believed too much in literature.
It may sometimes have seemed to us that nothing else
was really important. Some of us can remember how
quite average Oxford undergraduates, who did not
get first classes or university scholarships, used to be
familiar with all the best English poetry, and even with
that of France. The names to conjure with then were
Arnold, Swinburne, Morris, and Rossetti—and now
where are they ? It was one-sided, no doubt, and the
making of verses is not the chief end of man ; but I do
not think any of us who came under that influence
would be willing to have had it otherwise, and I have
sometimes wondered in recent years, when I have been
privileged to inspect an undergraduate's collection of
books, what his interest in life can possibly be.

Even where we should least expect it, we find the
trail of βαναυσία. The school of *Literae Humaniores*
at Oxford, once so powerful an engine of liberal culture,

is in danger of becoming professionalized. It is amazing how much the young men know now about the administration of remote Roman provinces, and how they can pick holes in the Ἀθηναίων πολιτεία, but they don't appear to have read Thucydides or Tacitus. In philosophy too they know all sorts of marvellous things which I presume are useful to professional students of the subject, but they haven't read the great philosophers. The days seem to be past when a man in his third year would buy a big Plato and very likely read it through, or when two or three would go off together in the long vacation, and struggle with Kant in the mountains. Dreadful heresies were started on these occasions and we strayed far from the track, but it was, so to say, a grand experience. Nowadays, the young men all say the same things aboutKant and Plato. I suppose what they say about Kant is all right ; but I know it is very uninteresting. What they say about Plato has not even the merit of being right.[1]

Moderations, too, has become a lifeless thing. In the old days of set books, we all of us learnt what it was really to master a work ; nowadays, everything seems fragmentary. And, as it would of course be absurd to expect that the average first-class man should be able to write verses or even Greek prose, their place must be taken by technical details which are as easily crammed as they are easily forgotten.

And all this is because what is called ' research ' is ousting scholarship from its old place in the universities, and the acquisition of facts is considered more important in our schools than the cultivation of form. That is the subject I wished to speak of to-day ;

---

[1] The most living thing at Oxford just now seems to be a revived Aristotelianism of a somewhat scholastic type. I have grave doubts of the educational value of this, except for professional students. It is a remarkable symptom of the tendency to undo the work of the humanist Renaissance.

for here in Scotland we stand at the parting of the ways. The raising of the age of leaving school, which is the most satisfactory feature of recent changes,[1] has made liberal culture a possibility in Scotland in a way that it was not before. The full effect of that change has not yet been felt, and students still come to us at the age of eighteen, who know more facts, certainly, but are not better trained, so far as I can see, than those that used to come at the age of sixteen. But that I believe to be a temporary and passing condition. We could not expect all the schools to rise at once to their new opportunity, and it was inevitable at first that the additional years should mean at first more facts rather than a different training. For, if a boy is to be kept at school till he is eighteen, his whole education should be different from the very beginning. It is no solution of the problem to treat him in the old way till he is sixteen, and then to cram him for an Honours Leaving Certificate. I hope that, both in the schools and the universities, we shall soon rise to our new opportunities. If we can only do that, I think we need not make ourselves anxious about the future of classical education in this country. No substitute for it has yet been discovered, and our best teachers of modern languages are the first to insist that their work can only be thoroughly done on a classical foundation. But we must see to it that the old humanist ideal is not sacrificed to the pseudo-scientific one ; for, if that happens, classical education is doomed.

[1] In my own classes this year I have only one student under eighteen, and only six under nineteen.

THE RELIGIOUS AND MORAL IDEAS
OF EURIPIDES

*Read before the Classical Association of Scotland at St. Andrews,
March 14, 1908*

THERE are few questions on which it is easier to go
wrong than that of the moral and religious ideas of a
dramatist. No work of art can be interpreted unless
we have regard to its medium. A drama is no doubt
a written work, but that is an accident. It is written
primarily because actors have to learn their parts. If
it is a real drama at all, it is meant to be acted, not read ;
and everything in it must be judged from the point of
view of representation.

It is true, of course, that we can and do read plays.
There are even people who say they can appreciate
Shakespeare better by reading him than by seeing him
acted, and I can quite believe that this may be so in the
case of men endowed with a very vivid imagination and
a considerable knowledge of stage-craft. It is conceivable that such people should be able to set before
themselves an imaginative reproduction of a play which
should far surpass anything the actual theatre, with its
many limitations and frequent pursuit of false ideals,
can give. This is, I say, conceivable ; but I am
afraid that most people who prefer the written to the
acted play mean something quite different. They
read the play, not for itself, but for isolated passages
distinguished by ingenious character-drawing or striking reflections. These are the elements in a dramatic
composition which Aristotle called $\mathring{\eta}\theta o\varsigma$ and $\delta\iota\acute{a}\nu o\iota a$,
and which he rightly subordinated to $\mu\hat{v}\theta o\varsigma$, ' the soul
of the tragedy.' Or again, they read the play ' as

46

literature' or 'as poetry.' That aspect of it is what
Aristotle calls λέξις, and also regards as subordinate.
It is true, no doubt, on the other hand, that the ordinary
playgoer who will not read plays is also attracted chiefly
by a subordinate element of the drama, and that the
least artistic, what Aristotle calls ὄψις, but that is not
what I am speaking of now. A play is essentially the
imitation of an action, and unless we bear this constantly in mind we shall certainly miss its significance.

This is, I take it, the source of most modern misin-
terpretations of Greek Tragedy. We approach it too
much as literature, as something intended to be read,
and so we emphasize unduly the element of διάνοια or
reflection. We are apt to think of the plays as intended
mainly to illustrate or further some religious or philosophical idea, and to attribute to the dramatist himself
sentiments which are appropriate in the mouths of his
characters at a given moment in the action, but are not
in the least meant to have a wider application. The
leading instance of this is very familiar, but it is of
special interest as showing that the mistake to which I
am referring is not wholly modern, but goes back to the
time when there first came to be such a thing as a
reading public. We all know the famous verse of the
Hippolytus—

    ' 'Twas but my tongue, 'twas not my soul, that swore.'

From the time of Aristophanes downwards this has been
quoted to prove that the mind of Euripides was sophis-
ticated by the casuistry of mental reservations. Let us
suppose that the *Hippolytus* had been lost ; and how
could we have defended Euripides from the charge ? If
we had urged that the purpose of the verse was purely
dramatic, we should have been met by the answer that
Aristophanes was a dramatist, and could not have been
mistaken in the poet's intention. It would have been

hard to answer this ; but fortunately the title of the
Hippolytus begins with the letter I, and it has been
preserved.   If Euripides had happened to call the play
Phaedra, as Racine called his version of it *Phèdre*, it
would have been lost.[1]   We should not know that,
while Hippolytus does utter the sentiment in the thick
of an intolerable situation which he has not created, he
also, as a matter of fact, goes to meet a cruel death
rather than break this very oath.   As it is, we even
happen to know the origin of this misinterpretation
from a statement in Aristotle's *Rhetoric*.[2]   Euripides
was involved in an ἀντίδοσις action, and his opponent
tried to make light of his sworn testimony by saying
that no doubt, though his tongue had sworn, his mind
remained unsworn, like that of his own Hippolytus. It
was merely, then, a piece of forensic banter.   That
should be a warning to us not to construct Euripidean
philosophies out of detached fragments.

There can be no doubt that Euripides is peculiarly
liable to misinterpretation of this sort, and that for two
reasons which follow at once from the general considerations which I have just stated.   In the first place, he is
the most purely dramatic of the Greek tragedians ; and,
in the second, the element of διάνοια bulks larger in
his work than in that of his predecessors.   The consequence is that those who read plays in the undramatic
spirit which has been indicated are peculiarly liable to
be led astray, and a fallacious view of the poet's mind is
readily accepted.   That fallacious view, as I consider
it, has found its ablest expositor in Dr. Verrall ; but it
is implied also in most of the current criticism.

The problem is admirably stated by Dr. Verrall
himself.   Though Euripides was not popular during his
lifetime, all antiquity placed him in the highest rank as

---

[1] See Wilamowitz, *Analecta Euripidea*, pp. 136 sqq.
[2] *Rhet.*, iii. 15.

a tragic poet. Plato, who disapproved of his weakness for 'tyrants'—a point to which we shall return—admits that he was generally regarded as surpassing every one in tragedy. Aristotle, though he makes certain reservations with regard to his stage-craft, says that he is ' at any rate the most tragic of the poets.' Such was also the opinion of the Renaissance, and in the seventeenth century Milton and Racine have no doubt of it. It is not till the nineteenth century that his position is seriously questioned, and even then there is a strange divergence in men's estimate of him, which is conveniently represented for us by the names of two great poets. Mr. Swinburne has called Euripides ' a botcher,' while Browning gave some of his best work to the vindication of ' Euripides the human.' We are told of the late Sir Richard Jebb that ' he could not speak of Euripides without pain in his voice, and seldom, without necessity, spoke of him at all.' Sir Richard's successor at Glasgow took, we all know, a widely different view.

Dr. Verrall sees that there must be something wrong somewhere. Some one must have misunderstood Euripides completely, so he suggests a view of him which, in the extreme form in which he states it, has at least the merit of novelty. He tells us that the plays of Euripides were intended to subvert what he calls ' the Olympian religion ' by so presenting the sacred legends as to bring out their fundamental absurdity and immorality. It would not have been safe, however, he tells us, to do this openly. The performance of a tragedy was a religious service, and the Athenians at the end of the fifth century B.C. were very orthodox, as is shown by such things as the prosecution of Anaxagoras, and the excitement caused by the mutilation of the Hermae, and the profanation of the Mysteries. So the plays were made orthodox to the outer seeming by

D

a prologue, generally spoken by a god, and an epilogue
with a *deus ex machina*.   These parts of the play were
intended for the multitude ;   the enlightened inner
circle were to understand that the poet did not mean
them.   In fact, it is a canon of Euripidean criticism
that every statement made by a god at the beginning or
end of a play is to be taken as false.   The poet's true
meaning is generally just the reverse of what the god
says.

Now, in the first place, if this, or anything like it,
were true, it is hard to see how the character of Euripides as an artist would be saved by it.   Nothing could
well be more inartistic or undramatic ;   and, if Euripides had wished to undermine the Olympian mythology, there were many more suitable ways of doing
so.   A sacred oratorio would hardly be the place for
' The Higher Criticism ' or ' The New Theology,' and
no more would a Greek tragedy.   Of this Dr. Verrall
shows some consciousness when he says that the full
effect of the plays could only be realized by subsequent
reading and discussion.   From which it follows that
the actual performance of the plays was a more or less
irrelevant accident !   Could there be a severer criticism
of a dramatist than this, and would not Euripides
deserve every word his detractors have said of him were
it anything like the truth ?

But really the whole theory falls to the ground at
once if only we make clear to ourselves what was meant
by religious orthodoxy in the fifth century B.C.   Dr.
Verrall has transferred to antiquity a certain modern
view of orthodoxy which would have been quite unintelligible in these days.   According to this view, orthodoxy consists in believing in the historical narratives
contained in certain sacred books ;   but this is evidently
quite inapplicable to a religion which has no sacred
book and no creed.   A great deal of misunderstanding

has arisen from the saying that Homer was ' the Bible of the Greeks.' So far was that from being the case, that the Greek religious consciousness was in a perpetual state of revolt against the Homeric secularism with its humanized gods. It begins as early as Hesiod, who makes the Muses say that they know how to tell falsehoods like the truth about the gods, though they can tell the truth too when they will. Stesichorus was struck blind for saying with Homer that Helen went to Troy with Paris, and only recovered his sight when he had written the famous Palinode beginning : ' This is no true tale, nor didst thou ever enter the well-benched ships and visit the towers of Troy.' Pindar is counted a religious poet, but he will have nothing to do with the more unedifying parts of mythology—' I stand aloof, and will never call one of the blessed gods a glutton.' So he proceeds to invent a myth of his own. No one objects ; no one calls him ἀσεβής; the religious feelings of the Greeks are not touched at all by the free handling of mythology. The poets had made all that, and they might do as they pleased with it. If, then, Euripides had wished to undermine ' the Olympian mythology ' he would only have been following the example of the chief religious poets of the past. There was not the least reason for him to veil his meaning. Aeschylus had produced the *Prometheus* without, so far as we know, the slightest scandal. The position of the Pythian Apollo is almost as ambiguous in the *Eumenides* as it is in the *Ion*. These things were no part of religion. What Aeschylus did get into trouble for was a supposed revelation of the ' Mysteries,' that is, for representing in one of his plays certain acts or repeating certain words which most Athenians knew as well as he did, but which were held to be ἀπόρρητα. The defence was that he did not know they were ἀπόρρητα, and this shows us exactly where the gravity of the charge lay. The things which must not be touched are those upon which the intercourse of the city with its gods was held to depend, and not the fancies which poets might have about these same gods. These formed a pleasing enough ἀκρόαμα at the Panathenæa or elsewhere, but no one regarded them as a matter of faith.

It is the same with all the prosecutions for impiety of which we know anything. Anaxagoras was condemned (if he was condemned) for saying that the Sun was a red-hot stone and the Moon earth. There was no mythology to speak of connected with Helios and Selene, but there were rites and sacrifices of immemorial antiquity. The mutilation of the Hermae has nothing to do with belief or disbelief in certain stories. The charge against Socrates was, indeed, one of Atheism, but we see how remote the Greek meaning of this word was from ours by the fact that the indictment accused him of introducing ' new gods.' We know that to the Greeks Christianity appeared primarily as a form of Atheism, and that was just because it condemned what was of the essence of Greek religion.

Euripides, then, might have ' undermined the Olympian religion ' as much as he pleased, and he might have done it quite openly. As a matter of fact, he does make his Heracles say this :—

' I hold not that the gods cherish unlawful loves : I have never allowed nor will I ever believe a god has worn fetters on his hands, nor that one has ever been another's slave.'

That is from Xenophanes, and there is no concealment or secret undermining about it.

But there is another weak point in Dr. Verrall's theory, which can be made even clearer. If we suppose that Euripides wrote plays because that was a safe and convenient way of overthrowing mythology, we should at least expect that he would turn his attention to myths which were well known to his audience. Now Dr. Verrall reached his view mainly from the analysis of two plays, the *Alcestis* and the *Ion*, which are as far as possible from answering to this description. I think it is very doubtful whether many of the audience had ever heard these stories at all before they saw the plays. Admetus was, indeed, known as a pattern of hospitality from an old drinking song, but that was probably all. I doubt if Ion was known outside the small circle who took an interest in the ' scientific history ' which had been imported from Ionia. At any rate, we have the definite statement of Aristotle that even the myths that were known were known to only a few, and that is enough to make us hesitate to accept Dr. Verrall's conclusions. It is a perfectly clear statement and one which Aristotle had no interest in making if it had not been true. It is quite inexplicable that a poet —and Euripides was certainly that—should waste his poetry in discrediting stories which were known only to a few.

We can, however, take a further step. In the form which they take in his plays, the myths are really in many cases the invention of Euripides himself. We can still distinguish three stages in the growth of these stories, and, as it happens, they correspond very closely to the three stages which we can trace in the growth of more modern legends, such as those that centre round the figure of King Arthur.

First, we have the stage of genuine legend. At this stage, we find a number of wonderful tales about national heroes. Some of these are genuine tradition, some are mythology proper, while a large number are αἴτια, that is, explanations of ancient usages or of remarkable objects like monumental stones. These are the genuine legends of the people, and their chief characteristic is that each stands by itself.   They are, therefore, often inconsistent with one another, and still more so with the legends of other peoples.

The next stage is that of systematization.   In the early Middle Ages this task was undertaken by chroniclers, monkish and other, like Geoffrey of Monmouth. They believed all these legends, and they therefore felt obliged to weave them into a single whole, a task which they accomplished with marvellous ingenuity.   In the process, legends were welded together which had no original connexion with one another.   That of the Holy Grail, for instance, comes from the East, and has no original link with Arthur at all.   This work was accomplished for the Greek legends by the Ionic historians of the fifth century B.C.   Their method was that of genealogy, and they filled up all the gaps as best they could.   When we find a king called Creon or a queen called Creusa, we may be sure that we are on their traces.   Such figures as Ion are their invention altogether.   They firmly believed that they could construct history in this way, and they applied to legend the spirit of rationalism.

The last stage is when the poet takes the dry bones of the rationalist chronicle, and turns its figures once more into real human beings.   That process has been steadily applied to the Arthurian legend from the time of the early French *Chansons* to that of the *Idylls of the King* and *Parsifal*, and that is what Euripides did.   So it is really true that the plots of his plays are his own creation, and it is inconceivable that he should have set himself to make these plots seem incredible.   Such real inconsistencies and awkwardnesses as critics have discovered in them are wholly due to their source, the rationalist chronicle, and the worst we can say of Euripides is that he did not always quite succeed in making true human stories out of these arid combinations.   But

that is a very different thing from Dr. Verrall's view. It
was no part of an Athenian's faith to believe in Hellani-
cus, and it is not likely that many Athenians had read
him at all.

So far our conclusion has been negative. Can we
say anything about the actual religious views of Euripides ? We might, of course, string together a cento
of passages from the remains of his work which would
produce exactly the opposite impression to that which
has lately been current. This, for instance, from the
Helena : ' Naught is certain that men dream ; but the
words of the gods have I found true.' But that would
be to fall into the very same mistake we have criticized
in others. We have no right to infer a dramatist's convictions from the utterances of his characters. They
speak for themselves, and not for him.

There are, however, the choruses, and it is possible,
if we are very careful, to infer something from them.
The theory that the chorus represents the ' ideal spec-
tator ' is, of course, erroneous ; but it is, nevertheless,
the case that the Greeks were accustomed to the expression of personal feeling through a chorus. Pindar
speaks to us quite directly in this way. It is strange to
us, and we have no real parallel to it except the singing
of a certain type of hymn by congregations whom we
know quite well not to be uttering their own feelings.
Even so, we must be cautious ; for the chorus expresses a mood rather than a conviction. To infer
Euripides from his choruses is something like inferring
Shakespeare from his Sonnets ; but there too, as we
know, something can be done.

There is also the last play of Euripides, the *Bacchae*,
which is not so much a drama as the celebration of a
certain form of religious belief, the ecstatic worship of
Dionysus. This play has always been the great difficulty to the theory of Euripides as a rationalist. It

celebrates, in fact, the triumph of every element of religion which, from the common point of view, is held to be irrational. Its opponents are represented, not only as foolish or wicked, but as ridiculous, and though the god himself is pictured as something strange and remote, and even as vindictive, it is with the calm vindictiveness of an outraged natural law. If we had that play only, we should say that Euripides was an Orphic votary, and no doubt we should be wrong ; but it is, nevertheless, quite easy to show that, all through his life, he was deeply affected by that strange religion, the significance of which we are only now beginning to understand.

One of the lines which afforded most amusement to Aristophanes and the rest was the famous ' Who knows if life be death and death be life ? ' This has been strangely called ' sophistry,' but is really Orphicism. According to that doctrine the body is the tomb of the soul, which can only return to its true life with the gods after a long course of purification. Even in the *Alcestis*, we find already a preoccupation with Orphicism. There is nothing to be found stronger than Ἀνάγκη, Necessity, the great Orphic divinity, and there is no spell against her even in the Thracian tablets that Orpheus wrote. In Hippolytus we have a study of the Orphic saint, as is shown by the taunts of his father Theseus : ' Take Orpheus for thy lord and play the Bacchus, holding in honour the vapour of his many scriptures.' Instances could easily be multiplied, but these are enough. They do not entitle us to say that Euripides was an Orphic ; but they do entitle us to say that, like Plato after him, he was fascinated by that strange religion of original sin, purification, and redemption.

But, if that is so, we shall have to say that, so far from being an innovator, Euripides had at least a romantic

attachment to what was archaic and primitive.   Well,
there are other things which confirm this view.   He
is evidently very learned in religious antiquities of all
kinds.   A very small knowledge of Greek religion will
carry you through Aeschylus and Sophocles ; but,
when you come to Euripides, you find you are in the
hands of a specialist and have to know details.   His
latest play takes the drama back to its original theme,
the triumph of Dionysus.   The Prologue and the *deus
ex machina* are really archaisms ; for they must have
existed when there was only one actor.   The old
trochaic tetrameter is increasingly common in the later
plays.   And, if it is true that Euripides introduces the
vocabulary of common life into his plays, it is no less
true that he uses old words taken from the elegiac and
lyric poets which cannot be matched in Sophocles.

On the whole, I take it that Euripides was a man who
could find but little satisfaction in his own times, and
was very willing to look back to the past for it.   And
that, I believe, was in large measure because he was an
intensely patriotic Athenian, who shared the general
uneasiness as to the future of democracy which marked
the end of the fifth century B.C.   Here again, however,
we must be careful.   We must not try to construct a
moral and political creed by stringing together fragments of which the context is wholly conjectural, or
isolated expressions of feeling where the intention is
purely dramatic.   If we proceed in that way, we may
easily piece together a picture of Euripides as an oli-
garch or an extreme democrat, just as we please.   There
is, for instance, a fragment of the *Phoenix* which extols
the virtue of birth in a way which reminds us of Pindar
and his contempt for ' taught goodness.'   There are
other passages which breathe the spirit of Theognis.
But this is all beside the mark.   The real point is that,
being essentially a dramatist, and also a man very sensi-

tive to the disquiet of his age, he has over and over again given utterance to the feeling which many of the best men, and not a few of the worst, entertained with regard to the problems of the time.

That feeling was this. The democracy of Athens had become great just because it was ready and willing to obey the guidance of its best men ; but even before the death of Pericles a change had come over it in this respect. It had begun to be jealous of all superiority, whether of breeding or intelligence, and to be impatient of everything that went beyond the middling and the ordinary. Over and over again we hear of the φθόνος to which all higher natures are exposed. The fate of Alcibiades was the most striking instance of this. Alcibiades had his faults, of course, but the ruin of his career was due rather to his virtues. Had he been a worse man, he might very possibly have made himself tyrant of Athens. But the memory of Pericles and the influence of Socrates kept him from that, and he failed because he aspired to fill a position which no one would tolerate any longer. From this point of view, it is interesting to notice the prevailing tradition that Euripides wrote the Epinician ἐγκώμιον on Alcibiades's victory at Olympia. It may well be true, and it has a certain pathos. The days for that sort of thing were long gone by ; but Euripides, we have seen, was a man who lived, at least in spirit, in better times. In any case, he often gives dramatic expression to a state of feeling which must have been common among his friends. He makes Hecuba say : ' There is no mortal that is free. A man is either a slave to wealth or circumstance, or the voice of the majority and the written laws keep him from showing his character as he thinks right.'

It is this feeling which leads to utterances that sound immoral. As in all times of feebleness, the ' strong

man ' became the ideal.   In our own days we have
seen how the reaction against democracy inspired first
Carlyle and then Nietzsche with this conception.   The
deadening influence of contemporary mediocrity makes
men long for a ' hero ' or a ' superman ' who will
trample down all conventions and break the fetters of
custom.   The doctrine that ' Might is right ' appeals
to them more and more.   At such times, very unlikely
people are exalted into heroes.   Frederick the Great
was, in sober truth, not exactly that.   At Athens, a
still stranger ' hero ' was the fashion, Archelaus of
Macedon.   Plato has represented all this for us in the
Gorgias.   We do not know who Callicles was, or indeed
whether he was a real personage at all ; but Plato has
drawn in him the perfect embodiment of this view of
life, the view which Plato felt it most necessary to deal
with.   Archelaus is the ideal of Callicles, and it is not
without significance that Euripides ended his life at his
court.

This view easily passes into sheer immorality.   In
the *Heraclidae*, Iolaus says : ' Long ere this have I
learnt of my own experience and not from others that the
righteous man is there for his fellows, and not for himself ; he that seeks his own is useless indeed for the
State and hurtful to his fellow-man ; but for himself is
best.'   That is what Thrasymachus says in the *Republic*
—ἀλλότριον μὲν ἀγαθόν, οἰκεία δὲ βλάβη—and it
was a common belief in those days.   It is monstrous,
however, to accuse Euripides of immorality because he
has given dramatic expression to an extreme form of a
sentiment he knew only too well.   And, indeed, it can,
I think, be shown that Euripides had actually found
something like the same answer to the problem of the
' strong man,' as Plato found later on.

There is one play which, as it seems to me, is more
definitely intended to teach a lesson, to solve a moral

problem, than usual, though this is done by strictly
dramatic means. I infer this from the choice of the
leading characters.   The Dorian hero Heracles—a
very different person from the jovial Athenian god of the
same name, whom Euripides had brought before us in
the *Alcestis*—was the ideal figure of those who preached
the return to Nature in those days. Pindar had sung
how Heracles had driven the cattle of Geryones without
paying a price for them, as an instance of how the law
of Nature justifies the most violent deed, and the verses
are duly quoted by Callicles in the *Gorgias*, as they
doubtless were over and over again in such circles.
Euripides has left us an immortal study of this very
Heracles, and he has contrasted him with Theseus, his
Ionic counterpart, who had become the traditional representative of the best spirit of Athenian democracy,
an idealized Pericles. It is noticeable that, so far as
can be made out, the plot of the *Heracles* is altogether
the invention of the poet. Tradition did not bring
Theseus into connexion with Heracles at all. We
hear nowhere else of the tyrant Lycus who persecutes
Amphitryon, Megara, and the children of Heracles.
Above all, the madness of Heracles, in which he
slaughters his own children, is put at the end of his
labours, a thing that is never done elsewhere.

We note once more in passing the extremely free
handling of mythological subjects which was open to a
tragic poet. If an Athenian audience had had any definite views about the life of Heracles, such a plot would
have been impossible. It is clear, at the same time,
that this reconstruction of the plot must have been
undertaken with a purpose, and we can still, I think, see
what that was.

In the first place, Lycus is introduced to represent the
hatefulness of tyranny, a point which is still further em-
phasized by the character of Iris, the messenger of Hera.

Here Euripides reproduces an old Aeschylean piece of stage-craft. Lyssa, Madness, who is sent by Hera to work the ruin of Heracles, has no taste for her task. She comes of the older stock of gods, and she only acts with reluctance as the minister of oppression. We are reminded of Hephaestus in the *Prometheus*. Iris plays the part of Cratos and Bia. She sneers at Heracles and his alleged divine parentage. Now that Heracles has finished his labours, she tells us, the protection of Zeus is withdrawn from him, and Hera may work her will. She will send madness on him ; for she wishes him to kill his children and, as Iris says with insufferable arrogance, ' I will it too.'

The revolting picture of the character of Iris is due to a very deep feeling in the mind of Euripides. This has been quaintly expressed by the older critics. Euripides, they say, hated heralds, just as he hated women and athletes, and it is very certain that most of the personages of this class whom he has introduced are odious. The fact is that this is the favourite way of bringing out the hatefulness of absolute power or tyranny. There is a certain glamour about the tyrant himself, though in the case of Lycus it is reduced to a minimum ; but the essential lowness and vulgarity of tyranny comes out in its subordinate instruments. The tyrant's order, when conveyed through the mouth of a subaltern, is seen as the hateful thing it is. That is why the heralds in Euripides are so unpleasing, and Iris herself, as Hera's herald, shares their general character.

At the same time, it is just in the speech of Iris that we get the key to a great deal of the play. It is fundamental that Zeus protects Heracles so long as he is engaged in his labours, but that now he is exposed to the enmity of Hera. The wild and untamed character of the Dorian hero is only of value when it is engaged in the service of mankind. It has not that greater strength which can rest from its labours and be of service in peace as well as in war.

That, I think, is what Euripides meant us to understand by the Heracles. The strong man is only of value so long as he uses his strength in the service of mankind. When he is released from that service, his strength becomes a danger to himself and to those that are nearest and dearest to him.

And this is marked by the character of Theseus, the type of Athenian φιλανθρωπία.[1] Euripides takes advantage of the fact that Heracles was worshipped as a god in Attica to introduce Theseus as his protector and friend. Sophocles makes Theseus play a similar part in the *Oedipus at Colonus*, which, it is important to remember, was later in date than the *Heracles*. The idea was Euripides's own, and it is quite likely that Sophocles borrowed it from him. From the time of the *Eumenides* the ἐπιείκεια and φιλανθρωπία of Athens had often been celebrated, and the reception of the Heraclids in Attica was a favourite theme of patriotic orators. But there is more, I take it, in the *Heracles* than mere patriotism, and I have tried to show what that was.

In the study of Euripides I have been guided all through by Plato. That great dramatist has left us some marvellous studies of the spiritual unrest, not so much of his own time, as of the days of his early youth. It was to the questionings of those days that Plato sought to find an answer, and his artistic genius led him to embody the doubts and strivings of the last generation in his dialogues. Critics who look for contemporary controversies and personal references in Plato miss the point altogether. The dialogues are not directly concerned with Plato's own time at all.

[1] See p. 120, inf. (*Humanism in Education,* p. 106).

He did not think it possible fully to commit his own teaching to writing. But he did give us a marvellous picture of the generation that came before his own, and it is for that reason, I believe, that we may safely follow his guidance in the interpretation of Euripides.

LANGUAGE AND LITERATURE
STUDIES AT ST. ANDREWS, 1411 TO 1911

Reprinted from VOTIVA TABELLA, 1911

WITH the single exception of History, Philology, or the study of Language and Literature, is the youngest department in our Faculty of Arts. In some respects it is still in its infancy. Romance and Teutonic philology are not twenty years old, and English has only been recognized for half a century. Even classical study is comparatively recent. Latin was not firmly established till the second half of the seventeenth century, and no provision was made for the teaching of Greek till the eighteenth. During the latter century St. Andrews was more or less decadent, and it is substantially correct to say that real classical study only began with the revival of the University in the nineteenth century, and that its growth was slow because that revival was slow. Unless we take account of the long and bitter struggle which ended in the tardy and grudging recognition of humanistic studies, it is impossible to form a just estimate of their present state among us. It is certain that philology is more backward in Scotland than in many European countries ; but quite as certainly that is not due to any unfitness of the Scottish people for its pursuit. If we consider the amount and quality of the philological work done by Scotsmen trained in England or on the Continent, it would seem rather that we have a real gift for it. In proportion to its population, Scotland has produced as many learned men as any other country ; the trouble is that it has hitherto proved very difficult to raise a home-bred scholar. There can be no doubt, however, that this backwardness is due to definite historical causes which have almost ceased to operate at the present day, except as a deadweight of tradition. Some of these causes are common to all the Scottish Universities, and some are peculiar to ourselves.

I

St. Andrews was founded as a medieval University in the strictest and narrowest sense of the word. It was too late for the first revival of letters, and too early for the second. The *cursus philosophicus* which the Middle Ages had inherited from the Pythagoreans and Plato was exclusively scientific ; and, though efforts had been made to graft the study of ' the authors ' upon it, this was considered dangerous to orthodoxy in the early fifteenth century. There was therefore no place for the study of Languages and Literature in the University curriculum of that age. It is true that the Renaissance had begun in Italy ; but in 1411 Scotland was effectively cut off from Italy by its prolonged adherence to Benedict XIII. (Pedro de Luna, whose arms appear on our ancient seal). Even France had renounced his obedience after the Council of Pisa, and Scotland was in full communion with Spain alone among European countries. The University of Salamanca (which also displays the arms of Pedro de Luna) might have helped us, but it does not appear that it did. The new University had to be manned by ecclesiastics who had studied at Paris before the Council of Pisa, and these were the last people in the world to be touched by the spirit of Humanism. They had no idea beyond ' reading ' the *libri consueti*, that is, the Latin versions of certain works of Aristotle. This was done *more parisiensi*, that is to say, by dictating sections

E

of the text along with the paraphrases of whoever were the approved doctors of the time. In this respect, the beginnings of St. Andrews form a striking contrast to those of Aberdeen, which was founded in 1494, and was influenced by Humanism from the first. The Humanism of the North never reached us, and all we can boast in this connexion is that Hector Boece, the friend of Erasmus and the first Principal of Aberdeen, was a native of Dundee, a city in our province and now intimately associated with our University.

There was indeed a brief moment of hope for us in the short interval between the foundation of Aberdeen and the Battle of Flodden. Alexander Stewart, the natural son of King James iv., was made Archbishop of St. Andrews, and consequently Chancellor of the University, at an early age. However irregular his appointment may have been, his education was specially designed to fit him for the position. Above all, he enjoyed the instruction of Erasmus himself, who mentions the Greek compositions he wrote for him at Siena. He tells us, in the language of the time, that the Archbishop was dedicated to ' Christ and the Muses,' and we hear of a sort of pilgrimage to the cave of the Sibyl at Cumae. Had he lived it cannot be doubted that he would have found the means to introduce some tincture of Humanism into the University ; but his untimely death at Flodden put an end to any such projects, and the first century of our existence passed away without seeing even the beginnings of literary study.

II

Towards the middle of the sixteenth century there was another gleam of hope. Cardinal Beaton was not averse to Humanism, and it seems that he contemplated doing what his predecessor had been prevented from accomplishing. At any rate, in 1540, his cousin, Archibald Hay, addressed a *Panegyric* to him in which he showed a full sense of what the times required. He urged that Latin, Greek, and Hebrew should be taught, and even suggested readers in Syriac and Arabic. Hay became Principal of St. Mary's in 1546, but he only held the office for a year, and nothing was done.

It is true that in the New Foundation of St. Mary's College in 1553 a first attempt was made to make provision for ' the tongues ' by the appointment of an *orator* and a *grammaticus*. It does not appear, however, that these offices were conceived in a humanistic spirit. The University continued to express itself then and long afterwards in the uncouth and debased jargon which had practically disappeared from the rest of Europe. At this date, learning was mainly Protestant, both in France and in England. The tardy reception of the Reformation in Scotland now cut it off from real scholarship just as effectually as its fidelity to the Antipope had done at an earlier date.

The first Reformers were naturally brought into contact with Continental scholars, and this was to bear some fruit for a time before long. In 1534 Erskine of Dun brought a Frenchman, Petrus de Marsiliers, to teach Greek at Montrose, and Andrew Melville learnt that language from him before he came to St. Andrews as a student in 1559, and his nephew, James Melville, whose Diary is our chief source of information for this period, was told at a later date how his uncle had astonished the regents by reading Aristotle in the original. That, however, was only a passing portent, and no one seems to have followed his example. The country was now in the throes of the Reformation, and men had other things to think of.

III

It might be supposed that the establishment of the Reformed religion would lead to the introduction of classical studies, but nothing of the sort happened. In spite of the Reformation the curriculum remained thoroughly medieval in character. A few things were dropped as 'superstitious,' and the rest went on precisely as before. James Melville, who entered St. Leonard's College in 1571, eleven years after the official recognition of the new order of things, has fortunately left us an account of his course, which may be rendered as follows in modern language. In his first year he began with the Rhetoric of Cassander, the eminent divine of Louvain and Cologne, and in a note he adds that he ' heard ' one speech of Cicero, the *Pro rege Deiotaro*. That was the only concession made to modern ideas, and it will be seen that it is a very little one. After this the regent took his class through a compendium of philosophy, composed by himself, and covering the ground of the *Categories*, the *De interpretatione*, and the *Prior Analytics*. James did exercises in the conversion of syllogisms, and he must have begun geometry ; for he mentions that a fellow-student helped him with the *Pons asinorum*. The second year was occupied with the *Posterior Analytics*, the *Topics*, and the *Sophistici Elenchi*, along with Arithmetic and ' the Sphere,' that is to say, the astronomical treatise of Johannes de Sacrobosco, the most authoritative manual of the Ptolemaic system. This implies a fair knowledge of plane and solid geometry. In the third year he went through five books of the *Ethics*, and the Aristotelian works on Natural Philosophy, eight books of the *Physics* and the *De ortu et interitu*, better known as the *De generatione et corruptione*. The fourth year was entirely given up to Astronomy. The class went through Aristotle's *De coelo* and the *Meteorologica* with a more exact study of ' the Sphere.' A good deal might have been learnt from such a course as this if it had been conducted with any knowledge or intelligence, and if the teacher at least had been able to read his text-books in the original ; but this was not the case. No regent had ever lectured on a Greek book in Scotland at this date. James Melville himself was the first to do so later on, and that was at Glasgow, not at St. Andrews. It is important to observe that it was the same regent who took the class right through the course from beginning to end, according to a curious custom which had grown up in Scotland and long survived. Melville's regent was a kindly man, and he speaks of him with affection ; but when his almost legendary uncle re-turned from abroad, and he had the opportunity of listening to a real scholar, he was made to feel that ' all he had got was some terms of Art in philosophy with-out light or solid knowledge.' His final judgment on the regents of his day is that ' as for languages and the Arts and Philosophy, they had nothing at all but a few books of Aristotle which they learnt pertinaciously to babble and flyte upon, without right understanding or use thereof.' Even in his student days he felt there was something lacking. He says, ' I would gladly have been at the Greek and Hebrew tongues, because I read in our Bible that it was translated out of Hebrew and Greek ; but the languages were not to be gotten in the land. Our regent began and teached us the A, B, C of the Greek, and the simple declinations, and went no further.' The good man probably went as far as he could. The fact that the medieval curriculum survived both the Revival of Learning and the Reformation without substantial change is the cardinal fact in the history of St. Andrews Uni-versity. It is intelligible enough that it should have

survived even longer after weathering these two storms
successfully.

IV

There were, of course, attempts at reform, but they
were all defeated by the passive resistance of the regents,
which became active resistance upon occasion.   They
would probably have found little to quarrel with in the
First Book of Discipline, if that had ever been ratified.
As a scheme of national education it has been justly
praised, and it would have secured that students should
come to the University well prepared for humanistic
studies.   Unfortunately, they would have found no
humanistic teaching when they got there.   Knox was
not a humanist, and the proposals of the *First Book of
Discipline* for the organization of the Universities are
quite inadequate.   The leading idea of the scheme was
the specialization of the colleges to particular faculties.
That was a wise provision, and bore some fruit at
St. Andrews later on ; but the only faculties contemplated were the three traditional ' superior faculties ' of
Divinity, Law, and Medicine, with so much of the
quadrivium as was specially related to each.   It was
only in the divinity college that languages were to be
taught at all, and these were, of course, to be Greek and
Hebrew.   That was forced upon Knox by the practical
need of training a Reformed ministry ; but it was
confined to the first year of the course, and the only
profane author suggested was ' one book of Plato,'
whatever that may import.   It is possible that Knox had
some idea of counteracting the dominant Aristotelianism
in this way ; but Aristotle, or what passed for Aristotle,
was to remain supreme for a long time yet.   Such Arts
teaching as was to be given in the other two colleges
was to be of the traditional character ; for Knox and his

coadjutors were completely dominated by the medieval idea that ' the tongues ' and ' the authors ' are the province of the school and not of the university. All that can be said for the scheme is that, if the schools had been organized as the *Book of Discipline* proposed, the hand of the University would probably have been forced, and classical studies would have secured recognition at an earlier date than they actually did.

The next attempt at reform marks a great advance on humanist lines. In 1563 a petition was presented to the Lords of the Articles praying for a reformation of St. Andrews University on the ground of misappropriation of revenues and inadequacy of teaching. It is set forth that ' few sciences, and specially they that are most necessary, that is to say the tongues and humanity, are in any part taught in the said city.' We may trace here the hand of George Buchanan, who had returned to Scotland, and was reading Livy with Queen Mary. At any rate, Buchanan was one of the Commissioners appointed to visit the University, and an entirely new scheme was drafted. The idea of specializing the colleges was retained, but one of them was to be a College of Humanity, the other two being reserved for Philosophy and Divinity. That would have involved a complete breach with medieval tradition, and the course which was drafted for the humanity college embodied all the best features of contemporary humanism. Unfortunately this scheme too remained a dead letter, and even when Buchanan was made Principal of St. Leonard's (or, as the humanists preferred to call it, *gymnasiarcha*), it does not appear that he succeeded in doing anything. James Melville's description of his course of studies refers to a period just subsequent to Buchanan's principalship, and the ' hearing ' of the *Pro rege Deiotaro* with the perfunctory teaching of the Greek alphabet seem to be the only traces left of the great humanist's influence.

In these circumstances, a new Commission was called for in 1579, of which Buchanan was once more a member, but its recommendations mark a further advance on those of 1563. In the interval, Andrew Melville had returned to Scotland, and had been re-forming the University of Glasgow on lines which went rather beyond the ideas of Buchanan. Melville had been a pupil of Turnebus and Ramus, and had been closely associated with Joseph Justus Scaliger, and he therefore represented a more developed stage of humanism. He succeeded at Glasgow, but only by doing the work of three or four regents in his own person, and at this time graduates of St. Andrews were glad to enter as students at Glasgow. It is natural that Andrew Melville, as a St. Andrews man, should be called upon to undertake the reformation of his own University, but he was very reluctant to do so. It re-quired ' compulsators of Horning,' that is, the threat of outlawry, to make him give up his post in the west ; but he had to come, and in 1580 he became Principal of St. Mary's College. Troubles now began in real earnest. So far as we can see, the regents had been able to resist Buchanan by the simple method of ignoring his schemes ; but no such policy was possible with Andrew Melville, and open war broke out between the medi-evalists and the new learning. The regents were nomi-nally Protestants, but they had the souls of Dominican friars, and Melville's life was one of ' feghting and fasherie,' as his nephew tells us in words which it would be a shame to modernize.

Andrew Melville set himself to get rid of the system by which the regents took their class right through the course. The ' fixation ' of the regents was the key-stone of his whole scheme of reformation. One of the regents of St. Salvator's was to teach Greek ; and, what must have seemed a still more ominous proposal, the Principal of St. Leonard's was to lecture regularly on Plato. Melville had introduced the Logic of Ramus at Glasgow, and he ventured to dispute the infallibility of Aristotle. He had read Aristotle, and the regents only knew him through the traditional interpretation ; but Aristotle was their ' breadwinner,' and they raised the cry of ' Great is Diana of the Ephesians,' as James Melville puts it. He was, however, beginning to make some headway, and his nephew tells us that he had actually persuaded some of the regents to read Aristotle in his own tongue, when he became involved in ecclesiastical disputes which do not concern us here. Whatever the merits of these may have been, it is certain that they were fatal to the studies of our University, all the more so as they embroiled Melville with King James vi., who, with all his faults, was just the man to understand what he was trying to do. From 1584 to 1586 Melville had to take refuge in England. In 1590 he was made Rector, but was soon deprived of the office on the curious ground that he had not observed the reformation of the University. Subsequently he became Dean of the theological faculty ; but in 1606 the end of all things came. He was summoned to London, and the King threw him into the Tower, where he remained for four years. It is pleasant to think that the pupil of Turnebus and the friend of Scaliger was visited in his captivity by Casaubon. He was at last released in order to take up a professorship in the University of Sedan, where he spent the remaining eleven years of his life, not without troubles, and Scotland saw him no more.

It seems certain that Andrew Melville's schemes were never carried out except in the most imperfect way.

A little elementary Greek may have been taught for a time at St. Salvator's, but the flame soon flickered out.   The second century of our history ended like the first, without seeing any provision made for classical study at St. Andrews.   In 1621 the last vestiges of the reforms were swept away.   On the ground that it had ' bred confusion in the professions of sciences,' Parliament revoked the ratification of 1579, and ' restored the first foundations of the said colleges.'   It seemed that all hope was gone ; but the beginnings at least of better things were made in that very year.   To understand how this came about we must look a little further afield.

V

What the humanists and reformers had failed to achieve in the sixteenth century was attempted with rather more success by men of the world in the seventeenth.   The foundation of a new college at Aberdeen by the Earl Marischal in 1594 may be taken as the beginning of the new period.   It is true that the ideals of this period were less comprehensive and less lofty than those of Andrew Melville ; but, perhaps for that very reason, they were realized at least in part.   As we shall see, the resistance of the regents was determined, and even unscrupulous ; but it is true nevertheless that the foundations on which we are still endeavouring to build were laid at this time.

It must be remembered here that, though the University had successfully shut its doors to classical study, there was no lack of classical scholarship in Scotland. The king of Scots had to conduct the external affairs of the realm in the Latin tongue, and it was essential, even in the fifteenth century, that he should have secretaries capable of penning dispatches which would not excite the laughter of foreign courts. The great ecclesiastics before the Reformation were under the like necessity. Men like Reid, Bishop of Orkney, were scholars themselves and knew the value of scholarship. Further, it had more and more become the custom for young noblemen to travel abroad with a 'pedagogue,' and they soon learnt that they could not go far in the world without Latin. The ability to write a more or less Ciceronian epistle, and even to turn out a tolerable copy of verses, was as necessary as a passport to the best society in those days as skill in fence and horsemanship. We have seen something of this in the case of Archbishop Alexander Stewart, while, at a later date, St. Andrews has the honour of numbering the 'admirable' Crichton among her sons. However legendary his talents and virtues may be, it is of importance to realize that such an ideal was possible in Scotland. Nor were such ambitions confined to the great nobles. Many a Scottish soldier of fortune had a touch of scholarship. It will be remembered that Dugald Dalgetty got his Latinity from Marischal College in Aberdeen.

In the seventeenth century St. Andrews already attracted a number of young noblemen—Montrose and Argyll among the number—and they were naturally followed by the sons of the lesser nobility and the lairds. This would at once create a demand for classical teaching. It is, however, to the nobility of the robe that we owe our first endowment for classical scholarship, and it is pleasing to think that it may have been due in part to the influence of the banished Andrew Melville. The Aberdeen physician and scholar, Arthur Johnston, had resided for a time with Melville at Sedan after taking his degree at Padua, and his patron was Sir John Scot of Scotstarvit, who at a later date bore the expenses of publishing the *Deliciae*

Poetarum Scotorum. Besides this, Sir John had been a student at St. Leonard's in Melville's time, and he had enough scholarship to write a Latin poem on the departure of King James for his southern kingdom. It is possible, therefore, to trace a thread of continuity between the efforts of the sixteenth century and those of the seventeenth. In 1620 Sir John mortified a sum of 8000 merks ' or thereby ' to endow a ' regent and professor of humanity ' in St. Leonard's, being moved thereto ' for the love and favor I do carie to St. Leonards College in St. androis wher I and my umquhile father were educat in philosophie.' This foundation was ratified in 1621, in the very year that Parliament gave the *coup de grâce* to Melville's reformation. Sir John was a shrewd man, and it is to be supposed that he knew what was going on and resolved to counteract it so far as he could.

The regents of St. Leonard's were not at all likely to refuse an endowment of 8000 merks, though they had little intention of carrying out the founder's intention. In these days the misappropriation of endowments was a fine art among us, and long remained so. The first professors of Humanity, Mr. Alexander Scot and Mr. Norrie, were harassed in every way. The chair was cheated of its share in the Priory revenues when they were attached to the College, and the regents of St. Salvator's complained that it created an inequality between the Colleges and was likely to leave their schools of philosophy ' desolate.' It should have been founded, if at all, in a neutral place. The master of the Grammar School also complained later that the ' private school ' of Humanity at St. Leonard's damaged him by drawing away his best pupils. It is to be noted that the term ' private school ' at this date means ' tutorial class ' as opposed to the ' public schools ' or formal lectures. The fact

that the new professor taught instead of 'reading,' that
is, dictating in the medieval way, is regularly put in the
forefront of the complaints that were made.

In 1641 a Commission, consisting mostly of old St.
Salvator's men, was appointed, and they ordained that
the new professor should teach in some neutral part
of the town and that he should not be allowed to teach
'grammar' even in his chamber.   He was also to take
rank below the four philosophy regents.   All this
seemed very satisfactory, no doubt, but the regents
forgot that they had to deal with a Senator of the
College of Justice and 'Director of the Chancellary.'
He was a St. Leonard's man, and he knew the sort of
people they were.   We may be sure, too, that the author
of that *chronique scandaleuse*, *The Staggering State of
Scottish Statesmen*, had a keen eye for sinister intrigues.
In any case, he had very prudently inserted a 'clause
irritant' in the deed of foundation, and he now raised
a summons of declarator, and had the whole trans-
action made null and void.   The College had to
refund the money, and the chair was abolished.   That
was not enough for Lord Scotstarvit, however.   He
was determined that St. Leonard's should have a
chair of Humanity, whether the regents liked it or not,
and in 1644 he petitioned Parliament to re-establish
the chair in such a way as to exclude effectually the
possibility of his wishes being disregarded.   The
petition was granted and the Act was passed.   There-
upon the regents of St. Salvator's, who had been making much of the inequality between the Colleges, went
with Lord Cassilis, the representative of the Kennedy
family, to Parliament and asked that they too might
have a chair of Humanity.   Their prayer was granted,
and the result of all the opposition to the plans of Lord
Scotstarvit was that St. Andrews got two professors of
Humanity instead of one.   In the circumstances we

cannot feel surprised that the founder retained the patronage of the chair in his own hands and those of his heirs, an arrangement which had a curious result later on. The fourth Duke of Portland married the heiress of the family, the daughter of the celebrated General Scott, and four professors of Humanity were appointed by an English duke during the nineteenth century. The patronage of the chair was not transferred to the University till the Commissioners under the Act of 1889 abolished private patronage, and Professor W. M. Lindsay is the first occupant of the chair to be elected by the University itself.

VI

The regents were foiled in their endeavours to prevent the study of Latin in the University ; but before the seventeenth century closed they had to face the still more serious question of the study of Greek. It is impossible to understand the policy which was adopted in this matter unless we consider it in the light of what was going on elsewhere, and especially in the Town's College, now the University, of Edinburgh. This has been elucidated by Sir Alexander Grant, and in the light of his researches the meaning of many things otherwise obscure becomes plain. To put the matter briefly, the plan adopted was as follows. It was clearly no longer possible to resist the admission of classical studies to the University, but it was possible to render them comparatively innocuous by preventing the teaching of Greek in the schools. To establish a regent or Professor of Greek was to diminish the importance of the Professor of Humanity, who was in theory Professor of Greek as well as of Latin ; and, if Greek was not taught in the schools, there was no

danger of it becoming an important subject in the
Universities.

In 1672 the Privy Council was induced, 'in the
interests of the advancement of learning,' to forbid the
teaching of Greek in schools altogether. To teach
Greek at school, they said, prejudiced the Universities
'by rendering some of their professors altogether useless.' It is to be hoped that the Lords of the Council
saw the humour of this declaration ; but the regents
of St. Leonard's took it quite seriously. They were
favourable, for the reasons indicated above, to the
establishment of a Greek professorship, but they
coupled with this a demand for the suppression of Greek
in the school. The grounds they assign are that 'there
are a number of silly men who, having hardly a smatter
of Greek themselves, do take upon them to teach others
to the great disadvantage of many good spirits.' This
is the way in which the regents thought fit to speak of
the burgh schoolmasters of Scotland in 1695. We
can see now that, however defective these men's knowledge may have been, they were doing more for Scottish
education than their critics.

After the Revolution, though the General Assembly
and the Universities continued to oppose the teaching of
Greek in schools, and though the University of Edinburgh appealed to the Town Council to put an end to
it as late as the year 1772, a new spirit prevailed in the
counsels of the Government, which may probably be
traced to the influence of Carstairs. The Parlia-
mentary Commission, which decided in 1699 that the
Greek regent should be 'fixed and not ambulatory,'
affords an instructive glimpse of the way in which
Greek was treated, and explains the policy of St.
Andrews in the matter. It was considered necessary
to lay down that the Greek regent should teach 'only
grammar and the proper Greek authors ' ; he was not

to give instruction in ' even so much as any *structura syllogismi*.' Apparently there was a danger that he should be made use of to teach elementary Logic, which had been the subject of the first year in the medieval curriculum. Further, it was ordained that ' for the better encouragement of said fixed teacher of Greek no scholar bred at school in Scotland and not foreign bred ' was to be allowed to study philosophy unless he had learned Greek ' at least for the ordinary year ' under ' the said fixed Greek master.'

In 1699 Francis Pringle came to St. Leonard's as regent, and for three years he had to carry on the old system. In his first year he was regent of the Bachelors; in his second, regent of the Magistrands, and in his third, regent of the *Bajans*, or, as we now call them (no doubt from the analogy of the word ' regent '), the ' bejants.' In 1702 he appears for the first time as Professor of Greek, and in 1705 we find Patrick Haldane as Professor of Greek at St. Salvator's. For the first time, St. Andrews had something like full provision for the teaching of classics. Unfortunately it came too late to be of much use. We know something, from the letters of Pringle which have been preserved, of the decay of the University at his period, when St. Leonard's had ' one country minister after another ' at its head, and the most definite fact about his tenure of the chair which has come down to us is that he had to whip some students who had indulged in Jacobite demonstrations. The union of the Colleges in 1747 did something to arrest their rapid decay ; but we have extremely little information as to the studies of the University at this date. There are practically no eighteenth-century minutes of the Faculty of Arts, and it is impossible to obtain any trustworthy information for that period.

It will be seen that the separation of Greek and Latin, and their assignment to separate professors, is to be explained from the course of events just narrated. Originally Humanity included Greek, but it now meant Latin only.   This still obscures the essential unity of classical philology, and has given rise to the literally preposterous idea that Latin without Greek can be a profitable subject of study in a University.

VII

During the latter part of the eighteenth century, the classical chairs were in the hands of some of the leading members of the Moderate party in the Church.   They were cultivated and scholarly men as a rule, but it is not likely that they had the opportunity of doing work of a high order in their chairs.   John Hunter, who held the Humanity chair from 1775 till 1835, was not only a scholarly man but a scholar.   He produced several editions of Latin authors, but he is best known to the present generation by the beautiful portrait which hangs in the hall of the United College.

With Hunter's professorship we emerge once more into the light of history, and we find that at some unknown date in the eighteenth century the medieval curriculum had at last faded away.   After all that has been said, it is startling to find that it had become the custom for students to attend the Latin and Greek classes during the whole four years of their course. There appears to be no minute of the Senatus or of the College on the subject of this momentous change, and there are no minutes of the Faculty of Arts.   That the change took place is, however, quite certain, and in the early years of the nineteenth century we find that, for this reason, the Latin and Greek classes far out-number all the others.   This fact has had important consequences down to the present day.   It had been a

F

tradition for so long that classical studies were to be carried on throughout the course, that when at last provision was made for graduation with honours, the number of students who took advantage of this was very large in proportion to the size of the University. As early as 1853, seven years before graduation with honours was introduced, Professor Alexander started the Third Greek Class, which is the origin of the present Honours Class, and has gone on ever since.   If we remember that twenty years ago the Third Classes of Latin and Greek at Edinburgh met only in alternate years, it will be seen how important this was.   The tradition still lives, and St. Andrews has often had nearly as many students studying for classical honours as the larger Universities, and on a few occasions it has had a greater number than any of them.

In the early years of honours graduation, St. Andrews was extremely fortunate in its Professors of Greek. Men still living remember the impulse given to classical studies by W. Y. Sellar, who was succeeded in 1863 by Lewis Campbell, the value of whose contributions to Platonic study are only fully recognized now that he has gone.

The next period is marked by the Commission of 1889, which made Greek an optional subject.   That, of course, decreased the numbers of those who take Greek for a pass degree ; but certain other provisions in the Ordinance had the effect of more than doubling the number of those who take honours in Classics.   It was soon felt, however, that the new scheme had been insufficiently thought out, and the University, which has recovered its ancient power of autonomous legislation in these matters, adopted a new scheme of Arts graduation in the present academical year.   So far as can be foreseen, this will encourage the classical student ; but an even more important measure is the institution of a new degree of Bachelor of Letters on the model of the existing degree of Bachelor of Science. There can be no question as to the impulse the latter degree has given to scientific study, and it may reasonably be hoped that the B.Litt. will do as much for philology. On the whole, the outlook seems bright enough, and it must be said that the recent and present successors of our old enemies, the philosophy regents, have more than atoned for the sins of their predecessors, and have shown themselves ready to co-operate with the classical department in every possible way. In particular, there is no doubt that Plato has come to his own at St. Andrews in a way that would do Andrew Melville good to behold if he could witness it.

WHO WAS JAVAN?

*Read before the Classical Association of Scotland,
May 11, 1912*

In the tenth chapter of Genesis there is a list of the
descendants of Noah, that is to say, of all the peoples of
the earth known to the writer. Some of the names are
transparent enough, while others are obscure. It seems
pretty clear that the sons of Japheth represent the
nations of Asia Minor, and it has generally been
assumed that the fourth of them, Javan, stands for the
Greeks. It is certain, at any rate, that in historical
times many Oriental peoples called the Greeks by such
names as Yāvana, Yauna, and Yona. A scholium on
Aristophanes tells us that the barbarians called all
Hellenes Ἰάονες,[1] that is to say, Ionians, and this statement is amply confirmed by the documents which have
been preserved. It is obvious too, that, if Yāvana represents Ionian, it must be a very old name, going back
to the days before the letter *vau* disappeared from the
Ionic dialect, and when the Ionians were still called
Ἰάϝονες. All this would be parallel to the Oriental
use of 'Frank' for European generally. The peoples
of the east knew the Ionians best, and applied the name
to all Greeks indiscriminately.

This account of the matter has been accepted by
historians with a very few exceptions, but it is not quite
so satisfactory as it appears, and it has recently been
called in question by Mr. Edward Robertson of this
University.[2] He maintains that the Oriental references to the Yāvana people do not suit the Ionians as

---

[1] Schol. Ar., *Ach.* 106, πάντας Ἕλληνας Ἰάονας οἱ βάρβαροι ἐκάλουν.

[2] *Notes on Javan*, by the Rev. E. Robertson, B.D., Carnegie Research
Scholar. Reprinted from the *Jewish Quarterly Review*, 1908.

they are represented in our standard histories. There are references to them long before there were any Greeks in Ionia at all, and they are represented as a powerful seafaring people. In fact, they seem rather to occupy the place which tradition assigns to the Phoenicians. But, of course, Mr. Robertson is aware that the tradition regarding the maritime supremacy of the Phoenicians in early times is entirely unconfirmed by archaeological research, and that, even in Cyprus, there is no evidence of Phoenician domination in any part of the island till the time of Xerxes.[1] There is, in fact, no room for the Phoenician thalassocracy of tradition in the early Mediterranean world as we now know it. Mr. Robertson accordingly identifies the Yāvana with the people of Minoan Crete, and he hazards the conjecture that this people came from Babylonia or Southern Arabia. This view is unacceptable for a variety of reasons, of which I shall mention only one. As Mr. Farnell has rightly insisted,[2] incense was unknown in the Homeric age, though it was in common use among the Greeks of later times. It is surely incredible that, if the Yāvana people originated in the very home of frankincense, they did not bring it with them and spread the knowledge of it in the Mediterranean. Nevertheless, Mr. Robertson is certainly right in holding that what we know of the Yāvanas is quite inconsistent with the account of the Ionians given in our histories, and I therefore propose to re-examine that account in the light of recent discoveries. I think we shall find that Javan is Ion after all.

[1] See D. G. Hogarth, *Ionia and the East,* p. 86.
[2] *Greece and Babylon,* p. 306.

I

This is not merely a problem of Greek history ; it really concerns the origin of our own civilization. Everything that distinguishes the European of to-day from the non-European had its birth in Ionia except the Christian religion, and even that has come to us in a form largely moulded by influences which are, in the last resort, Ionian. In any case, it is certainly to Ionia that we must trace the beginnings of our science and our art, our commerce, industry, and politics. All these arose at a time when Athens was in a sort of backwater ; and, though it is true that the influence of this *printemps de la Grèce*, as it has been called, has reached us mainly through Athens, that is just because Athens at a later date concentrated in herself all that was best in the cities of Ionia. So far as we know, Miletus, once a great seaport, but now a poor village some distance from the sea, is the earliest home of the European spirit, while the foundations of exact science were laid by a refugee from the island of Samos. The world's debt to Thales, Anaximander, and Pythagoras is one that it would be difficult to over-estimate. It was Miletus too that explored and colonized the Black Sea, while another Ionian people, the Phocaeans, penetrated to the west. Trebizond and Marseille are both Ionian colonies. Pytheas of Marseille, the Phocaean colony, made the important discovery of Scotland, and may have sailed in sight of St. Andrews Bay long before St. Regulus. I need not remind you that European art also comes from Ionia, though we know now that there was also an early development of art at Sparta, which was too soon arrested. The significance of that fact will appear as we go on. On the whole, we are bound to admit that all that made

Greece what it was, and most of what makes Europe what it is, comes from Ionia in the end.

Are we to say, then, that Ionia was the seat of the earliest civilization in Greek lands ? It is only a few years since such an answer seemed possible. Homer was still supposed to be the beginning of all things, and he was regarded as an Ionian. Nowadays it is true that the date assigned to Homer tends to become earlier and earlier, but we look on him as comparatively modern for all that. The historians of the nineteenth century refused to go further back than the first Olympiad (776 B.C.) ; before that lay only what Grote called ' the past which was never present.' To-day we know a good deal about the third millennium B.C., and the second millennium B.C. is becoming quite familiar. We owe this widening of our outlook to the archaeologists, who have laid bare the remains of what it is safest to call simply the Aegean civilization. Tradition had, indeed, preserved vague memories of this ; but it was not till Schliemann excavated Troy, Mycenae, and Tiryns that it was proved to have had a real existence. Still more important have been the recent excavations at Cnossus and elsewhere in Crete. We now know for certain that the Aegean was the seat of a high civilization which had an unbroken development from the Stone Age down to about 1000 B.C. This civilization was at least as old as, and probably older than, those of Egypt and Babylon, and in all material respects it was at least as advanced. The drainage system of the palace of Cnossus would be hard to match anywhere else before the nineteenth century ; and, artistically, the Aegean civilization stood much higher than those of Egypt and Babylon. The more it is revealed to us, the more we are struck by the naturalism of its decorations, and its mural paintings are a marvel. The Cupbearer of Cnossus is more nearly akin to the figures of a fifteenth-century Italian fresco than to the conventional representations of the human form familiar to us in the Egyptian collections of our museums. The magnificence of the palace of Cnossus shows it to have been the residence of a monarch who was the peer of any Pharaoh, and the art by which he surrounded himself proves that the human spirit was freer here than elsewhere. Tradition has preserved the memory of these kings under the name of Minos, and of their craftsman under that of Daedalus. The intricate foundations of their ruined palace gave rise to the fable of the Labyrinth.

This civilization, which had its centre in Crete, extended as far north as Thessaly ; but, for our present purpose, the main facts are, first, that it included Athens, and secondly, that it did not, in its flourishing days, include Ionia. At Troy in the N.W. and at Rhodes in the S.W. of Anatolia we have abundant remains of a civilization akin to that of Cnossus ; but in what was afterwards known as Ionia there are no such remains of earlier date than what Sir Arthur Evans calls Late Minoan III., that is to say, the period of decadence. This fact, as Mr. D. G. Hogarth points out,[1] calls for explanation. The Aegean unites, it does not separate ; and its coasts form a natural unity with the islands. The only possible ground for the absence of Aegean civilization from Ionia is, he urges, that some great power was dominant there and closed the coast-line to all foreign influences. What that power was is now becoming clear. The people known as Hittites were by no means confined to Syria ; the chief seat of their power was in Cappadocia, and it extended to the shores of the Aegean, as is proved by the rock-hewn image of their great goddess at Mount Sipylus, the image which the Greek sailors of later

[1] *Ionia and the East* (1909).

days called Niobe. We know further that, about
1100 B.C., the Hittites were hard pressed by the
Assyrians, and it is shortly after that time that the late
Aegean remains in Ionia must be dated. The inference is clearly that the Hittites were the people who
kept the Aegean civilization at bay as long as they
could.

II

So far there is no serious divergence of opinion
among our authorities. It is quite another matter when
we come to the question who the men of this great
Aegean civilization were. The natural thing to ask is
' Were they Greeks ? ' ' Were they Hellenes ? ' but
that is not the right way to put the question. Apart
from the fact that these names are of much later date
and only came into use in historical times, the question
assumes that we know who the Greeks or Hellenes
were, which is far from being the case. It looks more
scientific to ask whether the Aegean people were of the
same race as the Hellenes of history, but even that is
hardly a legitimate question. We have no right to
assume that the Hellenes of history were a pure race at
all ; indeed it is highly improbable that they were.
Conquest and migration lead to race-mixture, and
pure races are generally savage. It is more to the
point to ask whether this great people spoke Greek
or a language akin to Greek. Of course we cannot
answer that question decisively till their inscriptions
have been deciphered, and that has not yet been
successfully done. On the other hand, I agree with
Professor Ridgeway in holding that all the probabilities
of the case point in the most distinct fashion to the conclusion that the people of Crete spoke what we should
call Greek in Minoan days. This is highly con-

troversial, of course, and we must now advance
warily.

III

In the first place, we must ask the archaeologists for
some additional facts of Cretan history. They will
tell us that the palace of Cnossus was twice sacked and
burnt down, first about 1400 B.C., and again about
1000 B.C., after which date it was not reoccupied.
This final destruction is attributed to the Dorians,
and no doubt rightly; for in historical times Crete was
mainly Dorian. Possibly the earlier invaders came
from the north too, and these are generally identified
with the Achaians, the people to which the heroes of
Homer belonged. That is possibly right too, but we
must observe that the word 'Achaian' means very
different things to different writers. As a rule, it is
assumed that the Achaians were the earliest 'Greeks'
in the proper sense of the word, and that they imposed
their language upon a non-Greek population, whom
some suppose to have come originally from Africa, and
who were the real authors of the Aegean civilization.
Professor Ridgeway, on the other hand, believes the
Achaians to have been a people of Celtic or Teutonic
origin, and thus accounts for the yellow or red hair of
the Homeric heroes, and for a number of other peculiarities. He holds also that the conquered Aegean
people were 'Pelasgians,' and that the Achaians
adopted their language, which was, therefore, the
language of Homer.

Now this theory of Professor Ridgeway's has been
severely criticized, but the attack has been directed
almost exclusively against his use of the name 'Pelasgians.'[1] In my opinion, the attack has been

[1] J. L. Myres in the *Journal of Hellenic Studies*, vol. xxvii. pp. 170 sqq.

successful from this point of view ; but it is not always observed that Professor Ridgeway's main contention does not depend in the least degree upon his unfortunate use of the name 'Pelasgian.' If we simply say 'Aegean,' which commits us to nothing, let us see how the case stands.

The archaeologists tell us, in the first place, that the Achaians—if we are to call them so—adopted the material civilization of the Aegean people. They rebuilt and reoccupied the palace of Cnossus, and Cnossian art goes on as before, though it is now of inferior quality. The invaders never reached the high level of civilization which had been attained before their coming, and the civilization they had was simply so much of that already existing as they could appropriate. In particular, they continued to use the Minoan system of writing. In such cases, we always find that the conqueror adopts the language of the conquered in a very short time. I need only refer to the Normans and the Franks in support of this view. Analogy seems to require us to assume that the Achaians adopted the existing Aegean language, and not *vice versa*. Invaders of this kind come in comparatively small numbers, and they generally have to take their wives from among the original inhabitants. That alone suffices to settle the question of language ; for children learn their mother-tongue from their mothers.

But we are not confined to any inference from analogy. The island of Cyprus was colonized from Greece in Aegean times, as the remains testify, and the Cypriotes never adopted the later Greek alphabet till the time of the Ptolemies. They continued to use a syllabic script which was doubtless derived from that of the Aegean peoples. Now the dialect of Cyprus is practically identical with that of Arcadia, and tradition

makes the original colonists come from Arcadia.   In
later times Arcadia was entirely cut off from com-
munication with the sea, so that Agamemnon had to
provide ships for the Arcadian warriors who followed
him to Troy.[1]   They were shut up in their mountains
like the Welsh, and it must have been long before the
Trojan War that they colonized Cyprus and Pam-
phylia.   So, too, Cyprus lay for centuries outside the
main stream of Hellenic life.   We have, then, as it
were, two voices—' one is of the sea, one of the mountains '—and they tell the same tale.   The Arcado-
Cypriote dialect is not only Greek, but it is essentially
the Greek of Homer.   It is only in this speech that
men spoke of dwelling in a πτόλις and ordering their
deeds and words according to αἶσα.   It is only in
Cyprus that Ϝάναξ and κασίγνητος have been found
as living words.   In other respects, too, these dialects
are closely akin, and have a marked affinity to the
Ionic of later days.   Kretschmer has recently been led
to postulate a pre-Achaian Greek dialect which ultimately gave birth to Ionic, and it is hard to see how
such a conclusion can be avoided.   I think Professor
Ridgeway is right in holding that this dialect is just
the Arcado-Cypriote, though I certainly should not
call that ' Pelasgian.' [2]

But, if that is so, it is almost an inevitable inference
that the inhabitants of Minoan Crete spoke this
language too.   Their inscriptions have not yet been
deciphered, as we have seen, and their language was
supplanted by Doric in later days ; but there are
abundant indications in their religion and their place-
names that they were in close intercourse with Arcadia
before the Achaians appeared on the scene and cut
their communications with the mainland people.
There is actually a place called Arcadia in Crete

[1] Il., B. 610.   [2] Kretschmer, in *Glotta*, vol. i. pp. 9 sqq.

between Cnossus and Gortyn, while there is a place called Cretea on Mt. Lycaion in Arcadia, which the later Arcadians maintained against the Cretans to be the true birthplace of Zeus. For the story of the birth of Zeus was as much at home in Arcadia as in Crete, and the Arcadian Rhea is plainly the Great Mother who was the chief divinity of the Aegean religion. Again, the Paphian Aphrodite of Cyprus has far more to do with this same Great Mother than with any Oriental goddess. At any rate, the Arcadians thought so ; for there was a temple of the Paphian Aphrodite at Tegea. Everything points to the conclusion that Arcadia, Crete, and Cyprus at one time shared a common civilization. It would be strange if the centre of this civilization differed markedly in language from the extremes.

About 1000 B.C., as we have seen, there was a second and a more serious catastrophe at Cnossus. The palace was once more burnt down ; but this time it was not rebuilt, and the Aegean civilization comes to an end in Crete. This means that the later invaders came in greater numbers than the earlier, and that the somewhat decadent civilization, to which the remains bear witness, was no longer able to absorb them. As Crete was almost entirely Dorian in later days, the greater part of the population must have been put to the sword or expelled. Where would they go ? Not certainly to that part of the Peloponnesus which was also in Dorian hands. The islands of the Aegean were open to them ; for these were never occupied by the Dorians. So was Attica and the coast of the Saronic Gulf, which was under its sway. The thin soil of Attica had saved it, as Thucydides tells us, from foreign invasion. Above all, the western seaboard of Asia Minor invited settlement ; for the Hittite power had decayed, and the Phrygians from Thrace had occupied the *Hinterland*. The Phrygians cared nothing for the sea-coast, and it was therefore perfectly open for emigrants.

IV

That the Ionians were, in fact, to a large extent, settlers from Crete is no mere speculation. Colonies are extremely tenacious of their foundation-legends, and these are usually commemorated in the public worship of the state. Now we know from Pausanias and Strabo that some of the most important Ionian States claimed a Cretan origin. There is a Miletus in Crete as well as in Ionia, and the Milesians of Ionia regarded it as their mother-city. Ion of Chios was a contemporary of Herodotus, and must have been familiar with the foundation-legend of his native state, and he ascribed its origin to Oenopion, the son of Ariadne. Erythrae traced its foundation to a son of Rhadamanthus. Magnesia held that its founder came from the region between Phaestus and Gortyn, and there are many traces of Cretan nomenclature scattered up and down in Ionia.

This is not really inconsistent with the importance of the rôle ascribed by tradition to Athens and Euboea in the settlement of Ionia. It has been mentioned that Athens was one of the seats of Aegean civilization; and, after the fall of Argos and Cnossus, it was doubtless one of the most important left. It is quite likely that the kings of Athens should have taken a part in directing the new colonization. That there was an old connexion between Athens and Cnossus is probable in itself, and that most tenacious of all things, religious custom, points to the conclusion that Athens had in some way acknowledged the religious authority of the Cretan monarchy. As we know from Plato's *Phaedo*,

even in the fourth century B.C., the Athenians sent a
sacred ship annually to Delos, which was then the
centre of Ionian worship. But every Athenian knew
that the original destination of that ship had not been
Delos at all but Crete, and that it had conveyed the
seven youths and seven maids for the Minotaur till
Theseus slew the monster. Does not this suggest
that the religious centre of Ionia had been shifted from
Cnossus to Delos in consequence of the Dorian
conquest of Crete ?

But we are no longer confined to tradition, however
respectable. The link between Aegean and Ionian
civilization has at last been found, and found just
where we should expect to find it, if the view which I
am laying before you is correct. Theodor Wiegand
has been excavating at Miletus for ten years, and has
laid bare much that is of the highest interest ; but
nothing of greater importance than the remains of the
original Aegean colony. These are thus described
by a competent authority [1] :—

' The oldest settlement on Milesian soil lay close to
the coast, about a kilometer from the archaic Acropolis;
. . . at the temple of Athena it was possible to ascertain the existence of a Mycenaean stratum under the
Old Ionic, and the slight but well-preserved walls of
its houses group themselves into a picture which has
many points of contact with late Mycenaean localities
in Crete, for instance, the little town of Gournia on the
Gulf of Mirabello. . . . The pure Aegean civilization without any sort of foreign admixture maintained
itself in continental Greece till about the end of the
second millennium, and considerably longer in the east
of the Mediterranean basin, to which it penetrated
later, and in consequence of external pressure. Here
in Ionia it passes over by a slow metamorphosis into

[1] A. v. Salis in *Neue Jahrbücher*, xxv. p. 129.

the archaic civilization of Eastern Greece. . . . The results gained at Miletus, combined with observations elsewhere, compel us to the conclusion that Ionian Asia Minor did not adopt the specially " geometrical " civilization. It is literally true that at Miletus the dwellings of the old Ionians stand on and among the *débris* of the Mycenaean period. The answer to the question of the relation between the archaic period and the prehistoric age of the second millennium has never yet been given in so clear and simple a form.'

Now, if this is right, the difficulties about Javan all disappear. We are at liberty to believe that Javan existed, and was a great seafaring power long before the Ionian migration, and that the Yāvanas really occupied the place which was usurped in later tradition by the Phoenicians. On the other hand, the early bloom of civilization in Ionia is amply accounted for if we regard it as the direct descendant of the earliest European civilization we know.

There are all sorts of curious pickings to be gathered by any one who cares to follow up this clue. I will only give one example, which has a certain interest. Dionysius of Halicarnassus tells us[1] that Atlas was king in what is now called Arcadia, and dwelt by the Caucasian hill. Of course, the text has been emended by editors who could not believe that the Caucasus was ever in Arcadia, but that is the MS. reading. Now there is also a harbour at Chios called Καύκασος or Καύκασα (Hdt., v. 33) and we know of a deme called Καυκασῆς, and a proper name Καυκασίων in the same neighbourhood.[2] It opens up a wide vista when we find that Atlas and Caucasus, the mountains at the two ends of the οἰκουμένη, both get their names from Arcadia. There may be a certain grim irony in Homer's remark that the Arcadians had naught to do

---

[1] A.R., i. 61. [2] Solmsen, *Beiträge*, pp. 88 sqq.

with the works of the sea.   He probably knew that it
had not always been so.

V

And this brings us to the most interesting part of
our subject—the bearing of all this on the Homeric
question.   As Professor Ridgeway divined, Homer
sings indeed of the Achaians, but he is no Achaian.
He sings in his own language.   We need not now make
him a ' Pelasgian ' for all that.   He belongs to the old
Aegean stock, and is the greatest singer of Javan, and
that perhaps throws light on his name, Ὅμηρος, ' the
hostage.'   As he knows nothing of Ionians in Ionia,
his date must fall before the Ionian Migration ; but
as he also knows of Dorians in Crete, alongside of the
Achaians, he must have seen the beginnings of the
Dorian Migration.   There was doubtless a smaller
body of Dorian settlers there before the final catastrophe.   Meantime his skill was at the service of the
Achaian princes, who had settled down and rebuilt the
palace of Cnossus, or of those who had taken up their
abode at Argos and Mycenae.   That is quite in
accordance with analogy.   We see also why it is that
Homer always looks back to a better time, when men
were stronger than now, and why he delights in de-
scriptions of what is clearly earlier Aegean art.   We
can also explain what has been supposed to be the
Ionian character of the description he gives of the land
of the Phaeacians and the palace of Alcinous.   Such
things have led some to bring him down as late as the
days when Gyges was reigning at Sardis.   If I am
right, it is certainly Ionian life of which he gives us a
picture here, but Ionian life of a time before there were
any Ionians in Ionia.   The court of Alcinous is the
court of a typical Aegean prince, and it is suggestive

that all the names of its inmates are transparent Greek.
It is one of Professor Ridgeway's most suggestive
remarks that, while the names of the earlier heroes are
all easily intelligible, those of the Achaian heroes are
not. Presumably they used the speech of the men
who gave the name κύμινδις to the bird which the
gods called χαλκίς. It is also to be noted that Homer
has little to say about the 'Ιάϝονες by name. That is
only natural in one of the conquered race. He only
lets us know that better men had preceded the Achaians.
When he does use the word 'Ιάϝονες, it is in speaking of
the Athenians. Solon still called Athens πρεσβυτάτην
γαῖαν 'Ιαονίης and the boundary stone between Attica
and Megaris continued to bear witness to the fact that
it divided Peloponnese from Ionia—

$$τάδ' ἐστὶ \ Πελοπόννασος, \ οὐκ \ 'Ιωνία.$$

VI

But it will be said, 'How can the Cretans have
spoken an Indo-European language in the third
millennium B.C., when the accepted view is that the
Indo-European peoples did not enter the Balkan peninsula from their northern home till late in the Bronze
Age, or even early in the Iron Age ?' As to that, I
would point out that the accepted view is a mere speculation which must yield to facts. There is not really
a scrap of evidence to show where the Indo-European
peoples came from or at what date. Indeed, there are
some new facts which suggest that, after all, the highlands of Central Asia were their original home, and
that some of them at least reached the Mediterranean
by way of Asia Minor. The first fact is that recent ex-
plorations in Eastern Turkestan have brought to light

a large number of Buddhist MSS., written in an Indo-
European language which is not closely related to the
Aryan languages, Indian and Persian, but rather to
the languages of Western Europe. The other fact is
that the rulers of the Mitani, on the middle Euphrates,
in the fourteenth century B.C., bore Indo-European
names. The Amarna letters and the inscriptions of
Boghaz-Keui in northern Cappadocia, make it quite
plain that there were Indo-European princes in Syria
and Mesopotamia as well as Hittite. It is too soon to
draw any definite conclusion from these new facts ;
but one thing at least is clear, namely, that they are
wholly inconsistent with the view that the Indo-
Europeans came exclusively from anywhere in the
north towards the end of the Bronze Age. There is a
well-marked route which connects the region of the
Mitani with the Aegean. It passes through the Cilician
Gates, and goes on by Derbe, Iconium, and Colossae,
to the valley of the Maeander, reaching the sea at
Miletus. An Aegean vase has been found between
Iconium and Tyana, and Sir William Ramsay has
discovered Aegean sherds at Derbe. Quite lately ob-
sidian flakes from Melos have been brought to light
on this route.[1] That means that, even in Hittite times,
Aegean art products were exported to the valley of the
Euphrates as they were to that of the Nile. Before
Hittite times the road was open for a migratory people.
These, however, are only possibilities, and my main
contention does not rest on them.

VII

I do not think that any one has yet ventured to say in
so many words that the Minoan Cretans were in fact

[1] See Mr. Ormerod's paper in *C.R.*, xxvi. p. 76.

Ionians ; but there is really no great originality in that
view.   It is remarkable how many recent writers have
just stopped short of stating it.   The late Mr. D. B.
Monro almost divined it.   But for his Pelasgian theory,
Professor Ridgeway would certainly have come to this
conclusion ; and, indeed, since he regards the Ionians
as ' Pelasgians,' he practically does.   Mr. D. G.
Hogarth insists upon the ' sub-Aegean ' character of
Ionian civilization, and there he stops.   Kretschmer
has been driven to postulate a pre-Achaian dialect
which was the mother of Ionic-Attic, but he hastily
adds that of course it was not *called* Ionic.   Why not ?
It seems to me that what we know of Javan settles the
point.   Let me recapitulate.

It is certain that, in historical times, many Eastern
nations gave the name of Yāvana to the people we call
Greeks.

It is also certain that these same nations knew of a
great maritime people called Yāvana long before there
were any Ionians in Ionia.

It is also certain that such a sea-power existed in
Crete, and that it had a continuous civilization from the
Stone Age onwards.

There is evidence that Minoan Crete belonged to
the same circle of civilization as Arcadia and Cyprus ;
the Arcadians must have colonized Cyprus before the
Achaian Age, and the Arcado-Cypriote dialect is
unquestionably Greek, and more nearly related to
Homeric Greek than any other form of the language
known to us.

The Ionians claimed Homer as their own, and their
local tradition was that some of their most important
cities were founded by refugees from Crete.   These
traditions have received important confirmation from
recent excavations at Miletus.

The natural inference from all this is surely obvious,

and I do not hesitate to draw it.   I am not a specialist in these matters, and I shall therefore submit to refutation with perfect equanimity, if my hypothesis can be refuted.   There are, however, cases where an onlooker may see most of the game, and this strikes me as one of them.   The archaeologists have very properly been preoccupied by their immediate business, that of revealing the Aegean civilization to us, and when they have attempted to frame a hypothesis to account for the facts which they had discovered, they have been apt to accept too readily certain theories with regard to what they generally call 'Aryan' immigration from the north, theories which are by no means demonstrated, and are, in fact, improbable.   Sometimes, too, they have allowed themselves to be unduly influenced by the hypothesis known as *Panbabylonismus*.   I see no reason to doubt that the Minoan script will be deciphered in time, and we shall then know for certain who the people were to whom we owe European civilization.   For the present I like to think of them as the men of Javan, and as the direct ancestors of the Ionians.

HUMANISM IN EDUCATION

Read before the Classical Association of Scotland,
May 30, 1914

WHAT do we really mean by education ? Not so long
ago it was considered a sufficient answer to say that to
' educate ' is to *draw out*, but such short-cuts are not
open to the Classical scholar. In the first place, he
knows from experience that etymologies prove nothing,
even when they are right ; and in the second place, he
will have grave doubts as to the particular etymology
here suggested. It will strike him as dangerous
doctrine to say that *educare* with a short *u* is the same
thing as *educere* with a long one, even though the same
root may be ultimately involved. Moreover, if he has
learnt the invaluable lesson that the articles in his
dictionary are generally to be read backwards, he will
be able to go a step further. The dictionary tells him
that *educare* properly means to bring up children, and
that it is figuratively used in poetry and late prose of
rearing plants and animals, but he will suspect that this
is putting the cart before the horse. He knows that the
early Romans were a people of farmers, and that many of
their commonest words were agricultural metaphors, and
so, when he finds Ovid writing from his Pontic exile—

Non ager hic pomum, non dulces educat uvas

our scholar will not conclude that he is speaking meta-
phorically of apples and grapes as children of the
Italian soil ; he will incline rather to the belief that he
is reviving the original sense of an old term of hus-
bandry, as the Augustan poets so often do.[1] In short,

---

[1] Ovid, *ex Ponto*, i. 3, 51. The original sense is well seen in Catullus,
62, 41—*quem (florem) mulcent aurae, firmat sol, edcuat imber.*

educare means ' to grow ' a crop, and it is only by a figure of speech that it is applied to the bringing up of children at all.   It is possible that this false etymology of education may have been useful in discrediting certain mechanical methods of imparting knowledge, but it is misleading in a far deeper way ; for it has led people to overlook the simple truth that you cannot draw anything out of a young soul that is not in it already.   Plato is often appealed to in support of the view that education is a process of ' drawing out,' and this has even been dignified with the name of ' the Socratic method ' ; but the whole point of the argument in the *Meno* is just that, since certain pieces of knowledge can be so drawn out, they must have been learnt by the soul before its birth in a mortal body, and it falls to the ground entirely unless this assumption, or some similar assumption of ' innate ideas,' is made. The Latin language had another word—*seminarium*— which is also an agricultural metaphor, and suggests the true point of view.   The Roman *paterfamilias* would have thought little of the husbandman who tried to grow a crop without sowing the seed and manuring the soil, but if that is properly done it is not even necessary to ' draw out ' the crop ; it will grow of itself.   Everything depends on the seed you sow, and no amount of ' method ' will produce something out of nothing.

A far sounder view of education has been suggested by President Nicholas Murray Butler of Columbia. According to him, it is ' the adjustment of the individual to the spiritual possessions of the race.'   That formula has obviously been suggested by biology, and we must remember that biological analogies are dangerous things.   In particular, we must always be on our guard against any confusion between the processes of organic and spiritual evolution.   The former is automatic in the main ; the latter is for the most part directed by conscious purpose. Still, it was a sound maxim of Greek medicine that ' Art imitates Nature.' It meant that the physician may often get valuable guidance from observation of the automatic processes by which the body defends itself against disease. Hippocrates taught that we should study the *vis medicatrix naturae* with a view to assisting or, if need be, replacing it, and, in the same way, we may perhaps get some light on our subject if we consider the process by which Nature secures the adaptation of the individual organism to its environment. It is possible that what happens automatically in the case of a new body may give us a hint for the proper treatment of a new soul. Now there is an interesting biological speculation—it can hardly, I take it, be called more than that—according to which the development of the embryo is a ' recapitulation ' of the evolution of the species to which it belongs, and that speculation has suggested a very striking theory of education. According to this, the best way of adjusting a new soul to the spiritual possessions of the race will be to guide it in such a way that it shall repeat for itself the processes by which the race acquired the goodly patrimony that is the heritage of every child born into a civilized community. I do not offer any opinion as to whether this recapitulatory theory of education is based on a sound analogy or not ; what I hope to show you is that it is only another way of putting the fundamental principle of Humanism.

I

It is still widely believed that the Humanists were interested only in the composition of Ciceronian prose and of elegant Latin verses, and it is true, of course, that they cared much for these things. On the other hand, every one who has had to become intimately acquainted with any of their work knows quite well that they regarded the revival of Classical Latin as a means and not as an end. It is obviously impossible for me in the time at my disposal to give anything like a complete account of so complex a thing as Humanism ; all I can do is to suggest some very general points of view, and to emphasize certain aspects of the movement that were of vital importance at the time, though they are apt to be overlooked at the present day. That is specially true of the relation between Humanism and science. It is not sufficiently realized that one of the first aims of Humanism was the recovery of Greek science, and that it was the work done by the fifteenth-century Humanists that alone made possible the scientific discoveries of the sixteenth and seventeenth centuries. That is a very important historical truth, and it is not one of purely antiquarian interest. It throws light on the true function of Humanism in a scientific age like the present, and I hope to show that there is something to be learnt from this quarter even with regard to the teaching we give in our schools.

The Humanists were sometimes unjust to the Middle Ages, but there is no need for us to follow them in this. The early medieval schools were by no means hostile to science in principle. In the Faculty of Arts nothing else was studied. The word ' trivial ' still bears witness to the comparatively low esteem in which grammar, rhetoric, and dialectic were held, and the four ' Arts ' of the *quadrivium*, proficiency in which was certified by the Master's *biretum*, were arithmetic, geometry, music (which meant harmonics), and astronomy. These were the ' liberal Arts ' recognized by the Faculty, and the reading of ' the authors,' or what we should call the study of Language and Literature, was regarded as something even lower than the *trivium*. Such things were *ludicra*, as opposed to the *seria*, the liberal Arts, and their pursuit was discouraged and even condemned. That was the orthodox theory and practice, though protests were not wanting. The University of Orléans in particular preserved some tradition of literature, but the final triumph of the Sorbonne made an end of all that. Science itself became more and more traditional, an affair of sums and catechisms, and such things are necessarily dead. There were always a few men, however, who knew that the key of true science had somehow been lost, and who even knew where it was to be looked for. In this place I may mention Michael Scot, whose legendary fame as a wizard still lingers in Fife. In England, John of Salisbury and Roger Bacon were quite aware that the science of antiquity had been far in advance of anything taught in the medieval universities, and they knew, too, that the key to it was to be found in the Greek tongue. The mistake they made was in supposing that they could approach this through the Arabic, instead of by the natural highway which leads through Rome. Even their attempts to approach it directly were doomed to failure, because they had not recovered the ancient way of looking at things, which again was only to be done through Rome. The gulf between medieval and Greek thought was too wide to be bridged. Some intermediary was required, and that could only be secured by the revival of Latin. Let us consider this point first ; it is of capital importance for a just estimate of Humanism.

It is, of course, only a popular error to date the recovery of the Greek language from the fall of Constantinople in 1453. That had nothing to do with it, except in so far as it made it easier to find Greek teachers and press readers. The revival of Greek was completed in Italy considerably before the fall of

Constantinople, and it had begun much earlier. In the first instance, the Renaissance of Greek learning took place in Constantinople itself. That was in the ninth century, under the Patriarch Photius, after the long and dismal iconoclastic controversy had come to an end. It is to be noted, too, that this was before the knowledge of Greek had quite died out in the West. Calabria in South Italy had a Greek-speaking population, and Greek was one of the languages spoken in Sicily, so that the effects of the Renaissance at Constantinople were soon felt at the Court of Syracuse. In proof of this I may mention a typical fact connected with my own studies. One of the best MSS. of Plato (now at Vienna, where it came from Florence [1]) was in Sicily during the twelfth century, and the *Meno* and the *Phaedo* were translated from it for King William the Bad by Enericus Aristippus, a Calabrian Greek who was archdeacon of Catania. He has been identified by some writers with the ' learned Greek ' who tried to teach John of Salisbury to read Aristotle in the original at Beneventum. This translation must have been highly prized, for some generations later a copy of it was sent to Humphrey, Duke of Gloucester, for his library at Oxford, the nucleus of the present Bodleian.[2] Nevertheless it does not seem to have produced much effect, and the reason is plain. It is written in the uncouth Latin jargon of the time, and that language was quite incapable of expressing the mind of Plato. The medieval versions of Aristotle suffer from the like defect, though, from the nature of the case, Aristotle lost less than Plato in the process of translation. The situation, in fact, was this. Greek science could only be made generally accessible in a Latin dress, and there existed no Latin which was capable of rendering it.

[1] The MS. generally known as W.
[2] This copy is now in the library of Corpus Christi College.

The Latin language had to be revived, and that was the first task of the Humanists. They had to create afresh a fitting vehicle for ancient thought.

In this the Humanists were guided by a much profounder psychology than is generally to be found in modern works on education. What had to be revived, if progress was to be possible, was above all a way of thinking, and the Humanists were very clear about the reaction of language on thought. It is a perfectly sound doctrine that a way of thinking can best be reproduced by imitation of the manner in which it originally found expression. You can make yourself feel indignant by frowning, and in the same way you may best learn to think like the ancients by trying to speak and write like the ancients. The Humanists held that the shortcomings of medieval thought were mainly due to the barbarous language in which it was expressed, and they were perfectly right. The language you use forces you to think in a certain way. Any one who has ever known two languages well enough to think in both is aware that his thoughts are different according as he uses one or the other of them. The groundwork of the psychology of imitation has been laid for all time in Plato's *Republic*, and it is of vital importance in education. That was, and is, the justification of all the labour spent then and since in composition. Composition holds exactly the same place in Humanistic teaching as the work of the laboratory does in the teaching of Physical and Natural Science, and it would be a strange thing if we were to give it up just when the principle on which it is based has been so triumphantly vindicated in other branches of learning. That is the first practical lesson we have to learn from the Humanists. On the assumption that it is worth while for us to assimilate the thought of the ancients at all, there is no other way of doing it than by repeated efforts, however unsuccessful, to express ourselves as they did. It is not merely that translations are useless for the purpose. It may be interesting and even helpful to know what impression Euripides makes on Professor von Wilamowitz-Moellendorff or on Professor Gilbert Murray, but we mistake that for Euripides himself at our peril. That I may fairly take for granted here, but I go further still and assert that even the originals will never reveal their secrets except to those who can read them, so to say, from inside, and the power of doing that can be gained in no other way than the way the Humanists pointed out. Of course, even the best of our compositions have little real worth in themselves, and most of them may well be committed to the flames when they have served their purpose, just as the materials of a chemical experiment go down the sink. Here, too, it is the process and not the result which is of value. I would not, however, give two straws for any one's opinion on the criticism or interpretation of Plato's text unless he can write tolerable Greek prose, and I believe that what has made English scholarship superior on the whole to that of any other nation is just its unbroken tradition of composition. Even the Aberdeen 'Version' has done more for us in Scotland than some people seem to think. The Humanist view of education, then, is that it is the regulation of imitation, and I think we shall find that formula helpful. The child—to speak of him as a separate species with the ' educationists '— is above all things an imitative animal, and all progress is due to that fact. Education, it seems to me, is in the main the art of guiding the child to imitate the right things and in the right way.

II

The Humanists did well to begin with Latin ; for Rome was the historical intermediary between Greece and the West.   They were entirely successful in what they attempted, but their very success showed that their task was still unfinished.   Latin pointed everywhere to something beyond itself, to the perennial fount of all that makes antiquity of real value to us. This was very early felt.   Petrarch, whom Renan called ' the first modern man,' had a manuscript of Homer in his house and one containing certain dialogues of Plato, and he regretted bitterly his inability to read them.   The immediate occasion for the revival of a first-hand knowledge of Greek was furnished by the unsuccessful negotiations for the reunion of the Eastern and Western Churches, and especially by the Council of Ferrara and Florence.[1]   Two learned Greeks, Gemistos Plethon and Bessarion (afterwards a Cardinal of the Roman Church and founder of St. Mark's Library at Venice), brought the knowledge of Plato to Italy, and the scales fell from the eyes of Western Europe.   That was what made modern science a possibility ; for men learnt at last that, in certain important respects, Aristotle and Ptolemy did not represent the genuine Greek tradition.   The study of Plato pointed in another direction.   Greek scientific works were eagerly sought after and multiplied.   The thirteen books of Euclid were printed in Latin as early as 1482, and in Greek by 1533, and, what was still more important, Archimedes was printed in the original in 1544.   Hippocrates appeared in Latin in 1525, and the next year in Greek.   No doubt these

[1] 1438-1442 A.D.   Observe that this is still before the fall of Constantinople.   Aurispa brought the first Greek MS. of Plato to Italy as early as 1423.

texts would not pass muster at the present day, but
men were eager to know them and could not wait for
the critics.   The results were soon seen.   Copernicus
tells us himself how he was led to think of the earth as
a planet revolving round a central luminary by reading
in a work ascribed to Plutarch that the Pythagoreans
had taught this doctrine.   Though Copernicus did
not know it, Aristarchos of Samos had announced in
the third century B.C. that the simplest hypothesis on
which the apparently irregular motions of the planets
could be accounted for was that the sun is the centre
of the system and the earth a planet.   He had further
opened up a new view of the immensity of the universe
by calling attention to the absence of observable
parallax in the fixed stars.   Galileo, too, learnt in the
same school.   He was a Platonist, and his attacks on
the authority of Aristotle are to be understood from
that point of view.   The great heresy of Aristotle was
his theory that the heavens were of an ' incorruptible '
substance differing from that of the sublunary world,
and Galileo was on strictly Platonic ground when he
refuted this by pointing to the new star in Sagittarius.
Kepler, too, owed much to the Greeks.   It is true that,
so far as we know, no Greek had ever suspected that
the planetary orbits were other than circular, but the
disciples of Plato had worked out the theory of conic
sections, so that Kepler had much of the necessary
mathematical work ready to his hand.   The same is
true of Harvey, who was helped in his discovery of the
circulation of the blood by his study of the Greek
authorities.   The bare fact of the circulation was quite
well known to them, and Hippocrates uses the very
phrase ' circulation of the blood ' ($\pi\epsilon\rho\acute{\iota}o\delta o\varsigma$ $a\H{\iota}\mu a\tau o\varsigma$).
Plato makes Timaeus the Locrian speak of the blood
' circulating rapidly through the body.'   The Greeks
were prevented, however, by their erroneous view of

the arteries from completing the theory, and the credit of this is due to Harvey alone. A little later, Isaac Barrow exchanged the Professorship of Greek at Cambridge for the newly-founded Lucasian Chair of Mathematics, from which he lectured on Archimedes and Apollonius of Perga. It was through him that the tradition of Greek higher mathematics reached his pupil Isaac Newton, whose theory of fluxions, by the way, owes its name and something more to a Greek source, for ' fluxion ' is a translation of ῥύσις, a term used of the process by which a line is generated from a point, a plane from a line, and a solid from a plane. These facts do not detract in any way from the origin- ality of these great men ; they only show that originality consists very largely in knowing just where to take up a partially solved problem and complete its solution, and these men were one and all quite conscious that they were carrying on the work of their Greek predecessors. On the other hand, Francis Bacon despised the Greeks and continued to write in barbarous Latin. He was therefore unable to think in the ancient way, with the result that he never found out anything himself and rejected with scorn the discoveries of Copernicus and Harvey. No one will regard Huxley as a blind advocate of the Classics, but he was well aware of the facts, and he has stated them thus—

> Since the revival of learning, whereby the Western races of Europe were enabled to enter upon that progress towards true knowledge which was commenced by the philosophers of Greece, but was almost arrested in subsequent ages of intellectual stagnation, or, at most, gyration, the human larva has been feeding vigorously and moulting in pro- portion.

III

It is not, of course, for me to say how far it is
desirable or possible to base the teaching of science on
its history.   I know that there is a way of regarding
scientific truth *in abstracto*, as we may suppose the
Seraphim to do.   I cannot, however, help thinking
that, from an educational point of view, it is very important to insist that, whatever else science may be, it
is one of the spiritual conquests of mankind.   I have
just read with much interest what must be one of the
very latest of the innumerable German projects for the
reform of mathematical teaching, since it dates only
from 1912.[1]   In this it is laid down, in somewhat
turgid phrase, that ' the arrangement of our material
should conform to the biogenetic law,' which apparently
means the theory of recapitulation I referred to at the
beginning.   It goes on to say, ' the arrangement of
the material should follow the order that results from
the historical development, or, in other words, the
young human being should traverse the same path in
the discovery of mathematical truths as humanity
traversed in its youth.'   We are told further that
' the history of mathematics is to be cultivated as an
important side of the history of human thought, and
the pupil should be introduced by the help of originals
to the way in which the great mathematicians discovered laws.'   I am not sure that a Humanist would
put the thing in language of this kind, which is
curiously like that of scholasticism, but there could be
nothing more humanistic in spirit.
But, however it may be with the teaching of science,
I am quite sure that it is of vital importance for the
Classical teacher to keep before his pupils' minds the
fact that all science is Greek in its origin, and that

[1] See *Neue Jahrbücher*, vol. xxx. pp. 223 sqq.

science is perhaps the chief gift of Hellas to mankind. People are ready enough to admit the importance of Greek art. They can partially see its greatness for themselves, and so the idea gains ground that the Greeks were a people who cared chiefly for art and took what is called an ' aesthetic ' view of life. It would lead me too far if I were to discuss this point fully, but I should like to call attention to the significant fact that the Greeks had not even a word for art. Their language, which is capable of expressing so many nice distinctions, has no means of distinguishing the activities of a Phidias or a Parrhasius from those of a cobbler or a blacksmith. All are alike τέχναι and in the same sense. Further, the art of sculpture, which seems to us characteristically Greek just because we still possess so many examples of it, receives only cursory and incidental mention in the Classical Greek writers. But Greek literature is full of references to science, and we still possess a great body of Greek scientific writing, not only mathematical and astronomical, but also medical, which is of the highest order, and of which the significance is not yet exhausted. It is surely not creditable that our Classical teaching should ignore this side of the Greek genius as it usually does. I have come across good Classical scholars, who were also fair mathematicians, but who were quite surprised to hear that the *Elements of Euclid* were written in Greek, and still more surprised when they were told that everything of value in that work was familiar to educated men in the days of Plato, and that trigonometry and conic sections belong to the same date. That is not as it should be. Surely every boy who is doing both Greek and geometry should have the opportunity of seeing at least a few geometrical propositions in the original. Even Euclid's Greek has a lapidary beauty of its own, and the mere sight of the familiar figures set in a Greek text tends to suggest the unity of human knowledge.   Even in dealing with the pre-scientific stage of Greek literature we can show, if we will, how the Greek gift of accurate observation prepared the way for the marvellous scientific development of the fifth, fourth, and third centuries B.C. Homer, it is true, knows nothing about the planets, but it would be well to dwell a little on what he says about the fixed stars.   Sirius, the Dog-star, is supposed to bring the summer heat, and we still talk of 'the dog-days,' though every Boy Scout in St. Andrews knows that Sirius is blazing at the end of Queen's Gardens in the depth of winter.   Why is that ?   It is because the Greek sailors watched for the first appearance of the constellations in the East just before sunrise, and so came to speak of the 'rising' of a constellation as falling on the date when it rises along with the sun and is consequently invisible.   Sirius became visible in the East for the first time at the end of July, and so his rising became connected with the hottest days of the year.   Or again, we may consider the strange statement Homer makes about the portion of the Great Bear which we call the Plough or Charles's Wain, and which, he tells us, was called the Waggon (ἄμαξα) by some in his own day.   He says that it 'turns where it is' or 'on the same spot,' and that 'it alone has no part in the baths of Ocean.'[1]   That seems, or ought to seem, odd.   There is no obvious sense in which the Plough can be said to turn in the same spot any more than Cassiopeia, for instance, just opposite to it ; and in the same way it is not true to say that it 'alone' does not share in the baths of Ocean.   Indeed, if we think, as we should, of the latitude of Greece, it

---

[1] *Iliad,* xviii. 487-489 = *Od.,* v. 273-275.   I take this example from P. Cauer, *Palaestra Vitae,* pp. 34 sq.   Every Classical teacher should know this book.

is hardly true at all to say that the Plough does not sink beneath the horizon. In these parts the star at the end of the tail at any rate appears to dip. Is Homer's observation wrong, then, or has he confused the Great and the Little Bear ? Not at all. It is the position of the celestial North Pole which has altered. In Homer's day the North Pole was a good deal nearer the Plough than it is now, and the star at the end of the tail never came within 11°, or more than twenty lunar diameters, of the horizon in the latitude of Smyrna or Chios.

Or again, let us take Homer's view of the earth. As we know, he regards it as a sort of island surrounded by the river Oceanus. That is certainly a primitive view, and it is worth while to point out to a class that Herodotus laughs at it and says he does not believe there is any river Oceanus at all. It should be pointed out at the same time, however, that even the Homeric view is a considerable advance on the still more primitive conception of sky and earth as the lid and bottom of a sort of box. It should also interest a class to be told in outline the story of how, in the course of a few generations, a truer view was reached. The steps are clearly marked, and we can still see how the solid earth was gradually torn from its ' roots ' and left to swing free in space, and how, in a generation or two, its spherical shape was discovered. That brings us at once to the discovery of the true nature of eclipses. It was soon ascertained that eclipses of the sun were due to the interposition of the moon, but eclipses of the moon were a more difficult problem. The first step was to note that they could only take place when the moon was full, and the inference was drawn that they were due to the earth's shadow, and from this it followed that the moon shone by reflected light and that the earth was spherical. All that had been discovered by the middle of the fifth century B.C. I cannot help thinking that many people at the present day accept these things as a sort of dogma, for which they can give no reasons at all, and that it would help them very much if they were shown the steps by which they were gradually reached. Next comes the question of the planets, which were not carefully observed by the Greeks till after these discoveries had been made. No writer earlier than Plato mentions them by name, though they must have been known rather earlier. We have nothing but vague expressions like ' morning star ' and ' evening star,' and Parmenides is credited with the identification of the two. He is thus the discoverer of the planet Venus. Now here there is certainly a problem, for the Babylonians had known the planets fairly well, in spite of the fact that in other respects their astronomy was infantile compared to the Greek. The solution of this problem is instructive. The Babylonian interest in the planets was purely astrological, and the Greeks, who must have known about it, resolutely declined to have anything to do with astrology. It was not till the third century B.C., when Oriental influences became stronger, that we hear of astrology among the Greeks, and even the Stoic philosophy was able to furnish at least a pseudo-scientific justification of it.[1] That is why the Romans succumbed at once. They had not what I may call the scientific tact of the Greeks, and Stoicism impressed them unduly. It was, in fact, only after the spherical shape of the earth had been discovered that the other planets were studied by the Greeks, and then they were studied very minutely. The problem was to account for the extreme irregularity of their apparent motions, and it was the study of these which led to the

---

[1] It is worth while to note that Posidonius, who did more than any one to make astrology acceptable, was a Syrian.

abandonment of the belief that the earth was the centre of the system, which the authority of Aristotle unfortunately riveted on mankind once more for another two thousand years.

The scientific genius of the Greeks can be brought home to schoolboys in other ways, too. They ought to know that in the sixth century B.C. Anaximander declared that man must be descended from an animal of another species, and gave a good scientific ground for his belief. The young of other animals soon find their food for themselves, that of the human species alone requires a prolonged period of nursing. Accordingly, if man had been originally such as he is now, he could never have survived. If time permitted, we might sketch the history of biological and medical investigation as we have sketched the early history of astronomy. The best of the works which go by the name of Hippocrates are a model of scientific method for all time, and even when judged by the standard of actual results, they go in many respects far beyond anything that had been attained till comparatively recent times. I cannot discuss this now, but there is one remark which ought in justice to be made. When we study Greek mathematics and astronomy, Aristotle is apt to appear as the villain of the piece, and it is only too true that he arrested the progress of these sciences. Even in his physiology he was reactionary. Hippocrates and Plato had taught that the central organ of sensation was the brain, and had given good anatomical grounds for that belief, but Aristotle reverted to the primitive view that the heart was the seat of sensation. The brain, he held, was only an apparatus for cooling the blood. When we come to zoology, however, the case is very different. George Henry Lewes made fun of Aristotle for his account of the cuttlefish, but it turns out that Aristotle was right and George Henry Lewes

wrong.   The statements of Aristotle about the *galeus
levis* seemed quite incredible till the facts were redis-
covered by Johannes Mueller in 1840.   Where he
is on his own ground, Aristotle, too, represents Greek
science at its best.   Things like these ought surely to
form part of a Classical education.   They are not
difficult, and they can be made very interesting.

IV

I have said enough to show you how it was that the
rediscovery of Greek meant also the rediscovery of
science ; but it may be said that, even so, Greek has
done its work, and that science can now get along without it.   That is true in a sense, but in a far deeper
sense I think it is untrue.   I think that science depends upon Humanism in quite another way, since it
is only the Humanist point of view that can furnish an
adequate motive for its pursuit or even a justification
for its existence.   Of course public opinion looks
favourably on science mainly because of its practical
results.   In connexion with it people think of things
like electric lighting, telephones, wireless telegraphy,
and aeroplanes.   No one will belittle these things, but
it is surely wrong to regard them as more than by-
products of true scientific activity.   Most science is
really quite useless in the popular sense of the word,
and requires to be justified on very different grounds
from these.   Now I believe that such a justification
can only be found from the standpoint of Humanism,
and that the decline of Humanism would mean now, as
it meant before, the decline of science too.   It is not,
of course, necessary that all scientific workers should
be conscious of the interdependence of science and
Humanism, though very many of the greatest have

been so. They are carried along by a great tradition which they have no time to analyse, and they may be quite unconscious that it is derived from Greece. And yet it is true even now that it is only from the Hellenic point of view that science can be justified ; from any other, it must seem a waste of time. Let us see, then, what this point of view is.

Greek Humanism was something higher and more austere than Roman, though that had its value too. I read, indeed, the other day that the Greeks had not even a word for humanity, but I confess I do not know what this means. If the writer was thinking of humanity as the feeling which regards all human beings as akin, and therefore alike entitled to our help and service, it is simply untrue. The Greek word φιλανθρωπία meant that and more ; for it had not been vulgarized like the English ' philanthropy.' If, on the other hand, it is meant that they had no word for humanity in the abstract, the *humanité* of Positivism, I can only say that they were better without one. They preferred to say, ' all men, Hellenes and barbarians alike,' and that saved them from much confused thinking. Perhaps, however, it is this very antithesis of Hellenes and barbarians that the writer had in view, but we must not make too much of that. In its origin it only referred to difference in language, and it never conveyed so sharp a distinction as that between Jews and Gentiles did to the Chosen People. Here, too, Aristotle is rather misleading with regard to Greek feeling generally. He was trying to justify slavery— an institution about which the Greeks had many doubts, and which they never pushed to its logical consequences as other peoples have done. So far as we can see, the average Greek slave was better off than myriads of ' free ' industrial workers to-day. Still, the rightfulness of the institution had been questioned,

and Aristotle justified it by saying that the barbarians
were 'slaves by nature,' and that it was therefore for
their own good to be reduced to servitude.   Observe
that, even here, slavery is only justified on the ground
that it is for the slave's own advantage.   Carlyle went
far beyond that.   And even so, the Greeks for the most
part had no such feelings about the 'barbarians,' and
Plato deliberately rejected this classification of mankind
as unscientific.   It is just, he says, as if some intelligent
race of birds—say cranes—were to divide all animals
into cranes and non-cranes.   And yet there is something in the distinction too ; the Greeks really were
more human than other peoples, and I must try to
make it clear in what sense they were so.   I can do this
best by appealing to their use of certain words.

V

If we start from the word ἄνθρωπος itself, we note
in the first place a strong and universal belief that man
occupies an intermediate position between the gods and
the beasts.   All three—gods, men, and beasts—were
alike called animals (ζῷα), and there were, no doubt,
beings intermediate between them too, such as the
δαίμονες and heroes on the one hand, and the
Centaurs, Satyrs, and Sileni on the other.   That was
natural, since all were akin, but man's place in creation
was in a special sense intermediate and was clearly
marked.   We can see this best from the double sense
of the adjective ἀνθρώπινος, of which humanus is a
translation.   On the one hand, τὸ ἀνθρώπινον is
contrasted with τὸ θεῖον, the divine, and from that
point of view it connotes above all liability to error and
to death.   The Latin phrases humanum est errare and
si quid humani acciderit are but translations from the

Greek.   On the other hand, τὸ ἀνθρώπινον is contrasted with τὸ θηριῶδες, the merely animal or bestial,
and from that point of view it is applied to those feelings
which raise man above the beasts.   Their ruthless
attitude towards their fellow-beasts is not appropriate
for a man who knows that he himself is subject to the
like weaknesses as his neighbours, and that therefore pity (ἔλεος) or forgiveness (συγγνώμη) is alone
ἀνθρώπινον with regard to their failings or errors.
All that was common ground to ordinary Athenian
citizens, as is proved by the fact that the orators appeal
to it freely.   We have to start, then, from the view that
man is lower than the gods (οἱ κρείττονες), while he
is raised above the beasts of the field.   A threefold
attitude of mind is, therefore, appropriate for him.
There is his attitude to what is above him, that towards
what is below him, and his attitude towards his fellows.
The striking thing is that the Greeks expressed the
feeling common to all these attitudes by a single word,
and it is from that word we can best learn the meaning of Greek humanity.   It is αἰδώς, and is literally
rendered by ' shame.'

The Greeks distinguished two kinds of shame,
αἰσχύνη and αἰδώς.   The seat of the former was the
cheek, and a red flush was its sign.   It might often
keep men from wrong.   As the Roman poet (doubtless translating from the Greek) has it, *erubescit, salva
res est*—' he blushes ; all is well.'   As this instance
suggests, it was considered especially becoming in the
young, and αἰσχύνη or, as the Romans called it,
pudor, was used too for the soldier's honour, which
makes him blush to play the coward.   But there was a
higher kind of shame than this.   The seat of αἰδώς
was not the cheek, but the eyes, and it meant above all
the feeling that makes us realize our true position with
regard to others.   It follows that, as man holds an

intermediate place in the world, there will be three kinds of αἰδώς. In the first place, it is the feeling which makes us cast down our eyes in the presence of what is above us, and it is regularly used of reverence for the gods and for parents. In the next place, it is the feeling appropriate for us in the presence of our equals, and it thus means alike modesty and self-respect. Lastly, αἰδώς is the feeling we should have for those beneath us, and it is used especially with reference to homeless strangers and suppliants. From that point of view it means Mercy, and even in legal language it was the proper word for the mercy shown to the involuntary homicide by the kinsmen of the dead. The very fact that the Greeks used the same word for all these things shows clearly that they knew they sprung from a common root. Of course they did not live up to this ideal ; on the contrary, they often sinned heavily against it. That does not impair the value of the ideal itself. Modern Europe is hardly a garden of the Christian graces, but we do not condemn them on that account. What good there is comes from the ideal ; but it is also ἀνθρώπινον to have an ideal we cannot attain.

VI

But what, you will ask, has all this to do with science ? In my judgment, everything. It was just because the Greeks had this ideal of humanity that they came to invent science, a thing hitherto unknown in the world. The ' barbarians ' confused men with gods and gods with beasts, but the Greeks shook all that off at an early date, and Man stood out clearly for the first time as what he is. The beasts are ignorant and are content to be so. God knows all things and has no need of science. Man is ignorant, but he knows that he is so, and he cannot rest in his ignorance. The Pythagoreans, who were the real pioneers of science, regarded it as ' a being likened unto God, so far as may be,' and they also spoke of it as a purgation (κάθαρσις) of all that was merely animal. The more we think of it, the more we shall see that it is only on grounds like these that science can be justified, though the particular phraseology of the Pythagoreans may not commend itself to all minds in an equal degree. At the very least, it is well to know that it was this temper which first gave science birth.

Indeed, it is just because Classical antiquity can teach such lessons as these that it will live so long as man is truly human. Is it not strange that the only languages that are still truly living after three thousand years should be called ' the dead languages ' ? No one troubles to call Egyptian or Babylonian dead languages, and yet they are so. Gothic is a dead language, and so are Old and Middle High German and ' Anglo-Saxon.' Even the French of the *Chanson de Roland* can hardly be said to live. Hebrew and Sanskrit have a certain vitality, and so have some other sacred languages, but it is of an esoteric kind. Latin and Greek alone, and above all Greek, seem to be ageless and deathless. It is only because those who use the term have an uncomfortable feeling that they ought to be dead and are not that they trouble to call them so.

The great lesson, then, that Greece has to teach us at the present day is just the folly of any estrangement between science and Humanism. That is a survival of the time when Humanism was mainly Latin in character ; for it is true, of course, that the Romans were almost without scientific interests. Their greatness lay elsewhere. The estrangement to which I refer has persisted even now that Greek has resumed its rightful place ; for a one-sided Classicism has been apt to lay too exclusive an emphasis on the artistic side of the Greek genius. We must avoid all extremes here, and we only half understand Hellas if we leave its science on one side. There are signs that twentieth-century Humanism is learning a better way, and indeed there is even a danger that it may fall into the opposite error and unduly neglect the great literature which is another expression of the same spirit. At any rate, the true Hellenist will never be hostile to science, for he cannot be so without being faithless to Hellenism, and the true student of science will not be hostile to Hellenism when he sees that his own work is the continuation of what was begun at Miletus and Croton. The spirit of science was the same then as now, and the methods of observation and experiment were the same in all essentials, however much they may have been perfected since. The educator who has assimilated the idea of Humanism will reject the whole notion of 'subjects' competing with one another and even hostile. Human knowledge, as the men of the Renaissance well knew, is one. Their only mistake— and it was a noble error—was to suppose that one man could know it all. The Admirable Crichton was a student of the College in which we are assembled, but we do not aim at producing Admirable Crichtons here now. Nevertheless we must try to remember that every department of knowledge has its universal side, the side on which it comes into touch with every other, and that this is the most important side of it for the educator. To insist upon this is the true function of Humanism in Education.

THE SOCRATIC DOCTRINE OF THE SOUL

Second Annual Philosophical Lecture.   Read to the British Academy, January 26, 1916

My Lords, Ladies and Gentlemen,

When the President and Council did me the honour of inviting me to deliver the Annual Philosophical Lecture, and when they asked me to take Socrates as my subject, they were, of course, aware that the treatment of such a theme must be largely philological and historical.   I, certainly, have no claim to be regarded as a philosopher, but I have tried hard to understand what Socrates was and what he did, and I conceive that to be a question of genuine philosophical interest.   Whatever else it is, philosophy, in one aspect of it, is the progressive effort of man to find his true place in the world, and that aspect must be treated historically, since it is part of human progress, and philologically, since it involves the interpretation of documents.   I am not afraid, then, of the objection that most of what I have to say to-day is history rather than philosophy.   We are men, not angels, and for many of us our best chance of getting a glimpse of things on their eternal side is to approach them along the path of time.   Moreover, some of us have what may be called a sense of loyalty to great men.   In a way, no doubt, it does not matter whether we owe a truth to Pythagoras or Socrates or Plato, but it is natural for us to desire to know our benefactors and keep them in grateful remembrance. I make no apology, therefore, for the historical character of much that I have to lay before you, and I shall begin by stating the problem in a strictly historical form.

126

I

In a letter to the philosopher Themistius, the Emperor Julian says :

> The achievements of Alexander the Great are outdone in my eyes by Socrates son of Sophroniscus. It is to him I ascribe the wisdom of Plato, the fortitude of Antisthenes, the generalship of Xenophon, the Eretriac and Megaric philosophies, with Cebes, Simmias, Phaedo and countless others. To him too we owe the colonies that they planted, the Lyceum, the Stoa and the Academies. Who ever found salvation in the victories of Alexander ? . . . Whereas it is thanks to Socrates that all who find salvation in philosophy are being saved even now.[1]

These words of Julian's are still true, and that is partly why there is so little agreement about Socrates. The most diverse philosophies have sought to father themselves upon him, and each new account of him tends to reflect the fashions and prejudices of the hour. At one time he is an enlightened deist, at another a radical atheist. He has been lauded as the father of scepticism and again as the high priest of mysticism ; as a democratic social reformer and as a victim of democratic intolerance and ignorance. He has even been claimed—with at least equal reason—as a Quaker. No wonder that his latest biographer, H. Maier, exclaims :

> In the presence of each fresh attempt to bring the personality of Socrates nearer to us, the impression that always recurs is the same : ' The man whose influence was so widespread and so profound cannot have been like that ! ' [2]

Unfortunately that is just the impression left on me by Maier's own bulky volume, though he has mastered

[1] 264 c.
[2] H. Maier, *Sokrates, sein Werk und seine geschichtliche Stellung* (Tübingen, 1913), p. 3.

the material and his treatment of it is sound as far as it
goes.   Unless we can find some other line of approach,
it looks as if Socrates must still remain for us the Great
Unknown.

That, to be sure, is not Maier's view.   He thinks
he knows a great deal about Socrates, or he would not
have written 600 pages and more about him.   The
conclusion he comes to is that Socrates was not,
properly speaking, a philosopher, which makes it all
the more remarkable that the philosophers of the next
generation, however much they differed in other
respects, all agreed in regarding Socrates as their
master.   Maier makes much of the differences between
the Socratic schools and urges that these could not have
arisen if Socrates had been a philosopher with a system
of his own.   There seems to be something in that at
first sight, but it only makes it more puzzling that these
philosophers should have wished to represent their
philosophies as Socratic at all.   In modern times the
most inconsistent philosophies have been called Car-
tesian or Kantian or Hegelian, but in these cases we can
usually make out how they were derived from Descartes,
Kant or Hegel respectively.   Each of these thinkers
had set up some new principle which was then applied
in divergent and even contradictory ways by their
successors, and we should expect to find that Socrates
did something of the same kind.   Zeller, from whom
most of us have learned, thought he knew what it was.
Socrates discovered the universal and founded the
Begriffsphilosophie.   Maier will have nothing to do
with that, and I rather think he is wise.   The evidence
does not bear examination, and in any case the hypothesis would only account for Plato (if it would even
do that).   The other Socratics remain unexplained.
If, however, we are to be deprived of this ingenious
construction, we want something to replace it, and for

this we look to Maier in vain. He tells us that Socrates was not a philosopher in the proper sense of the word, but only a moral teacher with a distinctive method of his own, that of ' dialectical protreptic.'   In other words, his ' philosophy ' was nothing more than his plan of making people good by arguing with them in a peculiar way.   Surely the man whose influence has been so great ' cannot have been like that ! '

II

Now it is clearly impossible to discuss the Socratic question in all its bearings within the limits of a single lecture, so what I propose to do is to take Maier as the ablest and most recent advocate of the view that Socrates was not really a philosopher, and to apply the Socratic method of reasoning from admissions made by the other side.   If we try to see where these will lead us, we may possibly reach conclusions Maier himself has failed to draw, and these will be all the more cogent if based solely on evidence he allows to be valid.   He is a candid writer, and the assumptions he makes are so few that, if a case can be made out on these alone, it stands a fair chance of being a sound one.   The experiment seemed at least worth trying, and the result of it was new to myself at any rate, so it may be new to others.

I resolved not to quarrel, then, with Maier's estimate of the value of our sources.   He rejects the testimony of Xenophon, who did not belong to the intimate Socratic circle, and who was hardly more than twenty-five years old when he saw Socrates for the last time. He also disallows the evidence of Aristotle, who came to Athens as a lad of eighteen thirty years after the death of Socrates, and who had no important sources of information other than those accessible to ourselves. That leaves us with Plato as our sole witness, but Maier does not accept his testimony in its entirety. Far from it. For reasons I need not discuss, since I propose to accept his conclusion as a basis for argument, he holds that we must confine ourselves to Plato's earliest writings, and he particularly singles out the *Apology* and *Crito*, to which he adds the speech of Alcibiades in the *Symposium*. In these two works, and in that single portion of a third, he holds that Plato had no other intention than ' to set the Master's personality and lifework before our eyes without additions of his own.' [1] This does not mean, observe, that the *Apology* is a report of the speech actually delivered by Socrates at his trial, or that the conversation with Crito in the prison ever took place. It simply means that the Socrates we learn to know from these sources is the real man, and that Plato's sole object so far was to preserve a faithful memory of him. Maier uses other early dialogues too, but he makes certain reservations about them which I wish to avoid discussing. I prefer to take his admissions in the strictest sense and with all the qualifications he insists on. The issue, then, takes this form : ' What could we know of Socrates as a philosopher if no other account of him had come down to us than the *Apology*, the *Crito*, and the speech of Alcibiades, and with the *proviso* that even these are not to be regarded as reports of actual speeches or conversations ?' I should add that Maier also allows us to treat the allusions in contemporary comedy as corroborative evidence, though they must be admitted with caution. Such are the conditions of the experiment I resolved to try.

III

In the first place, then, we learn from the *Apology* and *Crito* that Socrates was just over seventy when he was

[1] p. 147.

put to death in the spring of 399 B.C., and that means that he was born in 470 or 469 B.C. He was, then, a man of the Periclean Age. He was already ten years old when Aeschylus brought out the Orestean Trilogy, and about thirty when Sophocles and Euripides were producing their earliest tragedies. He must have watched the building of the new Parthenon from start to finish. We are far too apt to see Socrates against the more sombre background of those later days to which Plato and Xenophon belonged, and to forget that he was over forty when Plato was born. If we wish to understand him historically, we must first replace him among the surroundings of his own generation. In other words, we must endeavour to realize his youth and early manhood.

To most people Socrates is best known by his trial and death, and that is why he is commonly pictured as an old man. It is not always remembered, for instance, that the Socrates caricatured by Aristophanes in the *Clouds* is a man of forty-six, or that the Socrates who served at Potidaea (432 B.C.) in a manner that would have won him the V.C. to-day was about thirty-seven. On that occasion he saved the life of Alcibiades, who must have been twenty at least, or he would not have been on active service abroad. Even if we assume that Potidaea was his first campaign, Alcibiades was eighteen years younger than Socrates at the very outside, and his speech in the *Symposium* carries us still further back, to the time when he was about fifteen.[1] In reading the account he is made to give of the beginning of his intimacy with Socrates, we are reading of a boy's enthusiasm for a man just turned

---

[1] In passing from the story of his first intimacy with Socrates to that of Potidaea, Alcibiades says, ταῦτά τε γάρ μοι ἄπαντα προυγεγόνει, καὶ μετὰ ταῦτα κτλ., 'That was an old story, but at a later time, &c.' (*Symp.*, 219 e, 5).

thirty. The story makes a different impression if we keep that in view. What concerns us now, however, is that the 'wisdom' of Socrates is assumed to be matter of common knowledge in these early days. It was just because he had some strange, new knowledge to impart that Alcibiades sought to win his affection.[1] We shall see the bearing of that shortly.

From the *Apology* we learn further that Socrates conceived himself to have a mission to his fellow-citizens, and that his devotion to it had brought him to poverty. He cannot have been really poor to begin with ; for we have found him serving before Potidaea, which means that he had the property qualification required at the time for those who served as hoplites. Nine years later (423 B.C.), however, when Aristophanes and Amipsias represented him on the comic stage, it appears that his neediness was beginning to be a byword. They both allude to what seems to have been a current joke about his want of a new cloak and the shifts he was put to to get one. Amipsias said he was ' born to spite the shoemakers,' but Socrates may have had other reasons than poverty for going barefoot. In the same fragment he is addressed as a ' stout-hearted fellow that, for all his hunger, never stooped to be a parasite.' Two years later, Eupolis used stronger language. He calls Socrates a ' garrulous beggar, who has ideas on everything except where to get a meal.' Of course we must not take this language too seriously. Socrates was still serving as a hoplite at Delium, the year before the *Clouds* of Aristophanes and the *Connus* of Amipsias, and at Amphipolis the year after. Something, however, must have happened shortly before to bring him into public notice, or the comic poets would not all have turned on him at once,

---

[1] He thought it would be a stroke of luck πάντ' ἀκοῦσαι ὅσαπερ οὗτος ᾔδει (*Symp.*, 217 a, 4).

and it is also clear that he had suffered losses of some kind. Very likely these were due to the war in the first place, but the *Apology* makes him poorer still at the close of his life, and he is made to attribute that to his mission. We may infer, I think, that the public mission of Socrates had begun before the year of the *Clouds*, but was still something of a novelty then, so that its nature was not clearly understood. He was absent from Athens, as we know, the year before, and presumably in the preceding years also, though we do not happen to hear of any actual battle in which he took part between Potidaea and Delium. We are told, however, that his habit of meditation was a joke in the army before Potidaea, and that it was there he once stood wrapped in thought for twenty-four hours.[1] It looks as if the call came to him when he was in the trenches ; and, if so, the mission cannot have become the sole business of his life till after Delium, when he was forty-five years old. Now we have seen that he was known for his ' wisdom ' long before that, and the *Apology* confirms the speech of Alcibiades on this point. It was before Socrates entered on his mission that Chaerepho went to Delphi and asked the oracle whether there was any one wiser than Socrates, from which it follows that this ' wisdom,' whatever it was, was something anterior to and quite independent of the public mission described in the *Apology*. To sum up, the evidence Maier admits is sufficient to prove that Socrates was known as a ' wise man ' before he was forty, and before he began to go about questioning his fellow-citizens. Whatever we may think of the details, both the *Apology* and the speech of Alcibiades assume that as a matter of course, which is even more convincing than if it had been stated in so many words.

---

[1] *Symp.*, 220 c, 3 sqq. Maier says (p. 301 n.) that this obviously depends on trustworthy tradition.

On the other hand, it does not seem likely that the mission of Socrates stood in no sort of relation to the 'wisdom' for which he was known in his younger days. The *Apology* does not help us here. It tells us a good deal about the mission, but nothing as to the nature of the 'wisdom' which prompted the inquiry of Chaerepho, while Alcibiades is not sufficiently sober in the *Symposium* to give us more than a hint, which would hardly be intelligible yet, but to which we shall return. It will be best, then, to start with the account given in the *Apology* of that mission to his fellow-citizens to which Socrates devoted the later years of his life, and to see whether we can infer anything from it about the 'wisdom' for which he had been known in early manhood.

IV

We are told, then, that at first Socrates refused to accept the declaration of the Pythia that he was the wisest of men, and set himself to refute it by producing some one who was certainly wiser. The result of his efforts, however, was only to show that all the people who were wise in their own eyes and those of others were really ignorant, and he concluded that the meaning of the oracle did not lie on the surface. The god must really mean that all men alike were ignorant, but that Socrates was wiser in this one respect, that he knew he was ignorant, while other men thought they were wise. Having discovered the meaning of the oracle, he now felt it his duty to champion the veracity of the god by devoting the rest of his life to the exposure of other men's ignorance.

It ought, one would think, to be obvious that this is a humorous way of stating the case. For very sufficient reasons the Delphic oracle was an object of suspicion at

Athens, and, when Euripides exhibits it in an un-
favourable light, he only reflects the feelings of his
audience.   It is incredible that any Athenian should
have thought it worth while to make the smallest
sacrifice in defence of an institution which had distinguished itself by its pro-Persian and pro-Spartan
leanings, or that Socrates should have hoped to conciliate his judges by stating that he had ruined himself
in such a cause.   We might as well expect a jury of
English Nonconformists to be favourably impressed
by the plea that an accused person had been reduced to
penury by his advocacy of Papal Infallibility.

On this point recent German critics have an inkling
of the truth, though they draw quite the wrong conclusions.   Several of them have made the profound
discovery that the speech Plato puts into the mouth of
Socrates is not a defence at all, and was not likely to
conciliate the court.   They go on to infer that he
cannot have spoken like that, and some of them even
conclude that the whole story of the oracle is Plato's
invention.   That is because they start with the conviction that Socrates must have tried to make out the
best case he could for himself.   ' He only needed,'
says Maier,[1] ' to appeal to the correctness with which
he had always fulfilled the religious duties of an
Athenian citizen.   Xenophon's *Apology* makes him
speak thus.   And he certainly did speak thus.'   The
inference is characteristically German, but the Socrates
we think we know from the *Apology*, the *Crito*, and the
speech of Alcibiades would never have stooped to do
anything of the sort.   He was not afraid of the State,
as German professors occasionally are.   He certainly
admitted its right to deal with its citizens as it thought
fit, but that is a very different thing from recognizing
its title to control their freedom of thought and speech.

[1] p. 105.

The Socrates of the *Crito* insists, indeed, that a legally pronounced sentence must be executed, and that he must therefore submit to death at the hands of the State ; but we misunderstand him badly if we fail to see that he asserts even more strongly his right not to degrade himself by a humiliating defence, or to make things easy for his accusers by running away, which is just what they wanted him to do. No. Each party must abide by the sentence pronounced ; Socrates must die, and his accusers must lie under condemnation for wickedness and dishonesty. That is what he is made to say in the *Apology*,[1] and he adds that so it was bound to be.

Even Xenophon, who does put forward the plea of religious conformity on behalf of Socrates, shows rather more insight than the Germans. In his own *Apology* he admits that other accounts of the speech— Plato's, of course, in particular—had succeeded in reproducing the lofty tone ($\mu\epsilon\gamma\alpha\lambda\eta\gamma o\rho\iota\alpha$) of Socrates. He really did speak like that, he says,[2] and he was quite indifferent to the result of the trial. Unfortunately this is immediately spoilt by a complaint that no one had accounted for his indifference, so that it seemed ' rather unwise,' just as it does to the Germans. Xenophon's own view, which he modestly attributes to Hermogenes, is that Socrates wished to escape the evils of old age by a timely death. He did not want to become blind and hard of hearing. It has not been given either to Xenophon or to the Germans to see that the only thing to be expected of a brave man accused on a trumpery charge is just that tone of humorous condescension and *persiflage* which Plato has reproduced. As we shall see, there are serious moments in

---

[1] 39 b, 4 sqq.

[2] Xen., *Apol.*, 1, ᾧ καὶ δῆλον ὅτι τῷ ὄντι οὕτως ἔρρηθη ὑπὸ Σωκράτους. Plato was present at the trial, but Xenophon was ' somewhere in Asia.'

the *Apology* too, but the actual defence is rather a pro-
vocation than a plea for acquittal.   That is just why
we feel so sure that the speech is true to life.

We need not doubt, then, that Socrates actually gave
some such account of his mission as that we read in the
Apology, though we must keep in view the ' ironical '
character of this part of the speech.   Most English
critics take it far too seriously.   They seem to think
the message of Socrates to his fellow-citizens can have
been nothing more than is there revealed, and that his
sole business in life was to expose the ignorance of
others.   If that had really been all, it is surely hard
to believe that he would have been ready to face death
rather than relinquish his task.   No doubt Socrates
held that the conviction of ignorance was the first
step on the way of salvation, and that it was little use
talking of anything else to people who had still this
step to take, but even Xenophon, whom these same
critics generally regard as an authority on 'the historical
Socrates,' represents him as a teacher of positive
doctrine.   It ought to be possible to discover what
this was even from the *Apology* itself.

V

We must not assume, indeed, that Socrates thought
it worth while to say much about his real teaching at
the trial, though it is likely that he did indicate its
nature.   There were certainly some among his five
hundred judges who deserved to be taken seriously.
Even if he did not do this, however, Plato was bound
to do it for him, if he wished to produce the effect he
obviously intended to produce.   As a matter of fact,
he has done it quite unmistakably, and the only reason
why the point is usually missed is that we find it hard to

put ourselves in the place of those to whom such doctrine was novel and strange.

The passage which lets us into the secret is that where Socrates is made to tell his judges that he will not give up what he calls 'philosophy,' even though they were to offer to acquit him on that condition. Here, if anywhere, is the place where we look for a statement of the truth for which he was ready to die, and Plato accordingly makes him give the sum and substance of his 'philosophy' in words which have obviously been chosen with the greatest care, and to which all possible emphasis is lent by the solemnity of the context and by the rhetorical artifice of repetition. What Socrates is made to say is this :

> I will not cease from philosophy and from exhorting you, and declaring the truth to every one of you I meet, saying in the words I am accustomed to use : ' My good friend, . . . are you not ashamed of caring for money and how to get as much of it as you can, and for honour and reputation, and not caring or taking thought for wisdom and truth and for your soul, and how to make it as good as possible ? '

And again :

> I go about doing nothing else but urging you, young and old alike, not to care for your bodies or for money sooner or as much as for your soul, and how to make it as good as you can.[1]

' To care for their souls,' then, was what Socrates urged on his fellow-citizens, and we shall have to consider how much that implies. First, however, it should be noted that there are many echoes of the phrase in all the Socratic literature. Xenophon uses it in contexts which do not appear to be derived from Plato's dialogues. Antisthenes, it seems, employed the phrase too, and he would hardly have borrowed it

[1] 29 d, 4 sqq., and 30 a, 7 sqq.

from Plato. Isocrates refers to it as something familiar.[1] The Athenian Academy possessed a dialogue which was evidently designed as a sort of introduction to Socratic philosophy for beginners, and is thrown into the appropriate form of a conversation between Socrates and the young Alcibiades. It is not, I think, by Plato, but it is of early date. In it Socrates shows that, if any one is to care rightly for himself, he must first of all know what he is ; it is then proved that each of us is soul, and therefore that to care for ourselves is to care for our souls. It is all put in the most provokingly simple way, with the usual illustrations from shoemaking and the like, and it strikingly confirms what is said in the *Apology*.[2] I am not called upon to labour this point, however, for Maier admits, and indeed insists, that this is the characteristic Socratic formula. Let us see, then, where this admission will lead us.

Just at first, I fear, it will seem to lead nowhere in particular. Such language has become stale by repetition, and it takes an effort to appreciate it. So far as words go, Socrates has done his work too well. It is an orthodox and respectable opinion to-day that each one of us has a soul, and that its welfare is his highest interest, and that was so already in the fourth century B.C., as we can see from Isocrates. We assume without examination that a similar vague orthodoxy on the subject existed in the days of Socrates too, and that there was nothing very remarkable in his reiteration of it. That is why Maier, having safely reached this point, is content to inquire no further, and pronounces that Socrates was not a philosopher in the strict sense, but only a moral teacher with a method of his own. I

---

[1] For references see Maier, p. 333, n. 3.   The allusion in Isocrates (*Antid.*, § 309) was noted by Grote (*Plato*, vol. i. p. 341).

[2] [Plato] *Alc.*, i. 127 e, 9 sqq.

hope to show that he has left off just where he ought to have begun.

For it is here that it becomes important to remember that Socrates belonged to the age of Pericles. We have no right to assume that his words meant just as much or as little as they might mean in Isocrates or in a modern sermon. What we have to ask is what they would mean at the outbreak of the Peloponnesian War; and, if we ask that question, we shall find, I believe, that, so far from appearing commonplace, the exhortation to ' care for his soul ' must have come as a shock to the Athenian of those days, and may even have seemed not a little ridiculous. It is implied, we must observe, that there is something in us which is capable of attaining wisdom, and that this same thing is capable of attaining goodness and righteousness. This something Socrates called ' soul ' (ψυχή). Now no one had ever said that before, in the sense in which Socrates meant it. Not only had the word ψυχή never been used in this way, but the existence of what Socrates called by the name had never been realized. If that can be shown, it will be easier to understand how Socrates came to be regarded as the true founder of philosophy, and our problem will be solved. This involves, of course, an inquiry into the history of the word ψυχή, which may seem to be taking us a long way from Socrates, but that cannot be helped if we really wish to measure the importance of the advance he made. It will be obvious that in what follows I have been helped by Rohde's *Psyche*, but that really great work seems to me to miss the very point to which it ought to lead up. It has no chapter on Socrates at all.

VI

Originally, the word ψυχή meant ' breath,' but, by historical times, it had already been specialized in two distinct ways. It had come to mean *courage* in the first place, and secondly the *breath of life*. The first sense has nothing, of course, to do with our present inquiry, but so much confusion has arisen from failure to distinguish it from the second, that it will be as well to clear the ground by defining its range. There is abundant evidence in many languages of a primitive idea that pride and courage naturally expressed themselves by hard breathing, or—not to put too fine a point upon it—snorting. Perhaps this was first observed in horses. At any rate, the phrase ' to breathe hard ' (πνεῖν μέγα) survived in the sense of ' to be proud,' and warriors are said ' to breathe wrath ' and ' to breathe Ares.' So the word ψυχή was used, just like the Latin *spiritus*, for what we still call ' high spirit.' Herodotus and the tragedians have it often in this sense and Thucydides once.[1] From this is derived the adjective εὔψυχος, ' spirited,' ' courageous,' and the ' magnanimous ' man, the μεγαλόψυχος, is properly the ' man of spirit.' It is clear that, if we wish to discover what Socrates really meant by ψυχή, when he called the seat of wisdom and goodness by that name, we must eliminate all instances of the word which fall under this head.

The second meaning of ψυχή is the ' breath of life,' the presence or absence of which is the most obvious distinction between the animate and the inanimate. It is, in the first place, the ' ghost ' a man ' gives up ' at

---

[1] Thuc., ii. 40, 3. In Herod., v. 124, we are told that Aristagoras was ψυχὴν οὐκ ἄκρος. From the context we see clearly that this means he was poor-spirited. I mention this because Liddell and Scott are wrong on the point.

death, but it may also quit the body temporarily, which
explains the phenomenon of swooning (λιποψυχία).
That being so, it seemed natural to suppose it was also
the thing that can roam at large when the body is
asleep, and even appear to another sleeping person in
his dream.   Moreover, since we can dream of the
dead, what then appears to us must be just what leaves
the body at the moment of death.   These considerations explain the world-wide belief in the ' soul ' as a
sort of ' double ' of the real bodily man, the Egyptian
ka, the Italian *genius*, and the Greek ψυχή.

Now this ' double ' is not identified with whatever it
is in us that feels and wills during our waking life.
That is generally supposed to be blood and not breath.
Homer has a great deal to say about feelings, but he
never attributes any feeling to the ψυχή.   The θυμός
and the νόος, which do feel and perceive, have their
seat in the midriff or the heart ; they belong to the body
and perish with it.   In a sense, no doubt, the ψυχή
continues to exist after death, since it can appear to the
survivors, but in Homer it is hardly even a ghost, since
it cannot appear to them otherwise than in a dream.   It
is a shadow (σκιά) or image (εἴδωλον), with no more
substance, as Apollodorus put it, than the reflection of
the body in a mirror.[1]   Departed souls are witless and
feeble things.   Tiresias is the exception that proves
the rule, and in the *Nekyia* it is only when the shades
have been allowed to drink blood that consciousness
returns to them for a while.   That is not because death
has robbed the ψυχή of anything it ever had ; it had
nothing to do with the conscious life when it was in the
body, and cannot therefore have any consciousness

---

[1] Apollodorus περὶ θεῶν (Stob., *Ecl.*, i. p. 420, Wachsm.) ὑποτίθεται
τὰς ψυχὰς τοῖς εἰδώλοις τοῖς ἐν τοῖς κατόπτροις φαινομένοις ὁμοίας καὶ τοῖς
διὰ τῶν ὑδάτων συνισταμένοις, ἃ καθάπαξ ἡμῖν ἐξείκασται καὶ τὰς κινήσεις
μιμεῖται, στερεμνώδη δὲ ὑπόστασιν οὐδεμίαν ἔχει εἰς ἀντίληψιν καὶ ἀφήν.

when detached from it.   A few favourites of heaven
escape this dismal lot by being sent to the Isles of the
Blest, but these do not really die at all.   They are
carried away still living and retain their bodies, without
which they would be incapable of bliss.   This point,
too, is well noted by Apollodorus.[1]

VII

It is generally agreed that these views can hardly be
primitive, and that the observances of the mortuary
cult (τὰ νομιζόμενα), which we find practised at
Athens and elsewhere, really bear witness to a far
earlier stratum of belief.   They show that at one time
the ψυχή was supposed to dwell with the body in the
grave, where it had to be supported by the offerings of
the survivors, especially by libations (χοαί) poured
over the tomb.   It has been fairly inferred that the
immunity of the Homeric world from ghosts had a good
deal to do with the substitution of cremation for burial.
When the body is burnt the ψυχή has no longer a foot-
hold in this life.   At any rate, the early Athenian
ghost was by no means so feeble and helpless a thing
as the Homeric.   If a man's murder went unavenged,
or if the offerings at his grave were neglected, his
ghost could ' walk,' and the feast of the Anthesteria
preserved the memory of a time when departed souls
were believed to revisit their old homes once a year.
There is no trace of anything here that can be called
ancestor-worship.   It is something much more primitive than that.   Though less helpless, and therefore
more formidable, than the Homeric ' shade,' the early
Athenian ghost is dependent on the offerings of the

---

[1] Apollodorus, *ib.* (Stob., *Ecl.*, i. p. 422), τούτοις μὲν οὖν καὶ τὰ σώματα
παρεῖναι.

survivors, and they make these offerings, partly, no doubt, from feelings of natural piety, but mainly to keep the ghost quiet. That is hardly to be called worship.

It is plain, on the other hand, that these beliefs were mere survivals in the Athens of the fifth century B.C. We should know next to nothing about them were it not that the mortuary observances become of legal importance in cases of homicide and inheritance, so that the orators had to treat them seriously, and, moreover, they went on quite comfortably side by side with the wholly inconsistent belief that departed souls all went to a place of their own. We know now that Lucian's picture of Charon and his boat faithfully reproduces the imagery of the sixth century B.C. ; for it agrees exactly with the representation on a recently discovered piece of black figured pottery.[1] There we see the souls—miserable little creatures with wings— weeping on the bank and praying to be taken aboard, while Charon sits in the stern and makes all he has room for work their passage by rowing. The people who decorated a piece of pottery, obviously intended for use in the mortuary cult, with such a scene had evidently no living belief in the continued existence of the soul within the grave. We find the same contradiction in Egypt, but there both beliefs were taken seriously. The Egyptians were a business-like people, and got out of the difficulty by assuming two souls, one of which (the *ka*) remains in the tomb while the other (the *ba*) departs to the place of the dead. Similar devices were adopted elsewhere, but the Greeks felt no need for anything of the sort. We may safely infer that the old belief had lost its hold upon them.

Whichever way we take it, the traditional Athenian

---

[1] Furtwängler, *Charon, eine altattische Malerei* (*Archiv für Religionswissenschaft*, viii. (1905), pp. 191 sqq.).

beliefs about the soul were cheerless enough, and we
cannot wonder at the popularity of the Eleusinian
Mysteries, which promised a better lot of some sort
to the initiated after death.   It does not appear, however, that this was at all clearly conceived.   The obligation of secrecy referred to the ritual alone, and we
should hear something more definite as to the future
life, if the Mysteries had been explicit about it.   As it
is, the chorus in the *Frogs* of Aristophanes probably
tell us all there was to tell, and that only amounts to a
vision of meadows and feasting—a sort of glorified
picnic.   Of one thing we may be quite sure, namely,
that no new view of the soul was revealed in the
Mysteries ; for in that case we should certainly find
some trace of it in Aeschylus.   As a matter of fact,
he tells us nothing about the soul, and hardly ever
mentions it.   To him, as to most of his contemporaries,
thought belongs to the body ; it is the blood round
the heart, and that ceases to think at death.   The life
to come has no place in his scheme of things, and that
is just why he is so preoccupied with the problem of
the fathers' sins being visited on the children.   Justice
must be done on earth or not at all.

In any case, the promises held out in the Mysteries
are quite as inconsistent with the beliefs implied by the
mortuary cult as are Charon and his boat, and the fact
that the Eleusinia had been taken over by the State as
part of the public religion shows once more how little
hold such beliefs had on the ordinary Athenian.   I do
not mean that he actively disbelieved them, but I
should suppose he thought very little about them.
After all, the Athenians were brought up on Homer,
and their everyday working beliefs were derived from
that source.   Besides, Homer was already beginning
to be interpreted allegorically, and the prevailing notion
in the time of Socrates certainly was that the souls of

K

the dead were absorbed by the upper air, just as their bodies were by the earth.   In the *Suppliants* Euripides gives us the formula ' Earth to earth and air to air,' and that is no heresy of his own.[1]   It was so much a matter of course that it had been embodied in the official epitaph on those who had fallen at Potidaea some years earlier (432 B.C.).[2]   There is nothing remarkable in that.   There was no room in the public religion for any doctrine of immortality.   The gods alone are immortal, and it would be shocking to suggest that human beings might be so too.   The dead are just the dead, and how can the dead be deathless ?   In the heroic age, indeed, some human beings had attained immortality by being turned into gods and heroes, but such things were not expected to happen now.   The heroic honours paid to Brasidas at Amphipolis had a political motive, and were hardly taken seriously.

VIII

So far I have been dealing with the beliefs of the ordinary citizen and with the official religion of Athens, but it would have been easy to find people there who held very different views about the soul.   There were the members of Orphic societies in the first place, and there were also the votaries of Ionian science, who had become fairly numerous since Anaxagoras first introduced it to the Athenians.   On the whole, the Orphics would be found chiefly among the humbler classes, and the adherents of Ionian science chiefly among the enlightened aristocracy.   Even in the absence of

---

[1] Eur., *Suppl.*, 533— $\pi\nu\epsilon\hat{\upsilon}\mu\alpha$ $\mu\grave{\epsilon}\nu$ $\pi\rho\grave{o}s$ $\alpha\grave{\iota}\theta\acute{\epsilon}\rho\alpha$,
$\tau\grave{o}$ $\sigma\hat{\omega}\mu\alpha$ δ' $\grave{\epsilon}s$ $\gamma\hat{\eta}\nu$.

[2] *C.I.A.*, i. 442—
$\alpha\grave{\iota}\theta\grave{\eta}\rho$ $\mu\grave{\epsilon}\nu$ $\psi\upsilon\chi\grave{\alpha}s$ $\grave{\upsilon}\pi\epsilon\delta\acute{\epsilon}\xi\alpha\tau o$, $\sigma\acute{\omega}\mu\alpha\tau\alpha$ $\delta\grave{\epsilon}$ $\chi\theta\acute{\omega}\nu$.

direct testimony we should be bound to assume that Socrates, who was interested in everything and tested everything, did not pass by the two most remarkable movements which took place at Athens in his own generation, and if we wish to replace him among the surroundings of his own time we must certainly take account of these.   The religious movement was the earlier in date, and claims our attention first.

The most striking feature of Orphic belief is that it is based on the denial of what we have just seen to be the cardinal doctrine of Greek religion, namely, that there is an impassable, or almost impassable, gulf between gods and men.   The Orphics held, on the contrary, that every soul is a fallen god, shut up in the prison-house of the body as a penalty for antenatal sin.   The aim of their religion as practised was to secure the release (λύσις) of the soul from its bondage by means of certain observances directed to cleansing and purging it of original sin (καθαρμοί).   Those souls which were sufficiently purged returned once more to the gods and took their old place among them.

That is certainly not primitive belief but theological speculation, such as we find among the Hindus and, in a cruder form, among the Egyptians.   The trouble was till recently that there seemed to be no room for an age of such speculation within the limits of Greek history as we knew it, and many modern scholars have followed the lead of Herodotus in holding that it came from the ' barbarians,' and in particular from Egypt. On the other hand, Orphicism was closely bound up with the worship of Dionysus, which seems to have come from Thrace, and we can hardly credit the Thracians with a gift for mystical theology.   If, however, we take a wider view, we shall find that doctrines of a similar character are to be found in many places which have nothing to do with Thrace.   Zielinski has shown strong grounds for believing that the Hermetic theology, which became important in later days, originated in Arcadia, and especially in Mantinea, the home of the prophetess Diotima, who is certainly not to be regarded as a fictitious personage.[1] There were mystical elements in the worship of the Cretan Zeus, and a book of prophecies was extant in later days composed in the dialect of Cyprus, which is practically identical with the Arcadian.[2] The geographical distribution of the doctrine strongly suggests that we have really to do with a survival from the Aegean Age, and that the period of theological speculation we seem bound to assume was just the time of the power of Cnossus. If that is so, the priests of Heliopolis in the Delta may quite as well have borrowed from Crete as *vice versa*, if there was any borrowing at all. There is no need to look for remote origins.

However that may be, it is certain that such doctrines flourished exceedingly in the sixth century B.C., and that their influence on the higher thought of Greece was by no means negligible. We must, however, be careful to avoid exaggeration here ; for, while it is certain that the Orphics attached an importance to the 'soul' which went far beyond anything recognized in the public or private religion of the Greek states, it is by no means so clear that they went much beyond primitive spiritism in the account they gave of its nature. In so far as the soul was supposed to reveal its true nature in 'ecstasy,' which might be artificially produced by drugs or dancing, that is obvious ; but, even in its higher manifestations, the doctrine still bears traces of its primitive origin. The earliest state-

---

[1] *Archiv für Religionswissenschaft*, ix. (1906), p. 43.

[2] On Euclous the Cyprian, see M. Schmidt in *Kuhns Zeitschrift*, ix. (1860), pp. 361 sqq. The identity of the Arcadian and Cypriote dialects is the most certain and fundamental fact with regard to the Aegean Age.

ment in literature of the unique divine origin of the
soul is to be found in a fragment of one of Pindar's
Dirges,[1] but even there it is called an ' image of life '
(αἰῶνος εἴδωλον) surviving after death, much in the
Homeric way, and we are expressly told that it ' sleeps
when the limbs are active ' (εὕδει δὲ πρασσόντων
μελέων) and shows its prophetic nature only in
dreams.   In fact, as Adam said, it is rather like what
has been called ' the subliminal self ' in modern times,
and is quite dissociated from the normal waking consciousness.[2]   It may be divine and immortal, but it is
really no concern of ours except in sleep and at the
moment of death.   It is not identified with what we
call ' I.'

IX

The word ψυχή had also been used by the scientific
schools of Ionia in quite another than the popular and
traditional sense.   This appears to have originated in
the doctrine of Anaximenes, that ' air ' (ἀήρ), the
primary substance, was the life of the world, just as the
breath was the life of the body.   That doctrine was
being taught at Athens by Diogenes of Apollonia in
the early manhood of Socrates, who is represented as
an adherent of it in the Clouds of Aristophanes.   The
emphasis lies entirely on the cosmical side, however.
There is no special interest in the individual human
soul, which is just that portion of the boundless air
which happens to be shut up in our body for the time
being, and which accounts for our life and conscious-

[1] Pindar, fr. 131 Bergk.
[2] Adam, The Doctrine of the Celestial Origin of the Soul (Cambridge
Praelections, 1906).   Adam pointed out (p. 32) that Myers chose the
Pindaric fragment as the heading of his chapter on Sleep (Human Personality,
vol. i. p. 121).

ness.   There is a great advance on primitive views
here in so far as the ψυχή is identified for the first time
with the normal waking consciousness, and not with
the dream-consciousness.   This point is specially em-
phasized in the system of Heraclitus, which was based
precisely on the opposition between waking and sleeping, life and death.[1]   The waking soul is that in which
the elemental fire burns bright and dry ; sleep and
death are due to its partial or total extinction.   On the
other hand, the soul is in a state of flux just as much as
the body.   It, too, is a river into which you cannot step
twice ; there is nothing you can speak of as ' I ' or even
' this.'   Anaxagoras preferred to call the source of
motion he was obliged to postulate νοῦς instead of
ψυχή, but for our present purpose he meant much the
same thing.   The common feature in all these theories
is that our conscious life comes to us ' from out of
doors ' (θύραθεν), as Aristotle puts it, employing a
term elsewhere used in describing respiration.   Its
existence is of a temporary and accidental character,
depending solely on the fact that for the moment a
portion of the primary substance is enclosed in a
particular body.   It will be seen that this fits in well
enough with the view commonly accepted at Athens
and expressed in the formula ' Earth to earth and air
to air.'   That is why no one was shocked by the
scientific view.   The ' sophists ' were accused of
almost everything, but I do not remember any place
where they are blamed for failing to ' think nobly of
the soul.'   There was no doctrine of soul in the
received religion, or none worth talking about, and
there could therefore be no impiety in what the sophists
taught.   The Orphic doctrine was far more likely to
offend current prejudices.

The Pythagoreans might, perhaps, have developed

[1] See my *Greek Philosophy, Part I., Thales to Plato*, § 41.

a more adequate doctrine of the soul ; for they shared the religious interest of the Orphics and the scientific interests of the Ionians. As it happened, however, their musical and medical studies led them to regard it as a 'blend' (κρᾶσις) or 'attunement' (ἁρμονία) of the elements which compose the body, of which, therefore, it is merely a function.[1] Democritus went so far, indeed, as to distinguish the pleasures of the soul as more 'divine' than those of the 'tabernacle' (σκῆνος) or body ; but, since he held the soul to be corporeal, that was only a difference of degree.[2] On the whole, we must conclude that neither religion nor philosophy in the fifth century B.C. knew anything of the Soul. What they called by that name was something extrinsic and dissociated from the normal personality, which was altogether dependent on the body.

X

In the Athenian literature of the fifth century the idea of soul is still more unknown. We might have expected that the Orphic, if not the scientific theory, would have left some trace, but even that did not happen. In a matter of this kind vague general impressions are useless, and the observations I am about to make are based on what I believe to be a complete enumeration of all instances of the word ψυχή in the extant Athenian literature of the fifth century, including Herodotus, who wrote mainly for Athenians. I was much surprised by the result of this inquiry, which showed that, down to the very close of the century, there is hardly an instance of the word in any other than a purely traditional sense.

In the first place, as I have said before, it often means

---

[1] See *ib.* § 75. [2] See *ib.* § 155.

'high spirit' or courage, but that does not concern us
for the present. In a certain number of passages it
means 'ghost,' but ghosts are not often mentioned.
In a larger number of places it may be translated 'life,'
and that is where possible misunderstandings begin.
It has not, in fact, been sufficiently observed that ψυχή,
in the literature of this period, never means the life of
a man except when he is dying or in danger of death,
or, in other words, that the Attic usage is so far the
same as the Homeric. You may lose or 'give up'
your ψυχή or you may save it ; you may risk it or fight
or speak in its defence ; you may sacrifice it like
Alcestis or cling ignobly to it like Admetus. To
'love one's ψυχή' is to shrink from death, and φιλοψυχία
is a common word for cowardice. In the same sense
you may say that a thing is dear as 'dear life.' As for
the ψυχαί of other people, you may mourn them or
avenge them, in which case ψυχή clearly means *lost* life,
and may just as well be rendered 'death' as 'life.'
The one thing you cannot do with a ψυχή is to live by
it. When Heracles in Euripides[1] bids Amphitryon
'do violence to his soul,' he means 'Force yourself to
live,' and the literal sense of his words is 'Hold in the
breath of life by force' and do not let it escape. 'Refuse to give up the ghost,' comes near it. Similarly,
the expression 'Collect your ψυχή'[2] properly means
'Make an effort not to swoon,' and implies the same
idea of holding one's breath. You will search the
Athenian writers of the fifth century in vain for a single
instance of ψυχή meaning 'life,' except in connexion
with swooning or death.

The ψυχή is also spoken of in the tragedians as the

---

[1] Eur., *Herc.*, 1366, ψυχὴν βιάζου. Wilamowitz's interpretation of this is
singularly perverse.

[2] Eur., *Herc.*, 626, σύλλογον ψυχῆς λαβὲ | τρόμου τε παῦσαι. Cf. *Phoen.*,
850, ἀλλὰ σύλλεξον σθένος | καὶ πνεῦμ' ἄθροισον.

seat of certain feelings, in which case we naturally
render it by 'heart.'   What has not been observed is
that these feelings are always of a very special kind.
We saw that Pindar thought of the ψυχή as a sort of
'subliminal self' which 'sleeps when the limbs are
active,' but has prophetic visions when the body is
asleep.   In Attic tragedy this function is generally
attributed to the heart and not the 'soul,' but there is
one place at least where ψυχή seems definitely to
mean the 'subconscious.'   In the *Troades* the infant
Astyanax, when about to die, is pitied for having had
no conscious experience of the privileges of royalty.
'Thou sawest them and didst mark them in thy ψυχή,
but thou knowest them not.' [1]   This seems to be the
only place where knowledge of any kind is ever
ascribed to the ψυχή, and it is expressly denied to be
knowledge.   It is only the vague awareness of early
childhood which leaves no trace in the memory.   We
note the same idea in another place where something is
said to strike upon the ψυχή as familiar, that is, to
awaken dormant memories. [2]   That explains further
how the ψυχή may be made to 'smart' by being
touched on the raw, and also why certain griefs are said
to 'reach' the ψυχή.   We still speak of a 'touching'
spectacle or an appeal that 'reaches' the heart, though
we have forgotten the primitive psychology on which
the phrases are based.

If we follow up this clue we find that the feelings
referred to the ψυχή are always those which belong to
that obscure part of us which has most affinity with the
dream-consciousness.   Such are all strange yearnings
and forebodings and grief 'too great for words,' as we
say.   Such, too, is the sense of oppression and gloom
which accompanies the feelings of horror and despair,

[1] Eur., *Tro.*, 1171.   See B. H. Kennedy in Tyrrell's note.
[2] Soph., *El.*, 902.

and which is spoken of as a weight of which we seek to lighten our ψυχή. Anxiety and depression—what we call ' low spirits '—have their seat in the ψυχή, and so have all unreasoning terrors and dreads. Strange, overmastering passion, like the love of Phaedra, is once or twice said to attack the ψυχή.[1] Twice in Sophocles it is the seat of kindly feeling (εὔνοια), but that goes rather beyond its ordinary range.[2] It is safe to say that the ψυχή is never regarded as having anything to do with clear perception or knowledge, or even with articulate emotion. It remains something mysterious and uncanny, quite apart from our normal consciousness. The gift of prophecy and magical skill are once or twice referred to it, but never thought or character. It is still, therefore, essentially the ' double ' of primitive belief, and that is just why it can address us or be addressed by us as if it were something distinct from us. That, of course, became a mannerism or figure of speech, but it was not so at first. The ' soul ' of the Watchman in the *Antigone*, which tries to dissuade him from making his report to Creon, can claim kindred with the ' conscience ' of Launcelot Gobbo in Shakespeare's *Merchant*.

We shall now be able to see the bearings of some special uses of the word ψυχή. It is spoken of, for instance, as the seat of a guilty conscience. That is brought out clearly by a remarkable passage in Antipho,[3] where he is making his client argue that he would never have come to Athens if he had been conscious of guilt. ' A guiltless ψυχή will often,' he says, ' preserve both itself and an exhausted body, but a guilty one will leave even a vigorous body in the lurch.' It is from the same point of view that the law of homicide demands the forfeiture of the guilty ' soul '

---

[1] Eur., *Hipp.*, 504, 526.   [2] Soph., *O.C.*, 498, fr. 98.
[3] *De caede Herodis*, § 93.

(ἡ δράσασα or βουλεύσασα ψυχή),[1] a phrase in
which the use of ψυχή as the seat of conscience is
combined with its meaning of life as a thing to be lost.
Several passages of the tragedians are to be interpreted
in the light of this. Aeschylus, indeed, makes the
conscience reside in the heart, as was to be expected, but
he is emphatic in referring it to the dream-consciousness. It is 'in the night season' that the sore of
remorse breaks out.[2] Even the placid Cephalus of
Plato's *Republic* is wakened once and again from his
sleep by the fear that he may have some sin against
gods or men on his conscience.

Another mysterious feeling closely associated with
the subconscious element in our life is the sentiment
of kinship, what the French call *la voix du sang*. The
Greeks, too, usually spoke of blood in this connection,
but Clytemnestra in Sophocles addresses Electra as
'born of my ψυχή,'[3] and occasionally near kinsmen are
spoken of as having 'one soul' instead of 'one blood.'

Finally, we must notice a curious and particularly
instructive use of the word, which we know to have
been derived from popular language. The ψυχή is
the seat of wayward moods and appetites, and especially
of those unaccountable longings for certain kinds of
food and drink which sometimes emerge from the more
irrational and uncontrolled part of our nature. The
Cyclops in Euripides, who has not tasted human flesh
for ever so long, says he will do his ψυχή a good turn
by eating Odysseus up.[4] Even Aeschylus does not
disdain to make the ghost of Darius advise the Persian
elders to 'give their souls some pleasure day by day.'[5]
Just so the Romans said *animo* or *genio indulgere*, and
spoke of acting *animi causa*. It is a quaint piece of

---

[1] Antipho, *Tetr.*, Γ. a, 7. Cf. Plato, *Laws*, 873 a, 1.
[2] See Headlam, *Agamemnon*, p. 186.
[3] Soph., *El.*, 775.   [4] Eur., *Cycl.*, 340.   [5] Aesch., *Pers.*, 840.

primitive psychology, and it is certainly convenient to make a ' double,' for which you are not strictly responsible, the source of those strange yearnings for good living to which the best of us are subject now and then. The Egyptian *ka* had similar tendencies. Looked at in this way, the ψυχή is the merely ' animal ' element of our nature.

I have now covered practically all the uses of the word ψυχή in the Athenian literature of the fifth century. Even in Lysias, who belongs to the fourth, there is only one instance of the word in any but a traditional sense, which is the more remarkable as he had belonged to the fringe at least of the Socratic circle. The few exceptions I have noted are all of the kind that proves the rule. When Herodotus is discussing the supposed Egyptian origin of the belief in immortality, he naturally uses ψυχή in the Orphic sense.[1] Hippolytus in Euripides speaks of a ' virgin soul,' but he is really an Orphic figure.[2] Otherwise the word is used by Euripides in a purely traditional manner, even in the *Bacchae*. Aeschylus employs it very seldom, and then quite simply. Sophocles, as might be expected, is rather subtler, but I cannot find more than two passages where he really goes beyond the limits I have indicated, and they both occur in one of his latest plays, the *Philoctetes*. Odysseus tells Neoptolemus that he is to ' entrap the ψυχή of Philoctetes with words,'[3] which seems to imply that it is the seat of knowledge, and Philoctetes speaks of ' the mean soul of Odysseus peering through crannies,'[4] which seems to imply that it is the seat of character. These instances belong to the very close of the century and anticipate the usage of the next. There is no other place where it is even suggested that the ' soul '

[1] Herod., ii. 123.　　　　　　[2] Eur., *Hipp.*, 1006.
[3] Soph., *Phil.*, 55.　　　　　　[4] Soph., *Phil.*, 1013.

has anything to do with knowledge or ignorance, goodness or badness, and to Socrates that was the most important thing about it.

Now, if even the higher poetry observed these limits, we may be sure that popular language did so even more strictly.   When urged to ' care for his soul,' the plain man at Athens might suppose he was being advised to have a prudent regard for his personal safety, to ' take care of his skin,' as we say, or even that he was being recommended to have what is called ' a good time.'   If we can trust Aristophanes, the words would suggest to him that he was to ' mind his ghost.'   The *Birds* tell us how Pisander came to Socrates ' wanting to see the ψυχή that had deserted him while still alive,' where there is a play on the double meaning ' courage ' and ' ghost.'   Socrates is recognized as the authority on ψυχαί, who ' calls spirits ' (ψυχαγωγεῖ) from the deep.[1]   The inmates of his thought-factory (φροντιστή-ριον) are derisively called ' wise ψυχαί ' in the *Clouds*.[2] It is true that once in Aristophanes we hear of ' crafty souls ' (δόλιαι ψυχαί), which reminds us of the *Philoctetes* ; but the speaker is an oracle-monger from Oreos, so that is another exception that proves the rule.[3]   We may, I think, realize the bewilderment which the teaching of Socrates would produce, if we think of the uncomfortable feeling often aroused by the English words ' ghost ' and ' ghostly ' in their old sense of ' spirit ' and ' spiritual.'   There is something not altogether reassuring in the phrase ' ghostly admonition.'

XI

The novelty of this Socratic use of the word ψυχή is also indicated by the curiously tentative phrases he is

[1] Arist., *Birds*, 1555 sqq.   [2] Arist., *Clouds*, 94.
[3] Arist., *Peace*, 1068.

sometimes made to substitute for it, phrases like
'Whatever it is in us that has knowledge or ignorance,
goodness or badness.'[1] On the same principle I
should explain the reference of Alcibiades in the
Symposium to 'the heart or soul or whatever we ought
to call it.'[2] Such fine historical touches are much in
Plato's way, and the hesitation of Alcibiades is natural
if Socrates was the first to use the word like this. He
denied, if I am not mistaken, that the soul was any sort
of mysterious second self, and identified it frankly
with our ordinary consciousness ; but, on the other
hand, he held it to be more than it seemed to be, and
therefore to require all the ' care ' that the votaries of
Orpheus bade men give to the fallen god within them.
No doubt it is open to any one to maintain that, even
so, Socrates was not really original. He only combined the Orphic doctrine of the purification of the
fallen soul with the scientific view of the soul as the
waking consciousness. That is a favourite device of
those who make it their business to depreciate the
originality of great men. Against it it may be urged
that the power of transfusing the apparently disparate
is exactly what is meant by originality. The religious
and the scientific view might have gone on indefinitely
side by side, as we find them in fact simply juxtaposed
in Empedocles. It took a Socrates to see that they
were complementary, and by uniting them to reach
the idea best rendered in English by the old word
' spirit.' In that sense and to that extent he was the
founder of philosophy.

From the *Apology* alone it may, I feel sure, be inferred
that to Socrates the immortality of the soul followed
as a necessary corollary from this view of its nature, but

---

[1] Cf. *Crito*, 47 e, 8, ὅτι ποτ' ἐστὶ τῶν ἡμετέρων, περὶ ὃ ἥ τε ἀδικία καὶ ἡ δικαιοσύνη ἐστίν.

[2] *Symp.*, 218 a, 3, τὴν καρδίαν γὰρ ἢ ψυχὴν ἢ ὅτι δεῖ αὐτὸ ὀνομάσαι κτλ.

the important thing to notice is that this was not the point from which he started nor that upon which he chiefly dwelt. If, for a moment, I may go beyond the *Apology* and *Crito* for a negative argument, it is not a little remarkable that, both in the *Phaedo* [1] and the *Republic*,[2] Plato represents the closest intimates of Socrates as startled by his profession of belief in immortality. It does not seem, then, that this formed the ordinary theme of his discourse. What he did preach as the one thing needful for the soul was that it should strive after wisdom and goodness.

Of course, Maier is compelled by the evidence he admits as valid to recognize that Socrates called his work in life ' philosophy,' but he holds that this philosophy consisted solely in the application of the dialectical method to moral exhortation. That is why he says Socrates was no philosopher in the strict sense of the word. If he only means that he did not expound a system in a course of lectures, that is doubtless true ; but, even at the worst of times, philosophy never meant merely that to the Greeks. It is not correct either to say that the wisdom of which Socrates is made to speak in the *Apology* and *Crito* was merely practical wisdom. At this point Maier makes a bad mistake by importing the Aristotelian distinction between φρόνησις and σοφία into the discussion. No doubt that distinction has its value, but at this date φρόνησις and σοφία were completely synonymous terms, and they continued to be used quite promiscuously by Plato. It is wisdom and truth (φρόνησις καὶ ἀλήθεια) that the soul is to aim at, and it is an anachronism to introduce the Aristotelian idea of ' practical truth.' If the word φρόνησις is on the whole preferred to σοφία, it is only because the latter had rather bad associations, like our ' cleverness.'

[1] Plato, *Phaed.*, 70 a, 1 sqq.   [2] Plato, *Rep.*, 608 d, 3.

It is hardly worth while, however, to waste words on this point ; for the Socratic doctrine that Goodness is knowledge amounts to a denial that there is any ultimate distinction between theory and practice.

XII

The conditions of our experiment did not allow us to admit much evidence, and that seemed at first rather unpromising. Nevertheless, we have been able to reach a result of the first importance, which must now be stated precisely. We have found that, if the *Apology* is to be trusted in a matter of the kind, Socrates was in the habit of exhorting his fellow-citizens to ' care for their souls.' That is admitted by Maier. We have seen further that such an exhortation implies a use of the word ψυχή and a view of the soul's nature quite unheard of before the time of Socrates. The Orphics, indeed, had insisted on the need of purging the soul, but for them the soul was not the normal personality ;[1] it was a stranger from another world that dwelt in us for a time. The Ionian cosmologists had certainly identified the soul with our waking consciousness, but that too came to us from outside. As Diogenes of Apollonia put it, it was a ' small fragment of god,'[2] by which he meant a portion of the cosmical ' air ' which happens for the time being to animate our bodies. Socrates, so far as we could see, was the first to say that the normal consciousness was the true self, and that it deserved all the care bestowed on the body's mysterious tenant by the religious. The jests of

---

[1] The doctrine of παλιγγενεσία or transmigration, in its usual form, implies this dissociation of the ' soul ' from the rest of the personality. For this reason I do not believe that Socrates accepted it *in that sense.*

[2] A. 19. Diels, μικρὸν μόριον τοῦ θεοῦ.

Aristophanes made it plain that Socrates was known as a man who spoke strangely of the soul before 423 B.C., and this takes us back to a time when Plato was not five years old, so that there can be no question of him as the author of the view he ascribes to Socrates. We may fairly conclude, I think, that the ' wisdom ' which so impressed the boy Alcibiades and the impulsive Chaerepho, was just this.

I promised not to go beyond the evidence allowed by Maier, and I must therefore stop on the threshold of the Socratic philosophy. I cannot, however, refrain from suggesting the lines on which further investigation would proceed. In a dialogue written thirty years after the death of Socrates, the *Theaetetus*, Plato makes him describe his method of bringing thoughts to birth in language derived from his mother's calling, and we can prove this to be genuinely Socratic from the evidence of Aristophanes, who had made fun of it more than half a century before.[1] The maieutic method in turn involves the theory of knowledge mythically expressed in the doctrine of Reminiscence. The doctrine of Love, which Socrates in the *Symposium* professes to have learnt from Diotima, is only an extension of the same line of thought, and it may be added that it furnishes the natural explanation of his mission. If Socrates really held that the soul was irresistibly driven to go beyond itself in the manner there described, there was no need of an oracle from Delphi to make him take up the task of converting the Athenians. That, however, is transgressing the limits I had imposed on myself, and I do not wish to prejudice what I believe to be the solid result we have reached. That in itself is enough to show that it is of very little consequence whether we call Socrates a philosopher in the proper sense or not ; for we now see how it is due

---

[1] Arist., *Clouds*, 137.

L

to him that, in Julian's words, ' all who find salvation in philosophy are being saved even now.' That is the problem we set out to solve. I only wished to throw out a few hints to show that Maier would have to write another 600 pages at least to exhaust the implications of his own admissions. Some of us will prefer to think it has been better done already by Plato.

SHAKESPEARE AND GREEK PHILOSOPHY [1]

Reprinted from A BOOK OF HOMAGE TO SHAKESPEARE, 1916

SHAKESPEARE has given us the finest interpretation in any language of one of the central doctrines of Greek philosophy. That does not mean, of course, that he was a student of the subject in the ordinary sense. Though I am convinced that his classical attainments were far more considerable than is sometimes supposed, I do not suggest that he had read Plato's *Timaeus*. What I claim for him is something more than that, namely, that he was able to disentangle the essential meaning of the Pythagorean doctrines preserved in that dialogue, though these were only known to him through a very distorted tradition. Milton knew them well in their original form ; but his Platonism, nobly as it is expressed, yet lacks a touch which is present in Lorenzo's brief discourse on Music in Act v. of the *Merchant of Venice*. It may be worth while to add that such sympathetic interpretation of Greek thought was quite 'out of the welkin' of Francis Bacon.

The commentators fail to throw much light on Lorenzo's theory. They do not appear to have heard of Plato's *Timaeus*, though that dialogue has had more influence on European literature than almost any work that could be named, and though it is the ultimate source of so much that is best in English literature in particular. Above all, they do not possess the clue to the whole discourse, namely, the Pythagorean doctrine

[1] [See also *The Greek Strain in English Literature*, Pamphlet No. 45 of the English Association.]

of Music as the ' purgation ' (κάθαρσις) of the soul.
Let us see whether, with that clue in our hands, we
can follow Lorenzo's argument more closely, and state
his theory rather more fully than the exigencies of
dramatic art have allowed him to state it himself.

Let us start from the words ' Such harmony is in
immortal souls,' and note at once that the term ' harmony ' in this connexion does not bear its modern
meaning. Greek music had no harmony in our sense,
and ἁρμονία meant ' scale ' or ' octave.' Now the
sun, the moon, and the five planets, along with the
heaven of the fixed stars, were believed to form a
harmony in this sense, an octave scale, the intervals of
which were determined by the distances between the
planetary orbits. That octave has its counterpart in
the immortal soul of each one of us ; for the circular
motions of the soul of man only reproduce on a smaller
scale the mightier revolutions in the soul of the world,
which are just the paths of the heavenly orbs.[1] Were
it not for the earthly and perishable nature of the body,
our souls would therefore sound in perfect unison with
the grander music of the Cosmos. As it is, there is a
corporeal barrier between the Soul of Man and the
Soul of the World. The function of Music is to overcome this barrier, and it can do so because it is able to
reach the soul, while its scales reproduce the intervals
of the celestial diapason. It is thus an intermediary
between the universe and ourselves. So, when we
hear music, our nature is changed for the time, the
motions of our ' spirits ' are brought into accord with
those of the heavenly bodies, and we are at one with
what is highest. We see rudimentary traces of this
even in some of the animals. On the other hand, a

[1] [The celestial orbits were held to be circular, and accordingly, in the
Pythagorean theory, the life of the soul, *when it is in its best state*, consists
of circular motions.]

human soul from which music can elicit no response is altogether out of tune with the Soul of the World. It is not only the body in this case that bars the way ; the soul itself rings untrue. All that is Pythagorean doctrine, and in the light of it Lorenzo's speech becomes quite clear.

It is curious that Lorenzo says nothing about the ' crystal spheres.' As a matter of fact, these are a later addition to the doctrine, and are not to be found in the *Timaeus*. It almost looks as if Shakespeare saw them to be irrelevant, as in fact they are. He does, however, introduce one modification of the imagery, which gives us a valuable hint as to the channels through which it reached him. In the Myth of Er in Plato's *Republic* we read that there is a Siren on each of the planetary rings who sings in monotone her proper note of the octave. Lorenzo substitutes angels and cherubim, and that goes back in the long run to ' Dionysius the Areopagite.' We may fairly infer that the theory of the celestial ' harmony ' reached Shakespeare, as it reached Dante, in a medieval dress, and it is not hard to see how that may have come about.

Plato's *Timaeus* was never wholly lost to western Europe, as his other dialogues were ; for the greater part of it was accessible in the Latin version of Chalcidius (fourth century A.D.), with an elaborate commentary based mainly on Posidonius. In that commentary the doctrine is to be found, Sirens and all. It is, says Chalcidius,[1] the *consortium corporis* which causes the

---

[1] [Chalcidius, ed. Wrobel, p. 298. The passage is so important for our purpose that I give the original *in extenso*. ' Quia iuxta rationem harmonicam animam in superioribus aedificaverat, naturalesque eius actus rhythmis modisque constare dixerat, sed haec exolescere animae ob consortium corporis necessario obtinente oblivione, proptereaque immodulatas fore animas plurimorum. medelam huius vitii dicit esse in musica positam, non in ea qua vulgus delectatur, quaeque ad voluptatem facta excitat vitia nonnunquam, sed in illa divina, quae nunquam a ratione atque intellegentia

ratio harmonica in the human soul to fade away into oblivion, so that the souls of the many are 'unmodulated.' Music is the cure (*medela*) for this ; for it alone can recall the motions of our soul when they deviate from their orbits (*exorbitantes*) to the original concord (*ad veterem symphoniam*). In general, we may say that Posidonius, who was specially interested in early Pythagoreanism, made use of his knowledge to illuminate the obscurities of the *Timaeus*, and that Chalcidius handed on the torch to the Middle Ages.

The School of Chartres was the legitimate successor of Plato's Academy, and its teaching was based on the work of Chalcidius. In the twelfth century Bernard Silvester of Tours sought to rival the *Timaeus* itself in his *De mundi universitate*, and it was he that made the terms Macrocosm and Microcosm familiar. They are not to be found in Greek, though Philo and others speak of man as a μικρός or βραχὺς κόσμος, the *brevis mundus* of Chalcidius. It is here, too, that personified Nature makes her appearance practically for the first time. Then comes the *De planctu naturae* of

separetur. hanc enim censet exorbitantes animas a via recta revocare demum ad symphoniam veterem. optima porro symphonia est in moribus nostris iustitia, virtutum omnium principalis, per quam ceterae quoque virtutes suum munus atque opus exequuntur ; ut ratio quidem (i.e. τὸ λογιστικόν) dux sit, vigor vero intimus, qui est iracundiae similis (i.e. θυμός) auxiliatorem se rationi volens praebeat, porro ⟨cum⟩ haec provenire sine modulatione non possint, modulatio demum sine symphonia nulla sit, ipsa symphonia sequatur musicam, procul dubio musica exornat animam rationabiliter, ad antiquam naturam revocans et efficiens talem demum qualem initio deus opifex eam fecerat.' In an earlier passage (Wrobel, p. 140) we read : 'Pythagoreorum dogma est ratione harmonica constare mundum caelestiaque distantia congruis et consonis sibi invicem intervallis impetu nimio et velocitate raptatus edere sonos musicos.' And again (Wrobel, p. 166) 'septemque circulos instituit planetum eosdemque adversum se distare facit intervallis musicis, ut iuxta Pythagoram motu harmonico stellae rotatae musicos in vertigine modos edant : similiter ut in Politia Sirenas singulis insistere circulis dicens, quas rotatas cum circulis unam ciere mellifluam cantilenam atque ex imparibus octo sonis unum concordem concentum excitari.' (*The Greek Strain in English Literature*, p. 7 n.).]

Alan of Lille, to whom Chaucer refers his readers for a description of the goddess Nature, and from whom he borrows her designation as 'God's vicar general.' The Platonism of Chartres was popularized by Jean de Meung's continuation of the *Roman de la Rose*, and by the fifteenth century the leading doctrines of the *Timaeus* were common property, especially in England. There was an eager desire to know more of Plato, and Humphrey, Duke of Gloucester, procured a translation of the *Phaedo* and the *Meno* from Sicily. Inevitably this interest in Platonism was reflected in the Moralities of the next age, which betray their affiliation to the school of Chartres by the leading part they often assign to Nature, a personification practically unknown in continental literature till a later date, but of the highest importance for English poetry and English science. Obvious examples are the *Interlude of the Four Elements* (though that is Aristotelean, not Platonic), and *The Marriage of Wit and Science*, the very title of which is pure Plato. It is a probable conjecture that Shakespeare's Platonism first came to him from sources of this kind, which would account for the angels and the cherubim, though we must not exclude other possibilities. It is certain, at any rate, that there was a vast mass of floating traditional lore, of Pythagorean and Platonic origin, in the England of Shakespeare's youth, and that he was just the man to be influenced by it.

The ' muddy vesture of decay ' deserves a few words to itself. The Pythagoreans generally spoke of the body as the tomb or prison of the soul, but there was also an old Orphic doctrine that the body was the soul's garment (χιτών). At a later date this was revived in Gnostic circles, and the ' vesture ' was identified with the coats of skins (χιτῶνες δερμάτινοι) made by God for Adam and Eve. The image was adopted by Porphyry and his successors, and so passed into medieval Platonism. The epithets 'muddy' (χοϊκός) and 'of decay' (φθαρτός) reveal the origin of the phrase, however it may have reached Shakespeare. He can hardly have got it from St. Paul; for 'muddy' is a more accurate rendering of χοϊκός than the *terrenus* of the Vulgate or the 'earthy' of the English version.

The result of all this is that Shakespeare has picked out the pure gold from the dross with an unerring instinct. The Aristotelean and Scholastic accretions which disfigured the doctrine have all dropped away, and the thought of Pythagoras stands revealed in its original simplicity. We need not wonder at that. The sympathetic insight into another soul, which is the gift of the interpreter, is at bottom the same thing as dramatic genius. It is, after all, no great marvel that the creator of Hamlet and Falstaff could also recreate Pythagoras from stray hints tradition had preserved.

KULTUR

Reprinted from HIGHER EDUCATION AND THE WAR (1917),
pp. 1-37 (London : Macmillan & Co. Ltd.)

'Don't imagine for a moment that you can establish here something
satisfactory by merely following the pattern of a foreign country. Our
notions are entirely different from those of Germany.'
VISCOUNT HALDANE, *Education and Empire*, p. 57.

IN spite of Matthew Arnold's efforts to acclimatize
it, the word 'culture' is not very seriously taken
among us. We think of a cultured person as one who
pretends to appreciate things that seem meaningless
to most of us, and who is too impatient of the people's
untutored admirations. That is why, when the
Germans talk of their *Kultur*, we are apt to smile. Of
course we know they must mean something quite
different,[1] but we hardly care to inquire what it is.
That is a mistake. The Germans say and believe they
are fighting for the maintenance and expansion of
their *Kultur*, and we may fairly infer that to be the very
thing we are bound to resist. At the beginning of the
war we used to say that we were only fighting Prussian
militarism, but we had not long to wait for our answer.
A manifesto was issued, signed by ninety-three of
Germany's foremost scholars, theologians and men of
science, in which they declared amongst other things
that, but for militarism, German civilization would
have been destroyed long ago.[2] That surely gives us
something to think about. It does not do to ignore

---

[1] The German for 'culture' is *Bildung*, not *Kultur*.
[2] Similarly a manifesto published on October 10, 1914, and signed by
3200 university professors and teachers in the Higher schools, contains this
declaration : 'We firmly believe that the salvation of the whole of European
civilization depends on the victory of German militarism.'

the enemy's point of view, and there is a real danger
that the sacrifices we are making may prove to have
been made in vain unless we try to understand it.   It
would be little use to defeat the Germans in the field
if we were to fall under the influence of German
Kultur, and this danger is nowhere so great as in all
matters connected with education.   There is no
doubt that German 'organization' has a strange
fascination for many perfectly loyal Britons, while
there are others who say that, since the end the Germans
aim at can never be ours, it is a matter of indifference
what means they take to attain it.   I hope to show that
the question is not nearly so simple as either party
imagines.   There is a real breach between the *Kultur*
of modern Germany and the educational system she
has inherited from the early years of the nineteenth
century, and that is at the bottom of all recent educational controversies in that country.   We are too apt
to think that important paedagogical principles must
be involved, when as often as not the issues are purely
political.   That makes the whole question very hard
to deal with, but we cannot get away from it ; for
ever since the time of Matthew Arnold our own
controversies have taken shape under the influence of
German ideas, whether these were regarded with admiration or the reverse.   It is now high time for us to
make up our minds what our attitude towards German
education is to be.   The present state of the world
calls for a thorough examination of everything we have
been accustomed to take for granted, and I propose to
do what I can to prepare the way for such an examination in one of the most important departments of the
national life, that of Higher Education.   It is here
especially that Germany is held up to us as an example
or a warning, and we are bound to try to find out what
this means.   It will not do to accept or reject anything

simply because it is German ; we must ask what the German system actually is and what it is intended to do, and we cannot answer that question till we know exactly what is meant by German *Kultur*.

I

In itself, the word *Kultur* is innocent and even useful. According to the historian Eduard Meyer (one of the signatories of the manifesto), it means the inherited stock of bodily and mental peculiarities, ideas, customs, and social arrangements which characterize a given group of human beings, a stock which is handed down and increased from generation to generation,[1] so that *Kultur* may be roughly translated by our word ' civilization.' There is, however, an important difference in the use of the words. We usually think of Civilization as something which properly belongs to mankind as a whole, and in which different groups of men may participate more or less fully. It is the standard by which any particular *Kultur* in the German sense is to be judged. We are committed to this as soon as we say, as we often do, that one community is more civilized than another. It is true that the Germans also speak of certain forms of *Kultur* as superior to others, but not quite from the same point of view. They regard French *Kultur* as decadent and Russian *Kultur* as primitive in comparison with their own, but it does not come natural to them to judge any and every *Kultur*, their own included, by a universal human standard. No doubt this is primarily a question of emphasis. We ourselves speak quite freely, for instance, of Greek or American civilization, while German writers admit the possibility of a ' collective

[1] *Geschichte des Altertums, Einleitung,* § 4.

Kultur ' (*Gesamtkultur*), in which a number of separate national groups may participate. Still, there remains this difference, that, when we speak of Greek civilization, we are consciously restricting the application of the word, while the German feels he is stretching the natural meaning of *Kultur* when he speaks, as he sometimes does, of European *Kultur* as opposed to Asiatic. For the present, we may express this difference by saying that to the German *Kultur* is in the first place something national, while to the Frenchman or the Englishman Civilization is primarily something human.

It adds considerably to the difficulty of understanding these things that the Germans now use the word *Zivilisation* in the sense of material and technical progress (telephones, motor-cars, aeroplanes, etc.) to the exclusion of the moral and spiritual elements included in *Kultur*. That is what they mean when they say that in this country we have *Zivilisation* but no *Kultur*. It is no use telling a German that we are fighting for Civilization. He understands that to mean we are fighting for material comfort, which is exactly what he believes about us already. The confusion is increased still further by Professor Ostwald, who is a law to himself and defines *Kultur* as the power of transforming energy, which is only a scientific way of describing what most Germans call *Zivilisation* and not *Kultur*. We have to be on the look-out for ambiguities of this kind.[1]

From the German point of view, it follows at once

---

[1] The modern German use of these words seems to be of recent origin. At any rate, W. von Humboldt defined *Zivilisation* as ' the humanization of peoples in their external institutions and customs and in the inner sentiments relating to these,' while *Kultur*, according to him, ' adds Science and Art to this ennoblement of social conditions ' (*Ueber die Verschiedenheit des menschlichen Sprachbaus*, § 4). That is much more like the way in which the words are still used in English and in French.

that a *Kultur* can only be maintained by the State ; for nothing else is strong enough to adjust the conflicting claims which necessarily arise within the group. Neither the tribe nor the family is equal to the task. That is the origin of Right or Law, which is simply a declaration of the principles on which the State will employ its force, whether those principles are explicitly embodied in legislative acts or implicit in custom.   It follows that, where there is no State, there can be no Right, and that States can stand in no legal or juridical relations to one another.   That is why it is meaningless to talk of International Law.   No sovereign State can recognize any law above its own. The nations are still in the state of Nature, in which Might is the only Right.   I need not insist further on this, since recent events have made the meaning of the German theory sufficiently plain.

Now it cannot, I think, be doubted that this way of looking at the State arose from the spectacle presented by the Holy Roman Empire of the German Nation down to the day of its abolition by Napoleon.   Every one who has had to study the writings of German historians knows that to most of them there is something almost sacred in force as such.   The Germans are inordinately proud of their victory over the Romans in 9 A.D., and their school children are regularly regaled with the picture of Augustus exclaiming *Varus, Varus, gieb mir meine Legionen wieder*, but it was really a great misfortune for them, since it has stood in the way of their becoming a nation till the other day.   The so-called Holy Roman Empire was utterly impotent, and the allegiance of the Germans was divided for centuries among a host of anarchical sovereignties.   It is, in fact, just because they had suffered so much from the impotence of the State that they have come to exalt force above everything as they do now.   They believe that, but for the strong arm of Prussia, there would be no German nation, and therefore no German *Kultur*, to-day, and that is what the ninety-three ' intellectuals ' mean by saying that German militarism is the only safeguard of German *Kultur*. Of course it seems strange to us. A nation that has long enjoyed a high civilization is apt to take these things for granted. We are not foolish enough to deny that the State must rest on force, but since the seventeenth century we have advanced some way beyond such very elementary political notions. The memory of the Thirty Years' War seems to haunt the Germans still, and they are apparently afraid they might fly at each others' throats again if Prussia were not there to keep them in order. They may be right, and they ought to know best, so we must just take their word for it.

For our present purpose the application of the doctrine is this. Education in all its grades must be regulated in view of the national *Kultur*, and not with reference to any vague ideal of humanity. In the first place, Elementary education must be compulsory (*Schulpflicht*), because military service is universal (*Wehrpflicht*), and so is the Imperial franchise (*Wahlrecht*). These three things go closely together. It is necessary, in the interests of the State, that its soldiers should have a certain education, and it should be of a kind to increase their military value. It is also necessary that the electors should be educated in such a way as not to make a bad use of their votes. At the other end of the scale it is necessary, in the interests of the State, that its officers and functionaries of all kinds should be the best that can be got, and that can only be secured by a system of Higher education which will select the best and eliminate the unfit. It follows, of course, that the whole educational system should be regulated by the State, and so it is ; but here we come

to the first breach between the ideals of modern
German *Kultur* and the existing system of education.
The State which ought logically to have control of
education is the German Empire, but, in fact, the
twenty-six federated states have retained this control
almost entirely in their own hands.[1]   Not to speak of
free cities like Hamburg, even Anhalt and Reuss have
certain peculiarities of their own.   No doubt the
North German States follow the lead of Prussia in
most educational matters, but Saxony, Bavaria, Würt-
temberg and Baden are under no obligation to adopt all
the paedagogical ideas of the Kaiser, and as a matter
of fact they go their own way in many things.

II

When pushed to its extreme limit this ideal takes the
form of what is called Pangermanism, and it is worth
while to note that this substitution of the idea of race
for that of nationality is due to the fact that the Germans
are not a nation even now.   The deliberate exclusion
of Austria from the German Empire by Bismarck
amounted to a confession that a German nation was
impossible, and Pangermanism is the inevitable out-
come of Prussia's failure to create a real German unity.
Whatever the ultimate issue of the question here involved may be, it has led to the present insistence on
race, which is of the essence of Pangermanism.   Of

[1] The government of the Empire only comes into contact with Higher
education at a few points.   The conditions under which schools may grant
the certificate for military service for one year as a volunteer (*Einjährig-
Freiwilliger*) are determined by the Imperial Chancellor on the advice of the
Imperial School Commission.   The Federal Council (*Bundesrat*) regulates
the State examinations for the medical profession and the conditions of
admission to the study of medicine.   The Emperor decides upon the admission of officers to the Army (except that of Bavaria) and the Navy.
Everything else is left in the hands of the federated states.

course it is based on a fiction.   There is no German
race, or if there is, the majority of the German people
do not belong to it.[1]   There are German-speaking
peoples, but the German language is not conterminous
with the German Empire, and it is hard to see how it
can ever become so.   That is the inner contradiction
from which Pangermanism suffers.

The German Emperor is not, perhaps, a full-
blooded Pangermanist, but he is certainly inclined to
magnify the part Germany is called upon to play in the
world.   When he said at Bremen in 1902, ' We are
the salt of the earth !   God has called us to civilize the
world,' he was perfectly sincere.   His idea is that
Germany should do for Europe what Prussia has done
for Germany, and behind that there is a prophetic
vision of a Germanized Europe playing a similar part
on the wider stage of the world by dealing with the
Yellow Peril and the like.   What makes all this so
dangerous is just that it is based on religious and phil-
anthropic motives, which give a sort of sanctity to
Pangermanist ambitions.   The mass of the German
people are quite honestly persuaded that it is their task
to rescue Europe from anarchy, and they have been
taught in their schools and by their press to look on
this as a divine mission.

No one who ever reads German newspapers will
say that this is an exaggerated account of the doctrine
many of them preach, but it is important for us to
realize that it is shared by some of the foremost men in
the Empire.   Professor Ostwald is a distinguished
chemist and has a great reputation in other countries
than his own.   Shortly after the outbreak of the war he
announced that, after the victory, it would be the task
of Germany to secure that Europe should be able to
work in peace, and for that reason Germany alone

[1] See Ripley, *Races of Europe*, p. 214.

would remain armed. The work would not, however, be performed as hitherto ; it would be ' organized ' and every one would be assigned that share in it for which he is best fitted. Germany would decide as to these aptitudes, and would assign to each its task. She will be generous, however, in some respects. In particular, she will not impose either her language, her thought or her aesthetics on foreign nations by force, but once it is established, the predominance of Germany will soon get the better of all obstacles to the spread of Germanism arising from the particularism of the con-quered nations. On the other hand, Ostwald holds, the defeat of Germany would mean the supremacy of the lower instincts over the higher, of the brute over man, and a set-back to morality, which would herald the downfall of European civilization.[1]

These are not the ravings of a half-educated Panger-manist, but the deliberate utterances of one of the foremost representatives of German Science, who really believes that he is advocating what is for the good of mankind. He even regards himself as a ' pacificist.' In a letter to a friend in America he writes : ' We pacificists must only understand that unhappily the time is not yet sufficiently developed to establish peace in the peaceful way.' It is the English policy of World Dominion that counteracts ' the eminently peaceful sentiment of the greatest part of the people, and especially of the German Emperor.'[2] Similarly Professor von Wilamowitz-Moellendorff, in a lecture reported in the *Times* of September 11, 1914, de-plores the absence of any effective sanction for inter-

---

[1] A translation of this outburst appeared in the *Semaine littéraire* of Geneva for October 17, 1914. Ostwald is fond of insisting that the function of Science is to enable us to prophesy. This is no doubt a specimen.

[2] This is quoted by Mr. A. D. Lindsay in *Oxford Pamphlets*, No. 16, p. 14.

national law, and says the only hope is for Germany ' to dictate peace to the rest of Europe.' I do not quote these utterances merely for their absurdity. I wish to suggest at once that modern German *Wissenschaft* appears to produce a very curious way of thinking. I for one would not choose to know as much Greek as Wilamowitz or as much Chemistry as Ostwald at the price of having my mind work like that.[1]

III

The ideal of German *Kultur*, then, is a purely nationalist one ; it is what distinguishes the Germans from other nations, and it would naturally follow that German education should be directed solely to the inculcation of Germanism or *Deutschtum*. I understand that this is in fact the chief aim of Prussian elementary education, and that the ready acceptance of a narrow nationalist ideal by the mass of the public is due to that. The system of Higher education, however, is not the creation of modern German *Kultur*, and has been very imperfectly assimilated by it even now. It originated, in fact, at a time when there was no German State and when Prussia was under the domination of Napoleon, and there could therefore be no national *Kultur* in the modern sense. That is why the Pangermanists assail

---

[1] It is desirable to put on record the view held by Wilamowitz before the war with regard to the debt of German classical scholarship to this country. In the preface to his edition of the *Bucolici Graeci*, published at the Clarendon Press in 1905, he said : ' Germanum philologum, si potest, gratiam referre decet Britanniae, e qua ante hos centum annos accurata linguae Graecae cognitio nobis tradita est. imprimis autem viro bono et patriae et humanitatis amanti nihil sanctius est colendum communione illa bonarum artium, per quam quicumque inter omnes gentes vero investigando vitam impendimus, vel ut breviter dicam, quicumque γνησίως φιλοσοφοῦμεν, regibus populisque viam praeimus quae sola ad mundi salutem et concordiam ducit.' That is the voice of ' the other Germany.'

the German Higher schools so bitterly. They object
to the teaching of foreign languages as tending to
undermine patriotism, and especially to the teaching of
Classics, which has for its object what is common to
western Europe, the Graeco-Latin *Kultur*. As the
greater part of what is now Germany did not form part
of the Roman Empire, that is something alien to
it. Nor do they care about the classical literature of
Germany itself. The writings of Goethe and Schiller
are suspect of cosmopolitanism and should only be
studied (with due precautions) in the highest classes of
the school. In the lower division the literary part of
the curriculum will be confined to Gothic, Old High
German and Middle High German when the Pangermanists get their way.[1] As for Science, that is frankly
international, and is for the most part the work of
Frenchmen, Italians, and Englishmen, so there will
be as little of that as possible. Even the Christian
religion is dangerous because of its humanitarian
tendencies, and the Hotspurs of the party, the out and
out *Deutschtümler*, are all for reviving the cults of Odin
and Thor. Of course the German Emperor does not
go to these extremes, but he is undoubtedly accessible
to ideas of the kind, and he too advocates a ' national
German education.' That is the real meaning of his
famous outburst against the Gymnasium at the
December conference of 1890, when he accused it of
producing young Greeks and Romans instead of

---

[1] In the *Rheinisch-Westfälische Zeitung* (published at Essen) of July 18,
1911, a truly national curriculum was outlined by the Germanist Baesecke.
In this the only language to be studied in the two lowest classes of the school
is Gothic. Old High German begins the next year and Middle High
German two years later. Modern High German is confined to the three
highest of the nine classes when the boys have been rendered immune to the
cosmopolitan taint of Weimar and Jena by their previous study of the older
literature. The curious thing is that Latin and Greek are not dropped altogether (why not ?), though they too are confined to the three highest classes
when the boys are seventeen and over. French of course is eliminated.

young Germans.[1] We shall misunderstand his attitude unless we remember all this. We shall see that he afterwards felt he had gone too far and tried to undo the effect of what he had said, but the ' King's Peace,' as it is called, of 1900 is only a truce. The whole future of German Higher education depends on the issue of the struggle between Humanism and Nationalism.

To most people it cannot but seem that Germany has suffered a heavy loss in departing from the educational ideals of her great age, and that she will have to go back to them if she is ever to hold up her head again. At one time she was in a fair way to become the intellectual centre of Europe, and if that had happened she would have been irresistible. The change that has come over her is just that which Plato describes as the transition from Timocracy to Oligarchy,[2] and the educational system devised by von Humboldt for quite another purpose has been made to serve the ends of a society such as he never contemplated. No one can tell yet whether the war will bring about a reaction towards better things or whether it will increase the influence of the Pangermanists. In that case, we may write *finis Germaniae*, but it would be better for Europe in every way that it should not happen. The only thing that can prevent it is the German system of Higher education, and we cannot be sure that it is strong enough. There have been indications of late years that some of those who should have been champions of Humanism have been tempted to make terms with the unclean thing. It is an ill day for a people when it mistakes nationalism for patriotism.

---

[1] ' Wir sollen nationale junge Deutsche erziehen und nicht junge Griechen und Römer.'

[2] *Rep.*, viii. 550 a, sqq. Plato was thinking mainly of Sparta, but the parallelism with Prussia is very exact.

IV

Now a great deal of misunderstanding arises from the fact that men of a certain age and a certain education fail to realize that it is this nationalist *Kultur* which is alone familiar to the British public of to-day, and even to the younger generation of educated men, and that it is extremely repugnant to them.   No doubt it was the violation of Belgian neutrality that helped many good people to see that we were right in drawing our somewhat rusty sword, but that was only because it was a peculiarly glaring instance of something that went far beyond the particular case.   If we ask how it was that the whole nation was roused at once the moment a German soldier crossed the frontier at Visé, the answer is clear.   It was not merely the ' scrap of paper.'   That holds an important place in the diplomatic case against Germany, but most people had never heard of it.   Few of us knew anything about the history of Belgium and fewer still felt any particular sympathy for the Belgian people.   They had not yet proved they had the soul of a nation.   The response of our people would have been exactly the same on those memorable August days of 1914 if no treaty had ever been signed in 1839 ; for they had grasped something that had eluded them before, and there can be no doubt that what opened their eyes to it was the rhetoric of the German Emperor.   His picturesque phrases had become household words among us, and the least instructed of us felt there was something behind them which was incompatible with Western civilization and which we should have to resist if it tried to assert itself.   That something was just modern German *Kultur*, though our people did not learn the word till a week or two later.   They will never forget it now.   They knew too that the French people, in spite of all that had happened to estrange us in the past, spoke and thought of these things in a way that may have seemed over-emphatic to the ordinary English-man, but was in substance the same as our own. So we took to singing the Marseillaise with complete conviction, regardless of the fact that we had helped Prussia to get the better of the men who sang it first, and that the ' tyrants ' referred to in the song may fairly be held to include ourselves. At that date modern German *Kultur* had not been invented and the methods of the French Revolution did not appeal to us. This time it was different. The popular instinct is not very subtle but it is sometimes very sound.

Nowhere was the call of the nation more promptly answered than in the Universities. To some extent, no doubt, that may be attributed to the patriotic pugnacity and love of adventure happily characteristic of youth, but that was by no means all. Some of us know, indeed, that most of the talk which might have sug-gested such a superficial explanation was only a cloak for a deep seriousness. It was a high privilege to be a university teacher in those early days of the war, when one's best students came to say good-bye and revealed something of what they were really thinking. We, who were their teachers, know why these young men went at once without waiting to be fetched. It was certainly not that they might help to ' capture German trade.' They were not particularly interested in trade, and I do not remember that one of them ever referred to the economic aspect of the war. Nor was it that they had any strong objection to Prussian militarism as such ; they were more likely to fancy we should be all the better for a little more of that our-selves. What they really dreaded was the intellectual and moral influence of modern Germany, and being students they were extremely sensitive with regard to any proposals to ' Germanize our educational system,' as they put it. To understand their point of view, we must realize that they were born in the 'nineties of last century, and that Germany meant something quite different to them than it meant to the men of the Victorian age, when there was still a tradition that Germany stood for philosophy, learning, music, and simplicity of life. They had heard of that, to be sure, just as they had heard of the Reformation and the French Revolution, but it never occurred to them that it could have anything but a historical interest now. The name of Essen was a good deal more familiar to them than that of Weimar. If we forget the point of view of the younger generation, misunderstandings easily arise. Our late beloved Principal at St. Andrews, Sir James Donaldson, had known Germany in better days and owed much to German learning, and it was natural that he should often address our students on the excellences of German education. He did not know that, if anything could have destroyed the affectionate regard in which they held him, it would have been that. In October 1914, he had to address them at the opening of our College, and a voice was heard to murmur reproachfully, ' German education again ! ' Fortunately what he had to say was very different ; it was a call to the service of the country and was received with enthusiasm. One of my students, who has since given his life for the cause he believed in, said to me before he went that the war clearly meant the breakdown of German education. It could not have happened if the Germans had really been an educated people. It seems to me very important that statesmen and educational reformers should realize the extreme sensitiveness of the younger generation on this point. It is a factor in the case which it would be dangerous to ignore.

Even in Germany itself, the older generation does not appear to be fully conscious of the change that has taken place within the last half-century. That, at any rate, is the only way in which I can account for the fact that the ninety-three ' intellectuals ' refer us to Kant, Beethoven, and Goethe to show us what is meant by German *Kultur*. Kant died in 1807, Beethoven in 1827, and Goethe in 1832. The *Kritik of Pure Reason* and *Faust* (in its original form) are earlier than the French Revolution, and it would surely have been a good deal more convincing to adduce some rather more recent representatives of German *Kultur* than these. Besides, from what we know of the men, we may doubt whether they would have been altogether pleased by its later developments. Kant was a Prussian (though his grandfather was a Scotsman), but he busied himself among other things with a scheme for securing everlasting peace by a free federation of nations. Beethoven (whose family came from a village near Louvain in Belgium) originally composed the *Eroica* symphony in honour of Napoleon and only changed his mind when the First Consul made himself Emperor. Goethe too was an admirer of Napoleon and of French *Kultur*, and he undoubtedly threw cold water on the War of Liberation. He told the Germans they were hoping in vain to make themselves into a nation, and that it would be better for them to shape themselves more freely into human beings, a thing that was in their power.[1] The Kaiser, who once made a speech at the University of Koenigsberg without mentioning Kant, would not have tolerated any of these men for a day. As a distinguished German writer on education observes, ' It appears to us nowadays a sorry reputa-

---

[1] ' Zur Nation euch zu bilden, ihr hoffet es, Deutsche, vergebens.
Bildet, ihr könnt es, dafür freier zu Menschen euch aus.'

tion, that of having been a nation of thinkers and
poets.'[1]   That, surely, is the true note.

V

I do not doubt that there is a good deal of prejudice
and injustice in our young men's estimate of German
education.   I have said already that there is a real
breach between it and the *Kultur* of the modern
German State, and for that reason there is still a good
deal of the older and better Germany left, if you know
where to look for it.   Few people, however, have time
to do that.   They must be content with a general impression, and the Germans of the present day certainly
do not possess the art of making a good one.   One
thing at least is certain.   It is many years now since
any sort of inspiration has come to our young men
from over the North Sea, and we shall find it worth
while to keep that in view.   There also exists a very
decided feeling that we have gone to absurd lengths in
depreciating our own achievements in matters of this
kind.   That is our way, but it is apt to be misunderstood abroad.   Foreigners do not know that, when we
want to stir our countrymen up, we generally do so by
telling them that they do things better in—whatever
may be the fashionable country at the moment.   It is
by no means edifying to read German disquisitions on
our intellectual inferiority, and our exclusive devotion
to what they imagine we call ' Sport,'[2] and to find in
the footnotes at the bottom of the page a string of

---

[1] ' Heute erscheint es uns ein leidiger Ruhm, eine Nation von Denkern und
Dichtern gewesen zu sein.' Dr. Max Wiesenthal, *Neue Jahrbücher für
Pädagogik*, vol. x. (1902), p. 206.

[2] To be just to the Germans, they seem to have learnt the incorrect use of
the word ' sport ' for school games from the French.

references to English writers in support of the thesis.
Take the case of Science, which is so much to the fore
just now.   It is a simple matter of fact that very few
of the greatest scientific discoveries have been made by
Germans.   Let any one make a list of a score of men
whom he regards as being in the very first rank of
scientific discoverers, and he will be surprised to find
how few of them are German, and the same holds good
of the great inventors who have transformed modern
life. What is true, as Professor Ostwald would tell
us, is that the Germans have ' organized ' scientific
work in a wonderful way.   They have surveyed the
whole field, with the result that the scientific workers
of other nations, when they wish to know the actual
state of any problem in which they are interested, have
recourse to German publications for their information.
In this way the Germans have done a most useful and
meritorious work, and the strange thing is only that
their vaunted ' method ' has led them to so few discoveries of the first importance.   The men who have
revolutionized our view of the world have almost
always been Frenchmen, Italians, or Englishmen.[1]

VI

The average Englishman, however, when he speaks
of the achievements of German science, means something quite different from this.   He is thinking of the
extraordinary skill with which the Germans have
applied the results of scientific discovery to the needs

[1] Science was introduced into Prussia by the Huguenot refugees, and it is
interesting to note how strong that influence remained.   Dubois Reymond
had not a drop of German blood in his veins, for his family belonged to
Neufchâtel, and had never married outside the French Huguenot circle.
The father of von Helmholtz was a German, but his mother was the daughter
of a British officer and a Huguenot lady.

of industry and commerce, and he will probably refer
to the classical example of the aniline dyes.   That
brings us back to the question of Higher education.
It is certain that we have fallen behind the Germans
in this respect, and the so-called practical man finds it
convenient to blame our Universities for it.   That, I
fear, is what gives force to the cry of the ' neglect of
science ' and makes some people desire a sweeping
reconstruction of our educational system on what they
suppose to be German lines.   As I have said already,
that idea is utterly abhorrent to the younger generation, and what is wanted is a little plain speaking on
the subject.   To begin with, we must remember that
the advance of German industry in recent years is due
to the fact that it was preceded by a long period of
perfectly disinterested scientific research.   If the
Industrial Revolution had taken place in Germany as
early as it did with us, it is very doubtful whether that
would have been possible.   It is certain that Science
itself may be injured by being diverted from its proper
business to the furtherance of material aims, and I am
inclined to think that has happened in Germany of late
years.   I speak with hesitation on such a matter, but
it does not seem to me that German science is quite
what it was a generation ago.   In the second place, it
is altogether untrue that the German system is what it
is represented to be.   The German universities do not
yoke themselves to the chariot-wheels of commerce
and industry ; it is just the other way.   The German
manufacturer or industrial leader is, for reasons which
will appear, a good deal better educated than ours
usually are, and he therefore knows the value of the
expert, and is prepared to pay him well and give him
a free hand.   The very same thing might be done in
this country if there was the slightest desire to do it.
There is already far more trained scientific ability in

our Universities than any one will make use of, and it could be increased if necessary, but it is not the business of the Universities to relieve those who control our industries of the trouble and expense of employing scientific experts of their own. The war has shown what our laboratories are capable of when they are called upon, and there are some who are simple enough to believe they will go on at the same high pressure in time of peace in the interests of industrial production. They forget that what has been done in them for the last two years was done for the nation, and that it would be quite another thing to put them at the disposal of individual manufacturers or limited companies. The men who have worked so hard during the war are not likely to go on finding out things in order to make a present of their discoveries to the directors of industrial concerns. In the language of the day, that is not a ' business proposition,' and it may become necessary for us to remember that the original meaning of *universitas* was ' trades-union.' The universities are partly supported by public moneys, but still more by private endowments. The expenditure of public moneys cannot be justified when the profits accrue mainly to individuals, as would be the case if such schemes were carried out. A socialist State might conceivably claim that Universities supported by it should confine themselves to its service, but an industrial community organized as ours is can make no such demand. As to endowments, their purpose is to enable the sons of poor men to give themselves to the disinterested pursuit of knowledge, and they are none too great for the purpose. To divert them to that of paying for researches, the expense of which should properly fall on those who primarily profit by them, would be unpardonable, and I cannot believe it will be permitted. What is wanted is really a better

education for the leaders of commerce and industry,
so that they may gain a rather wider outlook than they
have at present.

VII

The truth is that the Prussians only understand
these things better than we do, because they came late
upon the scene and had to think them out seriously.
They had learnt from their experience in other direc-
tions, and especially from that of their army, that a
nation needs above all things an *élite* to do its highest
work, and that an expert *élite* can be trained.   From
the beginning they organized their educational system
in view of that, though the type of expert they first
aimed at producing was of another kind.   The same
methods were applicable, however, in the sphere of
commerce and industry as in other departments, and
there was no difficulty in adapting them accordingly.
We need such an *élite* just as much as the Germans do
or more, but we are inclined to think it will be forth-
coming without our having to trouble ourselves in the
matter.   That idea has arisen very largely because, in
many departments of our public life we have, in fact,
been furnished with an *élite* by the Public Schools and
the Universities of Oxford and Cambridge.   I do not
propose to criticize these institutions here.   They have
even more than their share of the national habit of
self-depreciation, and may safely be left to criticize
themselves.   As, however, I have known something of
them in the past, and have no private interest in them
now, I think it only right to state my opinion for what
it is worth, that there is enough *Wissenschaft* in Oxford
and Cambridge to set up three or four German universities, and that the English Sixth Form boy is much
superior, intellectually and otherwise, to the German

Primaner, in spite of his being about two years younger on the average, a fact which those who compare the two do not as a rule think worthy of notice.[1]   The older Universities and the Public Schools do much the best educational work that is done in this country to-day, and we should be very careful not to meddle rashly with institutions which are more and more becoming the admiration and envy of Europe and America.   But this is not enough.   For a variety of causes, of which their geographical situation is certainly the chief, the older Universities and Public Schools have come to be more or less associated with a certain class, though to nothing like the extent that is commonly supposed.   That class is neither the aristocracy nor the plutocracy.   There are more sons of country parsons at Oxford than of peers or millionaires, and I hardly know how to describe the class I mean, unless we may call it the well-bred class.   It is the class which thinks it right to spend a disproportionate part of its income on the education of its sons, so that they may be fit for the service of the country.   Of the still heavier sacrifices that class has made since August 1914 I do not speak, but it ought to be remembered in estimating its value to the nation.   The older Universities and the Public Schools do not receive a penny of the nation's money, and the patriotism and public spirit they foster is a direct gain to the whole people. But, as I say, it is not enough.   We cannot afford to draw our *élite* mainly from a single class, and it is certain that there is a large population, especially in the North of England, which is out of touch with the Public Schools and even with the older Universities. It is not that these institutions are exclusive.   Oxford is the most democratic place in the world.   No one

---

[1] The facts as to the ages of Prussian and English schoolboys are given [in *Higher Education and the War*], pp. 96 and 166.

there asks who any one is, and those who know Oxford
best know that the result of such an inquiry, if made,
would be very surprising to the public.   But the fact
remains that Oxford is in the southern half of England,
and that so far limits its range.

In Scotland the situation is different.   We have
nothing that can be compared for a moment with the
great educational institutions of the South, but we
have more nearly solved the problem of drawing our
élite from every class in the community, and it is therefore possible that our experience may be of use in
England.   The day schools and the newer Universities
of the North of England are not unlike those of Scotland, and have indeed been modelled on them to some
extent, so that we already have within our island a
system which is of native growth, and only wants, as I
believe, to be treated as an organic whole to give us
something far better than Germany has ever had.   The
war has taught us that we are capable of organizing our
military resources when we are called upon to do so,
and our first work in time of peace will be to organize
our spiritual resources.   It is a good deal more difficult
to do, and it will take longer.   As the French Minister
of Public Instruction put it, ' munitions can be im-
provised, but not a soul.'

VIII

It is, of course, just the appearance of superior
organization that fascinates so many people when they
compare the Prussian system with our own, and it is
true that we fall short in many ways.   On the other
hand, we must not forget that, in so far as education
has been organized in view of the Prussian ideal of
State *Kultur*, we cannot adopt its methods without

danger. The whole *Kultur* of modern Germany is based on the organization of society in fixed classes, each of them efficient in its sphere, but sharply separated from one another. It is possible for an English boy to make his way from the elementary school to Oxford, and it happens a good deal oftener than some people realize. In Prussia, on the other hand, there is a barrier between the elementary schools and those above them that can hardly be passed after the age of ten,[1] and those who do not pass it are marked off from the class above them by being compelled to serve in the army for two years. The Middle schools [2] are able, indeed, to secure for their pupils the privilege of serving for only one year with the colours, but their pupils, who have only had six years of what we call Secondary schooling, are excluded by law from the Universities, and therefore from the professions and the higher civil service. They are even excluded by growing custom from positions of authority and responsibility in commerce and industry. In this way the educational system has to act as a social sieve, and unless a certain stage has been reached by a certain age, a boy is classed for life. We shall see too that the process of selection is most rigorous at the early stages of education, and that it becomes laxer as we go higher in the scale. The result is a rigid system of class distinctions, which, from the point of view of the State, yields a high average of efficiency in each class, however little it may favour the development of exceptional individuals. That is German *Kultur*, and Ostwald is right in saying that its secret is organization. But

[1] It has been done, of course, by exceptional men like Virchow and Paulsen.

[2] I use the term in the Prussian sense of schools which have only six classes. In South Germany, it includes what are called ' Higher schools ' in Prussia.

organization, when the word is applied to human beings, means the treatment of them as tools or instruments and not as persons, a treatment which is often necessary in war, for instance, but which is by no means what German Higher education was originally designed to promote. That is what I meant by saying that there is a real breach between Prussian *Kultur* and the Humanistic education Germany has inherited from the past. *Kultur* is really a spiritual Mechanism, and is incompatible with an education which puts Man above Machinery.

GREEK PHILOSOPHY

Reprinted from THE LEGACY OF GREECE, pp. 57-95 (1921)

IF we consider the philosophical tendencies of the day,
we shall probably observe first of all that the artificial
wall of partition between philosophy and science—and
especially mathematical science—is beginning to wear
very thin.   On the other hand, we cannot fail to notice
a reaction against what is called intellectualism.   This
reaction takes many forms, the most characteristic
perhaps of which is a renewed interest in mysticism.
It leads also to a strong insistence on the practical
aspect of philosophic thought, and to a view of its
bearing on what had been regarded as primarily
theoretical issues, which is known by the rather unfortunate name of pragmatism.   Now it is just on
these points that we have most to learn from the Greeks,
and Greek philosophy is therefore of special importance
for us at the present time.   At its best, it was never
divorced from science, while it found a way of recon-
ciling itself both with the interests of the practical life
and with mysticism without in any way abating the
claims of the intellect.   It is solely from these points
of view that it is proposed to regard Greek philosophy
here.   It would be futile to attempt a summary of the
whole subject in the space available, and such a summary
would have no value.   Many things will therefore be
passed over in silence which are important in themselves and would have to be fully treated in a complete
account.   All that can be done now is to indicate the
points at which Greek philosophy seems to touch our
actual problems.   It will be seen that here, as elsewhere, 'all history is contemporary history,' and that

the present can only be understood in the light of the past.

The word ' philosophy ' is Greek and so is the thing it denotes. Unless we are to use the term in so wide a sense as to empty it of all special meaning, there is no evidence that philosophy has ever come into existence anywhere except under Greek influences. In particular, mystical speculation based on religious experience is not itself philosophy, though it has often influenced philosophy profoundly, and for this reason the pantheism of the *Upanishads* cannot be called philosophical. It is true that there is an Indian philosophy, and indeed the Hindus are the only ancient people besides the Greeks who ever had one, but Indian science was demonstrably borrowed from Greece after the conquest of Alexander, and there is every reason to believe that those Indian systems which can be regarded as genuinely philosophical are a good deal more recent still. On the other hand, the earliest authenticated instance of a Greek thinker coming under Indian influence is that of Pyrrho (326 B.C.), and what he brought back from the East was rather the ideal of quietism than any definite philosophical doctrine. The barrier of language was sufficient to prevent any intercourse on important subjects, for neither the Greeks nor the Indians cared to learn any language but their own. Of course philosophy may culminate in theology, and the best Greek philosophy certainly does so, but it begins with science and not with religion.

By philosophy the Greeks meant a serious endeavour to understand the world and man, having for its chief aim the discovery of the right way of life and the conversion of people to it. It would not, however, be true to say that the word had always borne this special sense. At any rate the corresponding verb (φιλοσοφεῖν) had at first a far wider range. For instance, Herodotus

(i. 30) makes Croesus say that Solon had travelled far and wide ' as a philosopher ' (φιλοσοφέων), and it is clear from the context that this refers to that love of travel for the sake of the ' wonders ' to be seen in strange lands which was so characteristic of the Ionian Greeks in the fifth century B.C. That is made quite plain by the phrase ' for the sake of sightseeing ' (θεωρίης εἵνεκεν) with which the word is coupled. Again, when Thucydides (ii. 40) makes Pericles say of his fellow-citizens ' we follow philosophy without loss of manliness ' (φιλοσοφοῦμεν ἄνευ μαλακίας), it is certainly not of philosophy in the special sense he is thinking. He is only contrasting the culture of Athens with the somewhat effeminate civilization of the Ionians in Asia Minor. Even in the next century, Isocrates tried to revert to this wider sense of the word, and he regularly uses it of the art of political journalism which he imparted to his pupils.

Tradition ascribes the first use of the term ' philosophy ' in the more restricted sense indicated above to Pythagoras of Samos, an Ionian who founded a society for its cultivation in southern Italy in the latter half of the sixth century B.C. It is notoriously difficult to make any positive statements about Pythagoras, seeing that he wrote nothing ; but it is safer on general grounds to ascribe the leading ideas of the system to the master rather than to his followers. Moreover, this particular tradition is confirmed by the fact, for which there is sufficient evidence, that the name ' philosophers ' originally designated the Pythagoreans in a special way. For instance, we know that Zeno of Elea (c. 450 B.C.) wrote a book ' Against the Philosophers,' and in his mouth that can only mean ' Against the Pythagoreans.' Now the Pythagorean use of the term depends on a certain way of regarding man, which there is good reason for ascribing to Pythagoras him-

self.   It has become more or less of a commonplace
now, but we must try to seize it in its original freshness
if we wish to understand the associations the word
' philosophy ' came to have for the Greeks.   To state
it briefly, it is the view that man is something intermediate between God and ' the other animals ' (τἆλλα
ζῷα).   As compared with God, he is ' mere man,'
liable to error and death (both of which are spoken of
as specially *human, ἀνθρώπινα*) ; as compared with
' the other animals,' he is kindly and capable of civilization.   The Latin word *humanus* took over this double
meaning, which is somewhat arbitrarily marked in
English by the spellings *human* and *humane*.   Now it
is clear that, for a being subject to error and death,
wisdom (σοφία) in the full sense is impossible ; that
is for God alone.   On the other hand, man cannot be
content, like ' the other animals,' to remain in ignorance.
If he cannot be wise, he can at least be ' a lover of
wisdom,' and it follows that his chief end will be
' assimilation to God so far as possible ' (ὁμοίωσις τῷ
θεῷ κατὰ τὸ δυνατόν), as Plato put it in the *Theaetetus*.
The mathematical studies of the Pythagoreans soon
brought them face to face with the idea of a constant
approximation which never reaches its goal.   There
is, then, sufficient ground for accepting the tradition
which makes Pythagoras the author of this special sense
of the word ' philosophy ' and for connecting it with
the division of living creatures into God, men and ' the
other animals.'   If the later Pythagoreans went a step
further and classified rational animals into gods, men
and ' such as Pythagoras,' that was due to the enthusiasm
of discipleship, and is really a further indication of the
genuinely Pythagorean character of this whole range
of ideas.   We may take it, then, that the word ' philosophy ' had acquired its special sense in southern
Italy before the beginning of the fifth century B.C.

It is even more certain that this sense was well known at Athens, at least in certain circles, not long after the middle of the fifth century. To all appearance, this was the work of Socrates (470-399 B.C.). Whatever view may be taken of the philosophy of Socrates or of its relation to that expounded in Plato's earlier dialogues (a point which need not be discussed here), it is at least not open to question that he was personally intimate with the leading Pythagoreans who had taken refuge at Thebes and at Phlius in the Peloponnesus when their society came to be regarded as a danger to the state at Croton and elsewhere in southern Italy. That happened about the middle of the fifth century, and Socrates must have made the acquaintance of these men not long after. At that time it would be quite natural for them to visit Athens ; but, after the beginning of the Peloponnesian War (431 B.C.), all intercourse with them must have ceased. They were resident in enemy states, and Socrates was fighting for his country. With the exception of the brief interval of the Peace of Nicias (421 B.C.), he can have seen nothing of them for years. Nevertheless it is clear that they did not forget him ; for we must accept Plato's statement in the *Phaedo* that many of the most distinguished philosophers of the time came to Athens to be with Socrates when he was put to death, and that those of them who could not come were eager to hear a full account of what happened. It is highly significant that, even before this, two young disciples of the Pythagorean Philolaus, Simmias and Cebes, had come from Thebes and attached themselves to Socrates. For that we have the evidence of Xenophon as well as of Plato, and Xenophon's statement is of real value here ; for it was just during these few years that he himself associated with Socrates, though he saw him for the last time a year or two before his trial and death.

Whatever other inferences may be drawn from these facts, they are sufficient to prove that Socrates had become acquainted with some of the leading philosophers of the Greek world before he was forty, and to make it highly probable that it was he who introduced the word ' philosophy ' in its Pythagorean sense to the Athenians.

So much for the word ; we have next to ask how there came to be such a thing as philosophy at all.   It has been mentioned that Pythagoras was an Ionian, and we should naturally expect to find that he brought at least the beginnings of what he called philosophy from eastern Hellas.   Now it has been pointed out that Greek philosophy was based on science, and science originated at Miletus on the mainland of Asia Minor nearly opposite the island of Samos, which was the original home of Pythagoras.   The early Milesians were, in fact, men of science rather than philosophers in the strict sense.   The two things were not differentiated yet, however, and the traditional account of the matter, according to which Greek philosophy begins with Thales (c. 585 B.C.), is after all quite justified.   The rudimentary mathematical science of which, as explained elsewhere in this volume,[1] he was the originator in fact led him and his successors to ask certain questions about the ultimate nature of reality, and these questions were the beginning of philosophy on its theoretical side.   It is true that the Milesians were unable to give any but the crudest answers to these questions, and very likely they did not realize their full importance.   These early inquirers only wanted to know what the world was made of and how it worked, but the complete break with mythology and traditional views which they effected cleared the way for everything that followed.   It was no small thing

[1] [i.e. *The Legacy of Greece.*]

that they were able to discard the old doctrine of what were afterwards known as the ' elements '—Fire, Air, Earth, and Water—and to regard all these as states of a single substance, which presented different appearances according as it was more or less rarefied or condensed.   Moreover, Anaximander at least (*c.* 546 B.C.), the successor of Thales, shook himself free of the idea that the earth required support of some kind to keep in its place.   He held that it swung free in space and that it remained where it was because there was no reason for it to fall in one direction rather than another.   In general these early cosmologists saw that weight was not an inherent quality of bodies and that it could not be used to explain anything.   On the contrary, weight was itself the thing to be explained.   Anaximander also noted the importance of rotary or vortex motion in the cosmical scheme, and he inferred that there might be an indefinite number of rotating systems in addition to that with which we are immediately acquainted.   He also made some very important observations of a biological character, and he announced that man must be descended from an animal of a different species.   The young of most animals, he said, can find their food at once, while that of the human species requires a prolonged period of nursing.   If, then, man had been originally such as he is now, he could never have survived.   All this, no doubt, is rudimentary science rather than philosophy, but it was the beginning of philosophy in this sense, that it completely transformed the traditional view of the world, and made the raising of more ultimate problems inevitable.

This transformation was effected in complete independence of religion.   What we may call secularism was, in fact, characteristic of all eastern Ionian science to the end.   We must not be misled by the fact that Anaximander called his innumerable worlds ' gods '

and that his successor Anaximenes spoke of Air as a
'god.' These were never the gods of any city and
were never worshipped by any one, and they did not
therefore answer at all to what the ordinary Greek
meant by a god. The use of the term by the Milesians
means rather that the place once occupied by the gods
of religion was now being taken by the great fundamental phenomena of nature, and the later Greeks
were quite right, from their own point of view, in
calling that atheism. Aristophanes characterizes this
way of speaking very accurately indeed in the *Clouds*
when he makes Strepsiades sum up the teaching he
has received in the words ' Vortex has driven out Zeus
and reigns in his stead,' and when he makes Socrates
swear by ' Chaos, Respiration and Air.' So too the
Milesians spoke of the primary substance as ' ageless
and deathless,' which is a Homeric phrase used to mark
the difference between gods and men, but this only
means that the emotion formerly attached to the divine
was now being transferred to the natural.

The Milesians, then, had formed the conception of
an eternal matter out of which all things are produced
and into which all things return, and the conception of
Matter belongs to philosophy rather than to science.
But besides this they had laid the foundations of
geometry, and that led in other hands to the formula-
tion of the correlative conception of Limit or Form.
It is needless to enumerate here the Milesian and
Pythagorean contributions to plane geometry ; it will
be sufficient to remind the reader that they covered
most of the ground of *Euclid*, Books I, II, IV, and VI,
and probably also of Book III. In addition, Pythagoras
founded Arithmetic, that is, the scientific theory of
numbers (ἀριθμητική), as opposed to the practical
art of calculation (λογιστική). We also know that
he discovered the sphericity of the earth, and the

numerical ratios of the intervals between the con-
cordant notes of the octave.   It is obvious that he was
a scientific genius of the first order, and it is also clear
that his methods included those of observation and
experiment.   The discovery of the earth's spherical
shape was due to observation of eclipses, and that of
the intervals of the octave can only have been based on
experiments with a stretched string, though the actual
experiments attributed by tradition to Pythagoras are
absurd.   It was no doubt this last discovery that led
him to formulate his doctrine in the striking saying
' Things are numbers,' thus definitely giving the
priority to the element of form or limit instead of to
the indeterminate matter of his predecessors.

Pythagoras further differed from his predecessors in
one respect which proved of vital moment.   So far was
he from ignoring religion, that he founded a society in
southern Italy which was primarily a religious community.   It is quite possible that he was influenced by
the growth of the Orphic societies which had begun to
spread everywhere in the course of the sixth century,
but his religion differed from the Orphic in many ways.
In particular, Apollo and not Dionysus was the chief
god of the Pythagoreans, and all our evidence points to
the conclusion that Pythagoras brought his religion, as
he had brought his science, from eastern Hellas,
though rather from the islands of the Aegean than from
mainland Ionia.   He was much influenced, we can
still see, by certain traditions of the temple of Delos,
which had become the religious centre of the Ionic
world.   There had, of course, been plenty of religious
speculation among the Greeks before Pythagoras, and
it was of a type not unlike that we find in India, though
there are insuperable difficulties in the way of assuming
any Aegean influence on India or any Indian influence
on the Aegean at this date.   It may be that the begin-

nings of such ideas go back to the time when the Greeks and the Hindus were living together, though it is still more likely that both the Greeks and the Indians were affected by a movement originating in the north, which brought to both of them a new view of the soul. The Delian legend of the Hyperboreans may be thought to point in this direction. However that may be, the main purpose of the religious observances practised by the Orphics and Pythagoreans alike was to secure by means of ' purifications ' (καθαρμοί) the ransom (λύσις) of the soul, which was regarded as a fallen god, from the punishment of imprisonment in successive bodies. There is no reason to suppose that Pythagoras displayed any particular originality in this part of his teaching. It all depends on the doctrine of transmigration or rebirth (παλιγγενεσία), which is often incorrectly designated by the late and inaccurate term ' metempsychosis.' There is no doubt that Pythagoras taught this, and also the rule of abstinence from animal flesh which is its natural corollary, but such ideas had been well known in many parts of Greece before his time. The real difficulty is to see the connexion between all this and his scientific work. Here we are of course confined to inferences from what we are told by later writers ; but, if the doctrine which Plato makes Socrates expound in the early part of the *Phaedo* is Pythagorean, as it is generally supposed to be, we may say that what Pythagoras did was to teach that, while the ordinary methods of purification were well enough in their way, the best and truest purification for the soul was just scientific study. It is only in some such way as this that we can explain the religious note which is characteristic of all the best Greek science. It involves the doctrine that the Theoretic Life is the highest way of life for man, a belief still held by Plato and Aristotle, and to which we shall have to return.   We may note at once, however, that it is not an ' intellectualist ' ideal.   There is no question of idle contemplation ; it is a strenuous way of life, the aim of which is the soul's salvation, and it gives rise to an eager desire to convert other men.   Just for that reason, the Pythagorean philosopher will take part in practical life when the opportunity offers, and he will even rule the state if called upon to do so.   The Pythagorean society was a proselytizing body from the first, and it tried to bring in all it could reach, without distinction of nationality, social position, or sex (for women played a great part in it from the first).   It was precisely its zeal for the reform of human life, and its attempt to set up a Rule of the Saints in the cities of southern Italy, that led to its unpopularity.   If the Pythagoreans had contented themselves with idle speculation, they would not have been massacred or forced to take refuge in flight, a fate which overtook them before the middle of the fifth century.

It soon proved, however, that the Pythagorean doctrine in its entirety was too high a one for its adherents, and a rift between Pythagorean religion and Pythagorean science was inevitable.   Those who were capable of appreciating the scientific side of the movement would tend more and more to neglect the religious rule which it prescribed, and we find accordingly that before the end of the fifth century the leading Pythagoreans, the men whose names we know, are first of all men of science, and more and more inclined to drop what they doubtless regarded as the superstitious side of the doctrine.   In the end they were absorbed in the new philosophical schools which arose at Athens.   The mass of the faithful, on the other hand, took no interest in arithmetic, geometry, music, and astronomy, and with them to follow Pythagoras meant to go barefoot and to abstain from animal flesh and beans.   These

continued the tradition even after scientific Pythagoreanism had become extinct as such, and they were
a favourite subject of ridicule with the comic poets of
the fourth century B.C.

It is easy for us to see now that all this indicates a
real weakness in Pythagoreanism. Science and religion are not to be brought into union by a simple
process of juxtaposition. We do not know how far
Pythagoras himself was conscious of the ambiguity of
his position ; it would not be surprising if he came to
feel it towards the end of his life, and we know for
certain that he lived long enough to witness the beginnings of the revolt against his society in Croton
and elsewhere. It is for this reason that he removed to
Metapontum where he died, and where Cicero was
able to visit his tomb long afterwards. We shall see
later what the weak point in his system was, and we
shall have to consider how the discord he had left
unresolved was ultimately overcome. For the present,
it is more important to note that he was the real
founder both of science and of philosophy as we
understand them now. It is specially true of science
that it is the first steps which are the most difficult,
and Pythagoras left a sufficient achievement in mathematics behind him for others to elaborate. The
Greeks took less than three centuries to complete the
edifice, and that was chiefly due to Pythagoras, who
had laid the foundations truly and well.

We have now seen how the two great conceptions
of Matter and Form were reached ; the next problem
Greek philosophy had to face was that of Motion. At
first the fact of movement had simply been taken for
granted. The Ionian tendency was to see motion
everywhere ; it was rest that had to be explained, or
rather the appearance of it. However, when the new
conception of an eternal matter began to be taken

seriously, difficulties made themselves felt at once.   If
reality was regarded as continuous, it appeared that
there was no room for anything else, not even for
empty space, which could only be identified with the
unreal, and it was easy to show that the unreal could
not exist.   But, if there is no empty space, it seems
impossible that there should be any motion, and the
world of which we suppose ourselves to be aware must
be an illusion.   Such, briefly stated, was the position
taken up by another Ionian of southern Italy, Parmenides of Elea (*c.* 475 B.C.), who had begun as a
Pythagorean, but had been led to apply the rigorous
method of reasoning introduced into geometry with
such success by the Pythagoreans to the old question
of the nature of the world which had occupied the
Milesians.   The remarkable thing about the earliest
geometers is, in fact, that they did not formulate the
conception of Space, which seems to us at the present
day fundamental.   They were able to avoid it because
they possessed the conception of Matter, and regarded
Air as the normal state of the material substratum.
The confusion of air with empty space is, of course,
a natural one, though it may be considered surprising that it should not have been detected by the
founders of geometrical science.   Such failures to
draw all the consequences from a new discovery are
common enough, however, in the history of scientific
thought.

Parmenides cleared up this ambiguity, not by affirm-
ing the existence of empty space, but by denying the
possibility of such a thing, even before it had been
asserted by any one.   He saw that the Pythagoreans
really implied it, though they were quite unconscious
of the fact.   He is interesting to us as the first philosopher who thought of expounding his system in verse.
It was not a very happy thought, as the arguments in

which he deals do not readily lend themselves to this mode of expression, and we may be thankful that none of his successors except Empedocles followed his example. It has the very great inconvenience of making it necessary to use different words for the same thing to suit the exigencies of metre. And if there ever was an argument that demanded precise statement, it was that of Parmenides. As it is, his poem has the faults we should look for in a metrical version of Euclid. On the other hand, Parmenides is the first philosopher of whom we have sufficient remains to enable us to follow a continuous argument ; for we have nothing of Pythagoras at all, and only detached fragments of the rest. We can see that he was ready to follow the argument wherever it might lead. He took the conception of matter which had been elaborated by his predecessors and he showed that, if it is to be taken seriously, it must lead to the conclusion that reality is continuous, finite, and spherical, with nothing outside it and no empty space within it. For such a reality motion is impossible, and the world of the senses is therefore an illusion. Of course that was not a result in which it was possible for men to acquiesce for long, and historically speaking, the Eleatic doctrine must be regarded as a *reductio ad absurdum* of earlier speculation. There is no reason to believe, however, that Parmenides himself meant it to be understood in this way. He believed firmly that he had found the truth.

Several attempts were made to escape the conclusions of Parmenides, and they all start by abandoning the assumption of the homogeneity and continuity of matter which had been implicit in the earlier systems, though it was first brought to the light of day by Parmenides. Here again the influence of contemporary science on philosophic thought is clearly marked. Empedocles of Agrigentum (*c.* 460 B.C.), the only citizen of a Dorian state who finds a place in the early history of science and philosophy, was the founder of the Sicilian school of medicine, and it was probably his preoccupation with that science that led him to revive the old doctrine of Fire, Air, Earth, and Water, which the Milesians had cast aside, but which lent itself readily to the physiological theories of the day. He did not use the word afterwards translated 'elements' ($\sigma\tau o\iota\chi\hat{\epsilon}\iota a$) for these. It means literally 'letters of the alphabet,' and appears to have been first employed in this connexion by the Pythagoreans at a later date, when they found it necessary to take account of the new theory. Empedocles spoke of the 'four roots' of things, and by this he meant to imply that these four forms of matter were equally original and altogether disparate. That furnished at least a partial answer to the arguments of Parmenides, which depended on the assumption that matter was homogeneous. He also found it necessary to assume two sources of motion or forces, as we might call them, though Empedocles thought of them as substances, one of which tended to separate the 'four roots' and the other to combine them. These he called Love and Strife, and he supposed the life of the world to take the form of alternate cycles, in which one or the other prevailed in turn. In all this he was plainly influenced by his physiological studies. He thinks of the world as an animal organism subject to what are now called anabolism and catabolism. The details of the theory make this quite clear. A similar doctrine was taught by Anaxagoras (*c.* 460 B.C.), who came from Clazomenae in Asia Minor to Athens after the Persian Wars, and was one of the teachers of Pericles. His doctrine of 'seeds,' in which the traditional 'opposites'—wet and dry, cold and hot—were combined in different proportions, is rather more subtle than that of Empedocles, and it is possible to see in it a curious anticipation of certain features in modern chemistry. Anaxagoras too felt it necessary to assume a force or source of motion, but he thought that one would suffice to account for the rotation (περιχώρησις) to which he attributed the formation of the world. He called that force Mind (νοῦς), but his own description of it shows that he regarded it as corporeal, though he thought it was something more tenuous and unmixed than other bodies. There is little doubt that he selected the term in order to mark the identity of the source of motion in the world with that in the animal organism. That again is in accordance with the scientific interests of the time. In his astronomical theories, however, Anaxagoras showed himself a true eastern Ionian, and lagged far behind the Pythagoreans. For him, as for the Ionians of the Aegean down to and including Democritus, the earth was flat, and the eddy or vortex which gave rise to the world was still rotation in a plane. A more satisfying answer to Parmenides was the doctrine of Atomism, which frankly accepted the existence of space, and asserted that it was just as real as body. The first hint of such a solution was given by Melissus (c. 444 B.C.), who was a Samian but a member of the Eleatic school. He said, ' If things are a many, then each of them must be such as I have shown the One to be.' That was meant as a *reductio ad absurdum* ; but, when Leucippus of Miletus (c. 440 B.C.), who had also studied in the school of Elea, ventured to assert the existence of the Void, there was no longer any reason for shirking the conclusion which Melissus had stated only to show its impossibility. The atoms are, in fact, just the continuous indivisible One of Parmenides multiplied *ad infinitum* in an infinite empty space. On that side, at least, the theory of body was now complete,

and the question asked by Thales was answered, and
it is of great interest to observe that this was brought
about by the renewal of intercourse between the Ionians
of Italy and those of the Aegean, a renewal which was
made possible by the establishment of the Athenian
Empire.   Nothing makes us feel the historical connexion more vividly than the re-emergence of the
names of Miletus and Samos after all these years.
There were, however, certain more fundamental
problems which Atomism could not solve, and which
were first attacked at Athens itself.   So far, it will be
noted, Athens has played no part at all in our story, and
in fact no more than two Athenians ever became
philosophers of the first rank.   It is true that they
were called Socrates and Plato, so the exception is a
considerable one.   It was the foundation of the
Athenian Empire that made Athens the natural
meeting-place of the most diverse philosophical and
scientific views.   It was here that the east and west of
Hellas came together, and that the two streams of
tradition became one, with the result that a new
tradition was started which, though often interrupted
for a time, continues to the present day.

   If we wish to understand the development of Greek
philosophy, it is of the first importance that we should
realize the intellectual ferment which existed at Athens
in the great days of the Periclean age.   It has been
mentioned already that Anaxagoras of Clazomenae had
settled there, and it was not long before his example
was followed by others.   In particular, Zeno of Elea
(c. 450 B.C.), the favourite disciple of Parmenides, had
a considerable following at Athens.   He made it his
business to champion the doctrine of his master by
showing that those who refused to accept it were
obliged to give their assent to views which were at
least as repugnant to common sense, and in this way he

incidentally did much for mathematics and philosophy by raising the difficulties of infinite divisibility and continuity in an acute form. All that is something quite apart from the influence of the ' sophists ' at a rather later date, though they too came both from the east and from the west, and though they had been influenced by the more strictly philosophical schools of these regions. It was into this Athens that Socrates was born (470 B.C.) about ten years after the battle of Salamis, and he was naturally exposed to all these conflicting influences, of which Plato has given us a vivid description in the *Phaedo*, from his earliest youth. He cannot, in fact, be understood at all unless this historical background is kept constantly in view. There can be no reasonable doubt that at a very early age he attached himself to Archelaus, an Athenian who had succeeded Anaxagoras, when that philosopher had to leave Athens for Lampsacus. Ion of Chios, a contemporary witness, said that Socrates had visited Asia Minor with Archelaus, and that appears to refer to the siege of Samos, when Socrates was under thirty. There is no reason whatever to doubt the statement, which Plato makes more than once, that he had met Parmenides and Zeno at a still earlier date. At any rate, the influence of Zeno on the dialectic of Socrates is unmistakable. We may also take it that he was familiar with all sorts of Orphic and Pythagorean sectaries. Aeschines of Sphettus wrote a dialogue entitled *Telauges*, in which he represented Socrates as rallying the extreme asceticism of the strict followers of Pythagoras. So far, however, as we can form a picture of him for ourselves, he was not the sort of man to become the disciple of any one. He was a genuine Athenian in respect of what is called his ' irony,' which implies a certain humorous reserve which kept him from all extravagances, however interested he might be in the extravagances of others.

Nevertheless, while still quite a young man, he had somehow acquired a reputation for 'wisdom,' though he himself disclaimed anything of the sort. He had also, it appears, gathered round him a circle of 'associates' (ἑταῖροι). The only direct evidence we have for these early days is the *Clouds* of Aristophanes (423 B.C.), which is of course a comedy and must not be taken too literally. On the other hand, a comic poet who knew his business (and surely Aristophanes did) could hardly present a well-known man to the Athenian public in a manner which had no relation to fact at all. It is fortunate that there is a passage in Xenophon's *Memorabilia* (i. 6) which seems to supply us with the very background we need to make the *Clouds* intelligible. It represents Socrates in an entirely different light from that in which he appears in the rest of the work, and it can hardly be Xenophon's own invention. It seems to refer to a time when Plato and Xenophon were babies, if not to a time before they were born, and it is probable that it comes from some literary source which we can no longer trace. We are told, then, that Antiphon the sophist was trying to detach his companions (συνουσιασταί) from Socrates, and a conversation followed in which he charged him with teaching his followers to be miserable rather than happy, and added that he was right not to charge a fee for his teaching, since in fact it was of no value. It will be seen that this implies a regular relation between Socrates and his followers which was sufficiently well known to arouse professional jealousy. Socrates does not attempt to deny the fact. He says that what he and his companions do is to spend their time together in studying the wisdom of the men of old which they have left behind them in books, and that, if they come upon anything which they think is good, they extract it for their own use, and count it great gain if, in doing this, they become friends to one another. It is obvious that this suggests something quite different from the current view of Socrates as a talker at street corners, something much more like a regular school, and that, so far as it goes, it explains the burlesque of Aristophanes.

The Socrates of whom we know most is, however, quite differently engaged. He has devoted his life to a mission to his fellow-men, and especially to his fellow-citizens. If we may so far trust Plato's *Apology*, the occasion of that was the answer received from the Delphic oracle by Chaerepho, whom we know from Aristophanes as one of the leading disciples of Socrates in the earlier part of his life. Chaerepho asked the god of Delphi whether there was any one wiser than Socrates, and this of course implies that Socrates had a reputation for ' wisdom ' before his mission began. The oracle declared that there was no one wiser, and Plato makes Socrates say in the *Apology* that this was the real beginning of that mission. He set out at first to prove that the oracle was wrong, and for that purpose he tried to discover some one wiser than himself, a search in which he was disappointed, since he could only find people who thought they were wise, and no one who really was so. He therefore concluded that what the oracle really meant was that Socrates was wiser than other people in one respect only. Neither he nor any one else was really ' wise,' but Socrates was wiser than the rest because he knew he was not wise and they thought they were. It ought to be clear that this is mostly ' irony,' and it is not to be supposed that Socrates attached undue importance to the oracle, which he speaks of quite lightly, but he could hardly have told the story at all unless it was generally known that his mission did in fact date roughly from that period of his life. Historically it would probably be truer to say that the outbreak of the Peloponnesian

War, in which Socrates served with great distinction as
a hoplite, marked the decisive turning-point.   It was
in the camp at Potidaea that he once stood in a trance
for twenty-four hours[1] (431 B.C.), and that seems to
point to some great psychological change, which may
very well have been occasioned or accelerated by his
experiences in the war.   At any rate we now find him
entirely devoted to the conversion of his fellow-citizens,
and we must try to understand what the message he
had for them was.

In the *Apology* Socrates declares that his mission was
divinely imposed upon him, so that he dare not
neglect it, even if it should lead to his death, as in fact
it did.   The tone here is quite different from the half-
humorous style in which he deals with the Delphic
oracle, and even the ' divine sign.'   That only warned
him not to do things, mostly quite trivial things, which
he was about to do, and never told him to do anything ;
this, on the contrary, was a positive command, laid
upon him by God, and there can be no doubt that Plato
means us to understand this to have been the innermost
conviction of Socrates.   It is hard to believe that Plato
could have misrepresented his master's attitude on such
a point.   He was present at the trial, and the *Apology*
must have been written not very long afterwards, when
the memory of it was still fresh in people's minds.
Now Plato tells us quite clearly that what Socrates tried
to get the Athenians to understand was the duty of
' caring for their souls ' ($\psi\nu\chi\hat{\eta}s$ $\dot{\epsilon}\pi\iota\mu\dot{\epsilon}\lambda\epsilon\iota\alpha$).   That
is confirmed from other sources, and indeed it is
generally admitted.   The phrase has, however, become so familiar that it does not at once strike us as
anything very new or important.   To an Athenian of
the fifth century B.C., on the other hand, it must have
seemed very strange indeed.   The word translated

[1] [See footnote, p. 133.]

'soul' (ψυχή) occurs often enough, no doubt, in the literature of the period, but it is never used of anything for which we could be called upon to 'care' in the sense evidently intended by Socrates. Its normal use is to denote the breath of life, the 'ghost' a man 'gives up' at the moment of death. It can therefore be rendered by 'life' in all cases where there is a question of risking or losing life or of clinging to it when we ought to be prepared to sacrifice it, but it is not used for the seat of conscious life at all. It is sometimes employed to signify the seat of the dream-consciousness or of what is now called the subconscious or subliminal self, but never of the ordinary waking consciousness which is the seat of knowledge and ignorance, goodness and badness.[1] On the other hand, that use of the word is quite common in the fourth century, and it may be inferred that this change was due to Socrates. More than once Aristophanes ridicules him for holding some strange view of the 'soul,' and these jests were made at a time when Plato was only a child. We cannot, of course, expect to get any very definite idea from them as to the real teaching of Socrates on this subject, but it is not impossible to see what it was, if we take into account the views of the soul which had been held by the philosophical schools of eastern and western Ionia.

The Ionians of Asia Minor had certainly identified the soul with that in us which is conscious, and which is the seat of goodness and badness, wisdom and folly ; but they did not regard it as what we call the self or treat it as an individual. Anaximenes and his school held that the soul was what they called Air, but that was just because they regarded Air as the primary substance of which all things are made. The soul was

---

[1] See my paper on ' The Socratic Doctrine of the Soul.' *Proceedings of the British Academy*, 1915-16, pp. 235 sqq. [Reprinted above, pp. 126-162.]

something, in fact, that comes to us from outside
(θύραθεν) by means of respiration. As Diogenes of
Apollonia expresses it, it is ' a small portion of the god,'
that is, of the primary substance, enclosed in a human
body for a time, and returning at death to the larger
mass of the same substance outside. The formula
' Earth to earth and air to air ' was accepted as an
adequate description of what takes place at death.
The western Ionians, and especially the Pythagoreans,
held a very different view. For them, the soul was
something divine. It was, in fact, a fallen god, im-
prisoned in the body as a punishment for antenatal
sin, and it deserved our care in this sense, that it was
our chief business in life to purify it so as to secure its
release from the necessity of reincarnation in another
body. But, during this present life, they held that
this divine element slumbers, except in prophetic
dreams. As Pindar puts it, ' It sleeps when the limbs
are active.' Neither of these views was familiar to the
ordinary Athenian, but Socrates of course knew both
well, and felt satisfied with neither. When he spoke
of the soul he did not mean any mysterious fallen god
which was the temporary tenant of the body, but the
conscious self which it lies with us to try to make wise
and good. On the other hand, his insistence on our
duty to ' care for ' it is quite inconsistent with the view
that it is merely something extrinsic, as all the eastern
Ionians down to Anaxagoras had taught. It is, on the
contrary, our very self, the thing in us which is of more
importance to us than anything else whatever. It was
to this doctrine of the soul and our duty to it that
Socrates felt he must convert mankind and especially
his fellow-citizens. It was a strange and novel
doctrine then ; and, if it has become a commonplace
since, that only shows that he was successful, if not in
persuading his fellow-men to act on this knowledge, at

least in making them aware of it. It was in this way that Socrates healed the rift between science and religion which had proved fatal to the Pythagorean society, and it may be suggested that the significance of his teaching is not exhausted yet. As has been indicated above, it is to be found clearly stated in Plato's *Apology of Socrates*, and it furnishes the only clue to a right understanding of the great series of Platonic dialogues down to and including the *Republic* in which Socrates is represented as the chief speaker. Whether Plato added much or little of his own to the doctrine of his master in these dialogues is an interesting historical problem, but it need not concern the ordinary reader, at least in the first instance. We know from the allusions of Aristophanes that Socrates himself taught a new doctrine of the soul when Plato was a child, and no sympathetic reader can fail to see that the passage of the *Apology* to which we have referred is intended to be a faithful account of that doctrine. All the rest is simply its legitimate development, and it is not of very great importance for us to determine whether that development is due to Socrates or to Plato. The inspiration which has been derived from these writings by many generations will not be lessened by any decision we may come to on this point, so long as we keep clearly in mind that the new doctrine of soul is their principal theme, and that this must be understood in the light of the doctrines which had prepared the way for it. What Socrates did was really this. He deepened the meaning of the eastern Ionian doctrine by informing it with some of the feeling and emotion which had characterized the Pythagorean teaching on the subject, while on the other hand he rationalized the Pythagorean theory by identifying the soul with our conscious personality.

Now if this is a correct account of what Socrates

taught, he must be regarded as inaugurating an entirely
new period in the history of philosophy.   That is
implied in the common term ' Presocratics ' generally
applied to his predecessors, though the ordinary text-
books are by no means clear as to the grounds for
assigning this pre-eminent position to Socrates.   We
can also see how natural it was for him to lay such
emphasis on the conversion of souls as he certainly
did.   That purpose continued to dominate Greek
philosophy to the very end.   No doubt successive
schools varied in their conception of what conversion
meant, but that is the link which binds them all together.   In fact, it gave rise to a new literary form, the
' hortatory discourse ' ($\pi\rho o\tau\rho\epsilon\pi\tau\iota\kappa\grave{o}\varsigma$ $\lambda\acute{o}\gamma o\varsigma$), which
was more and more cultivated as time went on, and
was at last taken over by the fathers of the Christian
church along with much else of a more fundamental
character.

It has been noted already that Socrates had followers
among all the leading philosophical schools of the time,
and the possibility is not to be excluded that we may
still learn more of him from the discovery of new
sources.   For the present, the recovery of some new
and fairly extensive fragments of the *Alcibiades* of
Aeschines of Sphettus is the chief addition to our
sources of information.   We know that Aeschines
was a disciple of Socrates, and the tradition of antiquity
was that his dialogues gave the most faithful picture
of the man as he really was.   If so, that was probably
because Aeschines had no philosophy of his own.
For us the chief importance of the new fragments is
that, if we read them along with those already known
(and it is unfortunate that the old and the new have not
yet been printed together), they strongly confirm the
impression we get from Plato of the manner of Socrates
and his method of argument, and that helps to reassure

us as to the essentially historical character of the Platonic Socrates. The fragments of Aeschines also corroborate Plato by showing that the conversion of Alcibiades (whose life he had saved when a young man) was one of the things that lay nearest his heart.

But the real successor of Socrates was, of course, Plato himself (427-347 B.C.). It is not possible to give even an outline of Plato's philosophy here. Indeed the time has hardly come for that yet, though much admirable work is now being done, especially by a French professor, M. Robin, which promises more certain conclusions than have yet been possible. All that can be attempted here is to indicate the attitude of Plato to some of the problems we have been discussing. His very great contributions to the theory of knowledge will be passed over, as they are beginning to be well understood, and the *Theaetetus* in particular, with its sequel the *Sophist*, is more and more coming to occupy its rightful place as the best introduction to philosophy in general. It is necessary, however, just to notice in passing a fundamental question of method which the Platonic dialogues themselves suggest. It is this. While Socrates is present in every one of them except the *Laws*, he takes practically no part in some of them, and the dialogues in which this is the case are known on other grounds to belong to the later years of Plato's life. There must be some reason for this, and it is obviously prudent to treat these later dialogues in the first instance as our primary evidence for Plato's own views. Indeed, it is only after his philosophy has been reconstructed from these sources and from the sometimes obscure references to it in Aristotle, that it will be safe to attempt an answer to the question of how much there may be in the dialogues of his early life which is properly to be assigned to Plato himself rather than to Socrates. That is a historical question of great interest ; but, as has been said, the solution of it, if that should ever prove possible, would not greatly affect the impression that Athenian philosophy leaves upon us as a whole.

Now, if we consider Plato's later, and presumably therefore most independent writings, we find, just as we should expect from a disciple of Socrates, that the doctrine of soul holds the first place, but that it has certain features of its own which there is no sufficient ground for attributing to Socrates. We are too apt to think of Plato as mainly occupied with what is called the ' theory of Ideas,' a theory which is discussed once or twice in his earlier dialogues, and which is there ascribed to Socrates, but which plays no part at all in his mature works. There the chief place is undoubtedly taken by the doctrine of the soul, and we can see that it is of the first importance for Plato. Soul is regarded as the source of all motion in the world, because it is the only thing in the world that moves without being itself moved by anything else. It is this and this alone that enables Plato to account for the existence of the world and of mankind, and to avoid the theory of ' two worlds ' into which, as he points out in the *Sophist*, ' the friends of the Ideas,' whoever they may have been, were only too apt to fall. In Plato this view of the soul culminates in theology of a kind which he nowhere attributes to Socrates. He represents him, indeed, as a man of a deeply religious nature, but we do not gather that he had felt the need of a formal doctrine of God. Plato, on the other hand, has left us the first systematic defence of Theism we know of, and it is based entirely on his doctrine of soul as the self-moved mover. But the highest soul, or God, is not only the ultimate source of motion, but also supremely good. Now, since there are many things in the world which are not good, and since it would be blasphemy to attribute these to God, there must be other souls in the world which are relatively at least independent.   God is not, directly at least, the cause of all things, but it is not easy to discover the relation in which these other souls are thought of as standing to God.   In the *Timaeus* the matter is put in this way.   The soul of the world, and all other souls human and divine, are the work of the Creator, who is identified with God, and they are not inherently indestructible, since anything that has been made can be unmade.   They are, however, practically indestructible, since God made all things because He was good and wished them also to be as good as possible. His goodness, therefore, will not suffer Him to destroy what He has once made.   That of course is mythically expressed, and Plato is not committed to it as a statement of his own belief, since it is only the account which Timaeus puts into the mouth of the Creator.   We can see, however, what was the problem with which he was occupied, and it is not perhaps illegitimate to infer that he approached the question which still baffles speculation from the point of view that God's omnipotence, as we should call it, is limited by His goodness.   This is a much more important limitation than that imposed by the existence of matter, to which Timaeus also refers.   In that, he is simply following the tradition of the Pythagorean society to which he belonged, as is shown by his identification of matter with space, or rather with ' room.'   So far as can be seen at present, we are not entitled to ascribe this view to Plato without more ado, but that is a point on which the last word has not yet been said.

The description of the creation given by Timaeus is of course to be regarded as mythical in its details, but it has features from which we may learn a good deal as to the direction taken by Plato's thoughts about the world. In particular, while the important part played by geometry is quite intelligible in the mouth of a Pythagorean, he makes use of certain theories which we know to belong to the most recent mathematics of the day, in particular the complete doctrine of the five regular solids, which was due to Theaetetus, who was one of the earliest members of the Academy, and whom Plato represents as having made the acquaintance of Socrates just before the master's death. Theaetetus died young, but we know enough of him to feel sure that he was one of the few great original mathematicians who have appeared in history. In the *Timaeus* the theory of the regular solids is used to get rid once more of the doctrine of four ultimate ' elements.' These, Timaeus says, are so far from being elements or letters of the alphabet, that they are not even syllables. The way in which the so-called elements are built up out of molecules corresponding in their configuration to the regular solids, and the explanations of their transmutation into one another based on the geometrical construction of these figures, is apt to strike the average reader as fantastic, but one of the most distinguished living mathematicians and physicists has stated that he is struck most of all by their resemblance to the scientific theories of the twentieth century. It will be well, therefore, to avoid hasty judgments on this point. It is at any rate easy to understand how the study of mathematics came to hold the preponderating place it did in the Platonic Academy.

In accordance with the plan of this paper, something must now be said of Plato's attitude to the practical life, a point on which it is very easy to make mistakes. No one has insisted more strongly than he has on the primacy of the Theoretic Life. The philosopher is the man who is in love with the spectacle of all time

and all existence, and that is what delivers him from
petty ambitions and low desires.   He has made the
toilsome ascent out of the Cave in which the mass of
men dwell, and in which they only behold the shadows
of reality.   But, even in this enthusiastic description
of the philosophic life, an equal stress is laid on the
duty of philosophers to descend into the Cave in turn
and to rescue as many of their former fellow-prisoners
as may be, even against their will, by turning them to
the light and dragging them up into the world of
truth and reality.   It is quite easy to understand, in
view of this, that Plato devoted some of the best years
of his life to practical affairs and that he relinquished
the studies of the Academy for a time in order to direct
the education of Dionysius II.   The thing appeared
well worth doing ; for Greek civilization in Sicily,
and consequently, as we can now see, the civilization
of western Europe, was seriously threatened by the
Carthaginians.   They had been held at bay by
Dionysius I., but after his death everything depended
on his successor.   Now the education of Dionysius II.
had been completely neglected, but he had good
natural abilities, and his uncle Dion, who was Plato's
friend, was ready to answer for his good intentions.
Plato could not turn a deaf ear to such a call.   Unfortunately Dionysius was vain and obstinate, and he
soon became impatient of the serious studies which
Plato rightly regarded as necessary to prepare him for
his task.   The result was a growing estrangement
between Plato and his pupil, which made it impossible
to hope for a successful issue to the plans of Dion.   It
is unnecessary to tell the whole story here, but it is
right to say that there was nothing at all impracticable
in what Plato undertook, and that he was certainly
justified in holding that the education of Dionysius
must be completed before it would be safe to entrust

him with the championship of the cause of Hellenism in the west.

His failure to make anything of Dionysius did not lead Plato to abandon his efforts to heal the wounds of Hellenism. One of the studies most ardently pursued in the Academy was Jurisprudence, of which he is the real founder. It was not uncommon for Greek states to apply to the Academy for legislators to codify existing law or to frame a new code for colonies which had just been founded. That is the real explanation of the remarkable work entitled the *Laws*, which must have occupied Plato for many years, and which was probably begun while he was still directing the studies of Dionysius. It appears to have been left unfinished ; for, while some parts of it are highly elaborated, there are others which make upon us the impression of being a first draft. Even so, it is a great work if we regard it from the proper point of view. It is, in the first place, a codification of Greek, and especially Athenian law, of course with those reforms and improvements which suggest themselves when the subject is systematically treated, and it formed the basis of Hellenistic, and through that of Roman law, to which the world owes so much. There is no more useful corrective of the popular notion of Plato as an unpractical visionary than the careful study of the dullest and most technical parts of the *Laws* in the light of the *Institutes*.

No attempt has been made here to describe the system of Plato as a whole, and indeed the time has not yet come when such an attempt can profitably be made. We have no direct knowledge of his teaching in the Academy ; for we only possess the works which he wrote with a wider public in view. In the case of Aristotle (384-322 B.C.) a similar reservation must be made, though for just the opposite reason. We have only fragments of his published works, and what we possess is mainly the groundwork of his lectures in the Lyceum. It will be seen that there is still very much to be done here too. From the nature of the case, notes for lectures take a great deal for granted that would be more fully explained when the lectures were delivered, and some of the most important points are hardly developed at all. Nevertheless there are certain things which come out clearly enough, and it so happens that they are points of great importance from which we can learn something with regard to the philosophical problems of the present day.

In the first place, it is desirable to point out that Aristotle was not an Athenian, but an Ionian from the northern Aegean, and that he was strongly influenced by eastern Ionian science, especially by the system of Democritus (which Plato does not appear to have known) and by the medical theories of the time. That is why he is so unsympathetic to the western schools of philosophy, and especially to the Pythagoreans and the Eleatics. Empedocles alone, who was a biologist like himself, and the founder of a medical school, finds favour in his eyes. He is not, therefore, at home in mathematical matters, and his system of physics can only be regarded as retrograde when we compare it with that of the Academy. He did indeed accept the doctrine of the earth's sphericity, but with that exception his cosmological views must be called reactionary. Where he is really great is in biology, a field of research which was not entirely neglected by the Academy, but which had been treated as secondary in comparison with mathematics and astronomy. The contrast between Plato and Aristotle in this respect seems to repeat on a higher plane that between Pythagoras and Empedocles, and this suggests something like a law of philosophical development which may perhaps throw light on the present situation. It seems as if this alteration of the mathematical and the biological interest was fundamental in the development of scientific thought and that the philosophy of different periods takes its colour from it. The philosophy of the nineteenth century was dominated in the main by biological conceptions, while it seems as if that of the twentieth was to be chiefly mathematical in its outlook on the world. We must not, of course, make too much of such formulas, but it is instructive to study such alternations in the philosophy of the Greeks, where everything is simpler and more easily apprehended.

On the other hand, Aristotle had been a member of the Academy for twenty years, and that could not fail to leave its mark upon him. This no doubt explains the fact, which has often been noted, that there are two opposite and inconsistent strains in all Aristotle's thinking. On the one hand, he is determined to avoid everything ' transcendental,' and his dislike of Pythagorean and Platonist mathematics is mainly due to that. On the other hand, despite his captious and sometimes unfair criticisms of Plato, he evidently admired him greatly and had been much influenced by him. It may be suggested that the tone of his criticisms is partly due to his annoyance at finding that he could not shake off his Platonism, do what he could. This is borne out by the fact that, when he has come to the furthest point to which his own system will take him, he is apt to take refuge in metaphors of a mythical or ' transcendental ' character, for which we are not prepared in any way and of which no explanation is vouchsafed us. That is particularly the case when he is dealing with the soul and the first mover. On the whole his account of the soul is simply a development of eastern Ionian theories, and we feel that we are far removed indeed from the Platonist conception of the soul's priority to everything else. But, when he has told us that the highest and most developed form of soul is Mind, we are suddenly surprised by the statement that Mind in this sense is merely passive, while there is another form of it which is separable from matter, and that alone is immortal and everlasting. This has given rise to endless controversy which does not concern us here, but it seems best to interpret it as an involuntary outburst of the Platonism Aristotle could not wholly renounce. Very similar is the passage where he tries to explain how the first mover, though itself unmoved, communicates motion to the world. ' It moves it like a thing beloved,' he tells us, and leaves us to make what we can of that. And yet we cannot help feeling that, in passages like this, we come far nearer to the beliefs Aristotle really cared about than we do anywhere else. At heart he is a Platonist in spite of himself.

Aristotle's attitude to the practical life is also dependent on Plato's. In the Tenth Book of the *Ethics* he puts the claims of the Contemplative Life even higher than Plato ever did, so that the practical life appears to be only ancillary to it. He does not feel in the same degree as Plato the call for the philosopher to descend once more into the Cave for the sake of the prisoners there, and altogether he seems far more indifferent to the practical interests of life. Nevertheless he followed Plato's lead in giving much of his time to the study of politics, and that too with the distinctly practical aim of training legislators. He has often been criticized for his failure to see that the days of the city-state were numbered, and for the way in which he ignores the rise of an imperial monarchy in the person of his own pupil Alexander the Great. That, however, is not quite fair. Aristotle had a healthy dislike of princes and courts, and the city-state still appealed

to him as the normal form of political organization.
He could not believe that it would ever be superseded,
and he wished to contribute to its better administration.   He had, in fact, a much more conservative
outlook than Plato, who was inclined to think with
Isocrates, that the revival of monarchy was the only
thing that could preserve Hellenism as things were
then.   We must remember that Aristotle was not
himself a citizen of any free state, and that he could
hardly be expected to have the same political instincts
as Plato, who belonged by birth to the governing
classes of Athens and had inherited the liberal traditions of the Periclean Age.   This comes out best of
all, perhaps, in the attitude of the two philosophers to
the question of slavery.   In the *Laws*, which deals
with existing conditions, Plato of course recognizes
the *de facto* existence of slavery, though he is very
sensible of its dangers and makes many legislative
proposals with a view to their mitigation.   In the
Republic, on the other hand, where there is no need to
trouble about existing conditions, he makes Socrates
picture for us a community in which there are apparently
no slaves at all.   Aristotle is also anxious to mitigate
the worst abuses of slavery, but he justifies the institution as a permanent one by the consideration that barbarians are ' slaves by nature ' and that it is for their
own interest to be ' living tools.'   This insistence
upon the fundamental distinction between Greeks
and barbarians must have seemed an anachronism to
many of Aristotle's contemporaries and it had been
expressly denounced by Plato as unscientific.

The immediate effect of Aristotle's rejection of
Platonist mathematics was one he certainly neither
foresaw nor intended.   It was to make a breach
between philosophy and science.   Mathematical
science, whether Aristotle realized it or not, was still

in the vigour of its first youth, and mathematicians
were stirred by the achievements of the last generation
to attempt the solution of still higher problems.   If
the Lyceum turned away from them, they were quite
prepared to carry on the Academic tradition by themselves, and they succeeded for a time beyond all
expectation.   The third century B.C. was, in fact, the
Golden Age of Greek mathematics, and it has been
suggested that this was due to the emancipation of
mathematics from philosophy.   If that were true, it
would be very important for us to know it ; but it can,
I think, be shown that it is not true.   The great
mathematicians of the third century were certainly
carrying on the tradition of their predecessors who had
been philosophers as well as mathematicians, and it is
not to be wondered at that they were able to do so for a
time.   But the really striking fact is surely that Greek
mathematics became sterile in a comparatively short
time, and that no further advance was made till the
days of Descartes and Leibniz, with whom philosophy
and mathematics once more went hand in hand.

Nor was the effect of this divorce on philosophy itself
less disastrous.   Theophrastus continued Aristotle's
work on Aristotle's lines, and founded the science of
Botany as his predecessor had founded that of Zoology,
but the Peripatetic School practically died out with him
and had very little influence till the study of Aristotle
was revived long afterwards by the Neoplatonists.

For the present, the divorce of science and philosophy
was complete.   The Stoics and the Epicureans had
both, indeed, a scientific system, but their philosophy
was in no sense based upon it.   The attitude of
Epicurus to science is particularly well marked.   He
took no interest in it whatever as such, but he used it as
an instrument to free men from the religious fear to
which he attributed human unhappiness.   For that

purpose, the science of the Academy, which had led up to a theology, was obviously unsuitable, and, like a true eastern Ionian as he was, Epicurus harked back to the atomic theory of Democritus, adding to it, however, certain things which really made nonsense of it, such, for instance, as the theory of absolute weight and lightness, which Aristotle had unfortunately taught.   The Stoics too were corporealists, and found such science as they required in the system of Heraclitus, though they also adopted for polemical purposes much of Aristotle's Logic, taking pains, however, to alter his terminology.   Both these schools, in fact, while remaining faithful to the idea of philosophy as conversion, forgot that it had always been based on science in its best days.   It was this, no doubt, which chiefly commended Stoicism and Epicureanism to the Romans, who were never really interested in science. Both Stoicism and Epicureanism made a practical appeal, though of a different kind, and that served to gain credit for them at Rome.

The Academy which Plato had founded still continued to exist, though it was diverted from its original purpose not more than a generation after Plato's death.   Mathematics, we have seen, had made itself independent, and the most pressing necessity of the time was certainly the criticism of the new dogmatism which the Stoics had introduced.   That was really carrying on one side of Platonism and not the least important.   It is true indeed that the Academy appears to us at this distance of time mainly as a school of scepticism, but we must remember that its scepticism was directed entirely to the sensible world, as to which the attitude of Plato himself was not fundamentally different.   The real sceptics always refused to admit that the Academics were sceptics in the proper sense of the word, and it is possible that the tradition of Plato-

nism proper was never wholly broken.   At any rate,
by the first century B.C., we begin to notice that
Stoicism tends to become more and more Platonic.
The study of Plato's *Timaeus* came into favour again, and
the commentary which Posidonius (*c.* 100 B.C.) wrote
upon it had great influence on the development of philosophy down to the end of the Middle Ages.   It is this
period of eclecticism which is reflected for us in the
philosophical writings of Cicero.   It had great importance for the history of civilization, but it is far removed
from the spirit of genuine Greek philosophy.   That was
dead for the present, and it did not come to life again
till the third century of our era, when Platonism was
revived at Rome by Plotinus.

It is only quite recently that historians of Greek
philosophy have begun to do justice to ' Neoplatonism.'
That is partly due to the contemporary philosophical
tendencies noted at the beginning of this paper, and
partly to historical investigations into the philosophy
of the Middle Ages, which is more and more seen to
be dependent mainly on Neoplatonism down to and
including the system of St. Thomas Aquinas.   It was
indeed the most decisive fact in the history of western
European civilization that Plotinus founded his school
at Rome rather than at Athens or Alexandria ; for that
is how western Europe became the real heir to the
philosophy of Greece.   Every one knows, of course,
that Plotinus was a ' mystic,' but the term is apt to
suggest quite wrong ideas about him.   He is often
spoken of still as a man who introduced oriental ideas
into Greek philosophy, and he is popularly supposed to
have been an Egyptian.   That is most improbable ;
and, if it were true, it would only make it the more
remarkable that, though he certainly studied at
Alexandria for eleven years, he never even mentions
the religion of Isis, which was so fashionable at Rome

in his day, and which had fascinated so genuine a Greek as Plutarch some generations before. There is no doubt that what Plotinus believed himself to be teaching was genuine Platonism, and that he had prepared himself for the task by a careful study of Aristotle and even of Stoicism, so far as that served his purpose. No doubt he was too great a man to make himself the mere mouthpiece of another's thought ; but, for all that, he was the legitimate successor of Plato, and it may be added that M. Robin, who has taken upon himself the arduous task of extracting Plato's real philosophy from the writings of Aristotle, has come to the conclusion that there is a great deal more ' Neoplatonism ' in Plato than is sometimes supposed.

Plotinus is a mystic, then, though not at all in the sense in which the term is often misused. He sets before his disciples a ' way of life ' which leads by stages to the highest life of all, but that is just what Pythagoras and Plato had done, and it is only the continuation of a tradition which goes back among the Greeks to the sixth century B.C., nearly a thousand years before the time of Plotinus. His aim, like that of his predecessors, is the conversion of souls to this way of life, and he differs from such thinkers as the Stoics and the Epicureans in holding that the ' way of life ' to which he calls them must be based once more on a systematic doctrine of God, the World, and Man. The result was that the divorce which had existed for centuries between science and philosophy was once more annulled. We cannot say, indeed, that Plotinus himself made any special study of mathematics, but there is no doubt at all that his followers did, and it is due to them, and especially to Proclus, that we know as much of Greek mathematics as we do. Proclus was indeed the systematizer of the doctrine of Plotinus, though he differs from him on certain points, and his influence on later philosophy cannot be over-estimated. It can be distinctly traced even in Descartes, whom it reached through a number of channels, the study of which has recently been undertaken by a French scholar, Professor Gilson, of the University of Strasbourg. When his researches are complete, the continuity of Greek and modern philosophy will be plainly seen, and the part played by Platonism in the making of the modern European mind will be made manifest. We shall then understand better than ever why Greek philosophy is a subject of perennial interest.

The history of Greek philosophy is, in fact, the history of our own spiritual past, and it is impossible to understand the present without taking it into account. In particular, the Platonist tradition underlies the whole of Western civilization. It was at Rome, as has been pointed out, that Plotinus taught, and it was in certain Latin translations of the writings of his school that St. Augustine found the basis for a Christian philosophy he was seeking. It was Augustine's great authority in the Latin Church that made Platonism its official philosophy for centuries. It is a complete mistake to suppose that the thinking of the Middle Ages was dominated by the authority of Aristotle. It was not till the thirteenth century that Aristotle was known at all, and even then he was studied in the light of Platonism, just as he had been by Plotinus and his followers. It was only at the very close of the Middle Ages that he acquired the predominance which has made so strong an impression on the centuries that followed. It was from the Platonist tradition, too, that the science of the earlier Middle Ages came. A considerable portion of Plato's *Timaeus* had been translated into Latin in the fourth century by Chalcidius with a very elaborate commentary based on ancient sources, while the *Consolation of Philosophy*, written in prison by the Roman Platonist Boethius in A.D. 525, was easily the most popular book of the Middle Ages. It was translated into English by Alfred the Great and by Chaucer, and into many other European languages. It was on these foundations that the French Platonism of the twelfth century, and especially that of the School of Chartres, was built up, and the influence of that school in England was very great indeed. The names of Grosseteste and Roger Bacon may just be mentioned in this connexion, and it would not be hard to show that the special character of the contribution which English writers have been able to make to science and philosophy is in large measure attributable to this influence.

But the interest of Greek philosophy is not only historical ; it is full of instruction for the future too. Since the time of Locke, philosophy has been apt to limit itself to discussions about the nature of knowledge, and to leave questions about the nature of the world to specialists. The history of Greek philosophy shows the danger of this unnatural division of the province of thought, and the more we study it, the more we shall feel the need of a more comprehensive view. The ' philosophy of things human,' as the Greeks called it, is only one department among others, and the theory of knowledge is only one department of that. If studied in isolation from the whole, it must inevitably become one-sided. From Greek philosophy we can also learn that it is fatal to divorce speculation from the service of mankind. The notion that philosophy could be so isolated would have been wholly unintelligible to any of the great Greek thinkers, and most of all perhaps to the Platonists, who are often charged with this very heresy. Above all, we can learn from Greek philosophy the paramount importance of what we call the personality and they called the soul. It was just because the Greeks realized this that the genuinely Hellenic idea of conversion played so great a part in their thinking and in their lives. That, above all, is the lesson they have to teach, and that is why the writings of their great philosophers have still the power to convert the souls of all that will receive their teaching with humility.

IGNORANCE

The Romanes Lecture delivered in the Sheldonian Theatre,
Oxford, May 18, 1923

ABOUT seventy years ago a St. Andrews professor [1]
invented the word *Epistemology*. It has been immensely
popular, though we could perhaps have done without it.
He held, however, that this Epistemology, or Theory
of Knowledge, was a barren thing in itself, and would
not bring us a step nearer reality, unless it was supplemented by a Theory of Ignorance. That was, I think,
a suggestion much to the purpose. Unhappily he
thought proper to call this part of his system by the
repellent name of *Agnoiology*, with the result that it has
been overlooked and indeed forgotten. Yet it is
surely true that we have far more experience of ignorance than of knowledge, and also, as Aristotle puts it,
that we ought to start with what is ' more known to us.'
That, at least, was the conviction of Socrates, and it
certainly seems ' suitable to such a being as man, in
such a world as the present one.'

For us Platonists light is thrown on the problem of
Ignorance by the kindred, and at bottom identical,
problem of Sin. It cannot, I believe, be denied that,
on the whole, the theologians have been more successful in dealing with the question of Conduct than the
moral philosophers, and I think that is just because
they have approached it on this side. Disquisitions
on Virtue or the *Summum Bonum* leave us cold ; but
Sin is a thing of which we have intimate and personal
experience, so that, if we start from the sense of sin, we

---

[1] James Frederick Ferrier, Professor of Moral Philosophy in the United
College of St. Salvator and St. Leonard, 1845-64.

may reasonably hope to make some advance. Plato certainly thought so, and that is why we do not fully understand what the *Republic* is about till we come to Books VIII. and IX. which deal with Sin. I think it certain that these books were present to his mind, at least in outline, from the outset, and that everything else was intended to lead up to them. In the same way, I would suggest that our only chance of reaching a satisfying theory of Knowledge and Reality is to start from our immediate experience of Ignorance.

These, however, are high matters which it would be foolish to enter upon in a single lecture, even were I competent to deal with them. I only refer to them in order to put what I have to say in its proper setting. I am not going to develop an ' Agnoiology ' of my own, or even to expound that of Plato, though that is an attractive theme. All I have to offer is a contribution to a very pressing social problem, which I can illustrate from my own experience, illuminated by such light as I have been able to get from Plato, whom I have always found to be the surest guide in difficult places.

The problem I wish to discuss is the growth of ignorance at the present day, a problem which is generally overlooked just because, instead of beginning with ignorance, we fix our attention on knowledge, which at least appears to be increasing. Moreover, when I speak of the growth of ignorance, I am not referring specially to what are sometimes called ' the masses.' Among them we certainly find a great increase, if not of knowledge, at any rate of the desire for knowledge, and the Labour Party has a sincere belief in education. Unfortunately they are apt to speak as if there existed somewhere a stock of ready-made knowledge which has only to be doled out liberally to satisfy all needs. That was the view of Lord Brougham and other pioneers of popular education in the first half of the nineteenth century, but it is altogether wrong.   If we start, as we should, from a consideration of ignorance, we shall be struck first of all, I think, by its passivity and inertness, and this raises a presumption that knowledge is above all, as Plato held it to be, an activity of the soul.   But, if so, it follows that it cannot be communicated at all, except in so far as the active soul can induce other souls to share in its activity.   What can be supplied from stock is merely the sediment of dead knowledge, though even that is valuable, as I hope to show, since it furnishes us with the necessary tools for the real activity of knowing.   But it is not itself the real thing. The only knowledge worth distributing is living, first-hand knowledge, and that, from the nature of the case, can only be realized in its fullness by the few.   It is, however, the only reservoir from which the needs of the many can be supplied, and it is therefore important to consider from time to time whether it is being maintained at the proper level.   In the long run, everything depends on higher education, and so it remains true that the chief purpose of education is to form an *élite*, not for its own sake, but for that of society. That is Plato's doctrine.   The Guardians in the *Republic* are the hardest worked and least remunerated class in the community, and those who have ascended to the light of the true day must descend once more in turn to the Cave to release the prisoners from their bonds.   That is not to be done by lecturing to them, but only by overcoming their resistance to liberation.   Plato understood human nature much better than Lord Brougham.

The question I propose to ask, then, is this.   Are we taking the best way just now to secure the maintenance of that higher education on which all the rest depends?   The nineteenth century had a simple

faith in the progress of knowledge and enlightenment,
but we know too much history now to have any assured
confidence in that.   There have been Dark Ages
before, and they have generally supervened on periods
when knowledge of a sort was more widely distributed
than ever.   So far as we can see, the decay has always
set in at the top.   I am not thinking only of what are
specially known as the Dark Ages, the period from the
closing of the schools by Justinian in the sixth century
to the patriarchate of Photius in the ninth.   We know
vaguely too of dark ages even in prehistoric times,
and it sometimes looks as if oscillation rather than
progress were the law of history.   Nor can it be
denied that there are warnings and portents at the
present day such as have before now heralded an age
of darkness.   It is no wonder that some who are
skilled in reading the signs of the times should feel
uneasy.

No doubt it seems absurd at first sight.   Even since
1900, science of every kind has made advances hardly
to be matched at any other period of the world's
history.   In the course of a generation Physics and
Chemistry have been completely transformed, so that
those of us who tried to learn these things forty years
ago can hardly recognize them now.   I was present
the other day at a lecture on the structure of the atom,
and I felt very much as a Greek of the fifth century B.C.
might have done, if suddenly transported from the
rather crass air of Abdera to the sunnier climes of
Tarentum or the Epizephyrian Locri.   And the
advances in our knowledge of man have been as great
or greater.   Even in 1900 hardly any one knew anything worth knowing about Cnossus or the Aegean
civilization of the second and third millennia B.C., and
it still remains for us to adjust the rest of our historical
knowledge to that new world.   And we can go back

to millennia still remoter than that. The astounding revelations of prehistoric archaeology have hardly yet been grasped. What are we to make of a highly developed art at a date which it is not safe to fix even approximately, but of which we may say with confidence that the monuments of Egypt and Babylon are, in comparison, things of yesterday ?

There is, however, another side to the picture. The only true knowledge is living and first-hand knowledge, and such knowledge has no actual existence unless it is known by some one. Now it is plain that no one can possibly know more than a fraction of what is worth knowing. It seems rather that the more there is to be known, the less of it can we know, so that the growth of what, for any one of us, can only be potential knowledge, is necessarily to the same extent a growth of actual ignorance. Our knowledge bears a diminishing proportion to the mass. Libraries and museums are the great storehouses of potential knowledge ; but, if all possible knowledge were duly stored up in the Bodleian and the British Museum, what would it profit us ? The very existence of such an accumulation would discourage the best of us. What is the use of trying to make some fraction of the mass our own, when it can only have an infinitesimal ratio to the whole, and when it will be distorted besides by its detachment from the context which alone can make it intelligible ? I do not say that such a feeling is justified, but it is surely very natural.

We are told, to be sure, that specialism is the remedy, and that is no doubt true in a sense. But specialism has its drawbacks. Not long before the war I attended a congress of prehistoric archaeologists at Geneva. The whole proceedings were very interesting to me, but that was only because I had the advantage of knowing next to nothing about the subject. It was

impossible not to observe, however, that the interest
of the distinguished archaeologists present had curious
limits. We were chiefly concerned with the palaeo-
lithic age, though communications about the neolithic
were listened to with frigid politeness. When, however, an unfortunate gentleman tried to say something
about the bronze age, it was impossible to hear him
for the slamming of doors and the heavy tread of
archaeologists leaving the room. There must be
something wrong here ; for this system, if pushed to
its logical conclusion, would land us in a society where
no one knew anything that any one else knew. The
mass of men would take refuge in scepticism, and the
dark age would be upon us at once.

Now, even though that prospect may seem remote,
it must, I believe, be admitted that the recent enormous
growth of potential knowledge has been accompanied
by a corresponding growth of actual ignorance. It
will hardly be denied that those who have constantly
to do with young people, and who have sufficient
imagination to recall their own youth, are in the best
position to judge the tendency of the times. For that
reason I make no apology for drawing on my own
personal experience. I can only speak with any
authority on the youth of Scotland, but I do claim to
know something about that, and if we are to understand the growth of ignorance with any hope of finding
a remedy, it can only be by each stating our own experience and comparing it with that of others. In
the first place, then, I have no doubt that the young
men of the present day are, on the whole, healthier in
body and mind and more intelligent than those of my
own generation. I hope that we should have behaved
as well if the same call had come to us as came to them
in 1914, but frankly I am not sure. On the other
hand, I am certain that the young men of to-day are

absolutely and relatively more ignorant than those of forty years ago and, what is worse, that they have less curiosity and intellectual independence. In Scotland, at any rate, that is true. Every University teacher in that country whose memory can carry him back a generation knows that we have had to lower our standard of teaching and examination progressively for the last thirty years in every department except the physical and natural sciences. With that exception, no doubt a considerable one, I hear the same thing on every side. The complaints of teachers in the Department of English Literature are still more vocal than ours in the Department of Classics, though English is a compulsory subject in the schools, and no one can enter the Faculty of Arts without passing a Leaving Certificate Examination in that subject. Now I have said that my scientific colleagues do not seem to share the anxieties we feel in the Faculty of Arts, and the reason seems to be that they are not, to any extent worth mentioning, dependent on the schools for the subject-matter of their studies. A student who is to all intents and purposes a beginner can take up Chemistry, for instance, and be doing original research of a fairly high order in that department at the end of four years. It is different with the teachers of humanistic subjects. Whether we deal with the ancient or the modern humanities, we have been taught to depend on the schools for a foundation on which to build, and we find this growing more shaky every year.

I do not much blame the schoolmasters for that. They are no longer free agents, and the worst that can be said of them is that they are too ready to acquiesce in such a state of affairs, and even to claim that the requirements of the Universities should be modified in accordance with it. I do blame the system under which the teaching of the schools is determined by the necessities, real or imaginary, of an external examination, particularly when, as in Scotland, this is an identical written examination imposed on all schools alike by a government department. I blame still more the educational theorists of the last generation, whose theories are apt to find their way into departmental regulations and circulars just when they have been proved wrong even in theory. These notions were generally commended by a preposterous etymology of the word ' education,' which was supposed to mean ' drawing out,' just as if it were ' eduction ' and there were no difference between a long and a short u.[1] Etymologies prove nothing even when they are right, and they may work much mischief when they are wrong. The word *educare* is really, like so many other Latin words, an agricultural metaphor and means ' to grow ' a crop. It can also be used of breeding pigs and poultry. Now it does not take a profound knowledge of farming to see that, if you keep ' drawing out ' without putting anything in, you will end by exhausting the soil, and that, or something like it, is the chief explanation of the growth of ignorance we complain of. Here again I must draw on my own experience, and I make no apology for referring to some very elementary things. Nothing is so trivial that it may not illustrate the working of important principles.

That being so, I feel that I cannot illustrate my point better than by going back to my own early experiences of grammar. When I was at school we certainly thought it ' beastly,' as we called it, that we should have to learn such things as irregular verbs by heart. On the other hand, it was not particularly laborious for us at that age, and we could more or less

---

[1] Of course I am speaking of the proximate etymology. The prehistoric ' root ' *duc* no doubt occurs in both words, but that is irrelevant.

see the use of it.   It was clearly the way to get the
power of reading Homer and Virgil without constant
interruption, and I honestly believe that most of us
enjoyed that.   Of course we should not have dreamed
of confessing it to one another, and still less of admitting
it to 'old so-and-so,' our master, who was doing the
best he could for us with scant hope of reward and no
expectation of gratitude.   To do so would have
violated that mysterious schoolboy code, which is not
only a beneficent provision of nature to protect society
from juvenile prigs, but springs from a native instinct
of the young soul to preserve the solitude so needful for
the growth of its inner life.   Of course the time came
later when we were ready to admit, very shyly at first,
to one another that we did like Homer and Virgil, but
at first we were quite content to learn our irregular
verbs.   There is no great mystery in that.   Mere
memorizing comes natural to the young, and it does
not matter at all whether they understand what they
memorize or not.   Children have always invented
things—counting-out rhymes and the like—the main
purpose of which is to be memorized.   Think of the
undying popularity of *The House that Jack Built*.   We
may say, indeed, that they have a passion for rigmarole,
and small boys retain a great deal of this.   One would
think that our educational system would take advantage of that, and so it does in matters of absolute
necessity like the multiplication table.   Unhappily we
have not the same pressing need of declensions and
conjugations, so the educational theorist has a free
hand here.   He lays down certain canons, such as
that grammar should be taught 'inductively,' by which
he means that the phenomena of accidence and
syntax should be dealt with only as they occur and that
the rules should evolve themselves gradually out of the
examples.   That, of course, is how the mature scholar

goes to work, but it is something utterly alien to the
boy's mind.   No normal boy ever worked so, and no
normal boy ever will.   He knows that, for him,
grammar is only a disagreeable necessity, and he
rightly feels that he is not called upon to do over again
for himself what has been done once for all already.
He may not be able to formulate his protest clearly, but
he will probably tell you that it is ' all in the book,' and
he will refuse to work it out inductively to please you.
He has other employment for such reasoning powers as
he possesses, and he will not waste them on a thing like
grammar.   In this he shows a perfectly sound instinct,
and boys have a glorious power of resistance to what
they regard as the wrong way of doing things.   The
result is that he will not learn grammar at all, which is
no great loss in itself, but it will also be that he will not
learn to read Homer and Virgil, and that is a calamity.
The new plan of teaching grammar takes so much time
and leads to so little accomplishment that reading gets
crowded out altogether.   And then people complain
that boys who have had a classical education do not
read the classics in later life.   How can they ?   They
have never acquired the necessary facility.   They
often play games in later life, but that is because they
have acquired a certain automatism in them at an early
stage, which they could never have acquired on the
methods which are recommended to us for the teaching
of languages.   Fancy inductive cricket !

No doubt we memorized too much grammar in my
day.   The rhyme about the gender of *artifex* and *opifex*
was easily learnt indeed, but it conveys no very valuable
information, and, such as it is, might have been picked
up later, inductively if you care to call it so.   But it
remains true that nothing can ever take the place of
the instinctive and automatic responsiveness to grammatical forms which we certainly acquired on the old

method, and which can hardly be acquired otherwise. Of course it is perfectly true that Plato barely knew the difference between a noun and a verb, and that he had never heard of a subjunctive mood.   In the *Euthyphro* he takes nearly a page to explain the difference between the active and the passive voice, things for which he has no name, but which every elementary schoolboy knows now.   But then he had heard them used rightly from his childhood and so they had become instinctive and automatic to him.   We cannot reproduce that now (though anything that can be done in the way of making boys speak the language they are learning is to be eagerly welcomed), and we are driven to secure the automatism in another way.   That was the great discovery of Dionysius Thrax.   In his day the instinctive feeling for the living speech was dying, and many were beginning to speak it for whom it was a foreign tongue.   The whole apparatus of moods and tenses, declensions and conjugations, introduced by him was really a labour-saving device, and was eagerly adopted as such and applied to their own language by the practical Romans, who took little interest in grammatical theories, but wished to acquire the power of reading and speaking Greek in the quickest and easiest way.   Is it fair to deprive the modern boy of all this, seeing that he can acquire it quite easily and then go on to something more interesting ?   The multiplication table is acquired because it has, or can be made to have, a certain rhythm of its own which fixes it for ever in the memory.   Declensions and conjugations have a rhythm of the very same kind, or at any rate such a rhythm can be imposed upon them. That, by the way, is why boys so persistently make false quantities in repeating them ; they are only trying instinctively to adjust them to their own rhythmical scheme.   It was a great mistake when our grammars disturbed the traditional order of the cases. It was supposed that brevity was secured by placing the accusative next to the nominative, but that is based on a psychological fallacy. Within limits it is actually easier to memorize a longer series than a shorter, especially when the last term of the series makes a return, as it were, on the first. When the accusative came where Dionysius, for excellent reasons, put it, after the dative, it provided a satisfactory framework for the whole rhythmical pattern, and I feel sure that the declensions were easier to learn than they are now. In any case, you will never induce boys to learn grammar by any other process than this of rhythmical memorizing which I have tried to describe.

For the grown man, of course, grammar may be one of the most dangerously fascinating studies, but for the boy it is just what I have called the sediment of dead knowledge, to be acquired as speedily as may be for the sake of its results and not for itself. This is quite understood in many other branches of training. It is really a good deal easier to read Homer than it is to play the piano, and yet the proportion of people who learn to play the piano, at least to their own satisfaction, is far greater than that of those who learn to read Homer. In this case every one can see that the first thing to be done is to acquire the necessary automatism, and the methods of acquiring it have been more or less systematized. If you had to think of every chord, you would never play anything. On the other hand, no one imagines that the traditional scales and exercises are music. They are simply practice, directed to the acquisition of automatic power, and that is how grammar should be treated at school. It is an historical fact that, when this method was followed, a large number of people did acquire the power of reading

Homer, and that a very considerable number continued to read him all their days.

Moreover, it is just this acquisition of automatic power that can be quite precisely and accurately tested by a school examination, and I do not think that anything else can be fairly tested at all at this stage. As it is, we are prone to test schoolboys by setting them to do ' unseens,' which are the proper criteria of riper scholarship, but which really tell us nothing of what it is much more important for us to know, namely, whether the boy has ever read a complete book with understanding. What we really judge in this way is the power of guessing, a power not to be despised indeed, but a very unfair test for the purpose in view. The result of all this is that grammatical knowledge remains sloppy and inaccurate, and there is nothing at all to take its place. That is why we find our pupils more ignorant than they used to be.

Now this consideration of one minor but fundamental department of humanistic education suggests certain conclusions which I believe would be verified by a similar consideration of others, and equally by an examination of the foundations of scientific teaching. In the first place, we must learn to draw a hard and fast line between education and training. It is not a novel distinction, but its implications are by no means fully realized. The end of training is to secure automatic facility, and it is absolutely essential as a foundation for everything else. Where it is a matter of life and death we know that well enough. During the war most of us at least saw something of the training of platoons, companies, and battalions. The object of that was to secure automatic response to the word of command, and this was successfully accomplished by the system known as drill. Of course no one but an occasional sergeant-major ever imagined that drill alone would

make a soldier, but every one knew it was the necessary
first stage in the process.   It is exactly the same with
education.   Unless the power of spontaneous response
to certain stimuli has been acquired, so that no process
of conscious thinking is called for to deal with them, it
is useless to attempt anything further.   To face a boy
who has had no sufficient drill with Homer and Virgil
is as wicked as it is to send an untrained recruit into
the firing line.

And this suggests the further consideration that, if
ignorance merely means the absence of active and conscious knowledge, it may in certain cases be a good and
salutary thing.   It may be doubted, indeed, whether,
if knowledge is an activity, it is really possible for any
one to know more than one thing at a time in the full
sense of the word.   It seems rather as if the full light
of knowledge can only illuminate a single spot in the
field of consciousness at a given moment.   That spot
is surrounded by a sort of penumbra of potential knowledge shading gradually away into ignorance and utter
darkness, and it is this penumbra that makes all the
difference.   A great mathematician and a child may
both be said to know that two and two make four, and
it would not be easy to show that there is any actual
difference in the bare content of their knowledge at the
time.   The difference, which is really enormous,
seems to lie wholly in the surroundings by which it is
accompanied.   In the very same way, a schoolboy
and a great scholar may give a verbally identical translation of a passage, but here again there is a wide
divergence.   It is impossible to dispense with metaphors and analogies in a matter such as this ; for the
difference is not quantitative but qualitative.   It is
like the difference in *timbre* between two notes of
identical pitch sounded on different instruments.   It
is the presence or the absence of the over-tones that

makes the difference between the knowledge of the
educated and the uneducated man, and it is plain that
education in this sense is not a thing that can be handed
over ready-made. It is also plain that it depends
wholly on potential knowledge which may at a given
moment be very dimly realized or not realized at all.
I have never been able to discover what the Austrian
socialist Pernerstoffer meant when he defined education as ' the sum of all we have forgotten.' He may
only have intended a paradox, but he uttered a very
great truth. It is not only such things as grammar
and the multiplication table that can become automatic, but also such elusive things as taste and judgment. In the case of these, however, nothing is to
be achieved by drill. That is only suitable for bare
necessities which it is desirable to get out of the way as
quickly as possible. It is not easy—indeed it is impossible—to lay down rules for this higher spiritual
education. It consists above all in bringing the
youthful soul into contact with the really big things in
letters, science, and art, and letting it make what it can
of them. There is no need to tell it what it should
think about them ; it must find out that for itself.
Above all, it is wrong for a teacher to insult his pupils by
talking down to what he imagines to be the level of
their capacity. That is probably a good deal higher
than he supposes, and in any case his condescension is
sure to be resented. After all, it is very little that a
teacher can do by direct teaching. He can certainly
look after the preliminary drill, but beyond that it is
mainly by being himself that he can do any good. If
he cares for great things and if his pupils are capable
of caring for them too, there is every chance that they
will learn to do so. For the rest, we can add little or
nothing to what is written in the *Epistle to the Friends
and Companions of Dion*, where we are told, in a sentence

that surely no one but Plato can have written, that this kind of knowledge is a thing that comes in a moment 'like a light kindled from a leaping spark which, once it has reached the soul, finds its own fuel.' Finally, if it is true that what seemed to us an alarming growth of ignorance is mainly due to the confusion of training with education, and our neglect of the fundamental differences between the methods proper to each, we may find comfort in the reflection that it is not yet too late for us to retrace our steps.

Now these elementary pedagogical considerations have made it clear, I trust, that the value of all knowledge depends on something that is not actual knowledge. That presupposes, in the first place, an automatic facility of response to stimuli that can only be acquired by practice and drill. We have seen further that the quality of knowledge depends on a fringe of associations which is for the most part subconscious and belongs to what I have called the penumbra. But what of ignorance itself, the outer ring of darkness which surrounds the field ? Has it too a part to play ? It is easy to see that it may serve as a foil or background for knowledge, just as a light is thrown up by the surrounding darkness, but there is more in it than that. Ignorance is, after all, only another name for the possibility of knowledge ; it is essentially what Aristotle calls a στέρησις. No one can be taught anything of which he does not feel ignorant. We do not speak of a dog, or even a savage, as ignorant of Greek or of mathematics. Dogs know all they need to know and all they can know. In that sense of the word—and no other is really intelligible—man is more ignorant than any other animal, and it is just because he is so that he stands higher in the scale of being. It is the possibility of ignorance and sin that makes man what he is, and so he cannot wish it away without contradiction.   Huxley once said:

> I protest that if some great Power would agree to make me think always what is true and do what is right on condition of being turned into a sort of clock . . . I should instantly close with the bargain.[1]

Happily he was not taken at his word, and, if he had been, I do not believe he would have made any such suicidal choice.   No one can possibly wish to have anything on condition of being turned into something else.   Being what we are, we must regard liability to error and wrongdoing as our privileges, since it is only the sense of ignorance and the sense of sin that enable us even to conceive of righteousness and know-ledge.   Why we are such as we are, we are not bound, and probably not able, to say ; but I venture to think that here too Plato may help us to a partial under-standing.   Of course in his published writings he has only treated the problem by way of myth, but I think it a fair interpretation of his meaning to put it some-thing like this.   Plato believed in a Creator, but he did not believe in anything like foreknowledge or predestination.   These are Stoic inventions.   For Plato it was unworthy of the Creator to create souls which were not themselves creators in their degree.   Being creators they are free ; but, being also creatures, they may fall into sin and ignorance.   Something like that, I think, is what Plato meant ; but, however that may be, it is plain that such is indeed our nature, and that we must make the best of it we can.   If we try to do that we need not fear the return of the Dark Ages, which could only be brought about by our ignoring both the limits and the possibilities of beings such as we most undoubtedly are.

[1] *Collected Essays,* i. p. 292.

EXPERIMENT AND OBSERVATION
IN GREEK SCIENCE[1]

THE idea that Greek science was entirely *a priori* and chiefly consisted of more or less happy guesses is very deep-rooted. And yet there are obvious facts pointing to quite a different conclusion. It is certain, for example, that the very earliest beginnings of Greek science were closely connected with a great development of technical ability which could not have been acquired except by means of experiment.

Herodotus tells us (III. 60) that Eupalinus of Megara constructed a tunnel through the hill above Samos, and this tunnel, of which he has left us a description, was discovered in 1882. It is about half a mile in length, but the levels are nearly exact. Quite apart from the observations that we still have in the Hippocratean corpus, which are not later than the fifth century B.C., we can hardly believe that the anatomical exactitude of Greek sculpture was obtained by *a priori* methods. These facts undoubtedly presuppose experiment and observation of a truly scientific character.

It is true, doubtless, that we are told very little about observations and experiments in the accounts that have come down to us relative to the beginnings of science among the Greeks ; and it is quite justifiable to ask why this is so. As a matter of fact, the answer is simplicity itself. Nearly all that we know on this subject comes from compilations and manuals com-

---

[1] [This essay has been translated from an article which appeared in French in *Scientia*, vol. xxxiii. (1923), pp. 93-102. That article had been translated from an English original, but as that original has been lost, a retranslation has had to be made.]

posed centuries later, by men who were not themselves interested in science, and for readers who were even less so. What was even worse, these works were to a great extent inspired by the desire to discredit science by emphasizing the way in which men of science contradicted each other, and the paradoxical character of the conclusions at which they arrived. This being the object, it was obviously useless, and even out of place, to say much about the methods employed in arriving at the conclusions. It suited Epicurean and Sceptic, as also Christian, writers to represent them as arbitrary dogmas. We can get a slight idea of the situation by imagining, some centuries hence, contemporary science as represented by elementary manuals, second- and third-hand compilations, drawn up in a spirit hostile to science and scientific methods.

Such being the nature of the evidence with which we have to deal, it is obvious that all the actual examples of the use of sound scientific methods that we can discover will carry much more weight than would otherwise be the case. If we can point to indubitable examples of the use of experiment and observation, we are justified in supposing that there were others of which we know nothing because they did not happen to interest the compilers on whom we are dependent. As a matter of fact, there are a fair number of such examples, and I shall discuss one or two of them as briefly as possible.

One of the biggest discoveries of the fifth century B.C. was that of atmospheric air. Strange as it may seem to us, air up till then had been identified with water in a rarefied state, and even the founders of mathematics themselves had not made a clear distinction between air and empty space. It was then found out that air was a substance having its own distinctive character, and it can be shown that this discovery was brought about by experiment. It is true, certainly, that air was considered as a simple body or 'element,' but this does not seriously detract from the importance of the discovery that air consists neither of condensed fire nor of rarefied water. Now this discovery was made by means of a simple experiment that is still in use to-day in our elementary schools. It is Empedocles' experiment with the clepsydra. He has left us a description of the apparatus. The clepsydra was simply a metal cylinder with the base perforated in several places and a conical top with a single orifice. Empedocles showed that if the upper orifice is stopped with the finger, and the apparatus is then dipped in water, the air in the pipe prevents the water from entering through the lower holes, whereas if the finger is removed from the upper opening, the water immediately rushes into the pipe. There is nothing complicated about the experiment ; but, such as it is, it is completely scientific in character. All that is said of it in the compilation that is our principal source of information is : ' He reminds us what happens with the clepsydra.' Perhaps we might have made a guess as to what this meant, but we could never have been sure that our guess was right, if Aristotle had not quoted twenty-five verses of Empedocles in support of his theory of respiration, and if these verses had not contained a detailed account of this experiment with the clepsydra. The case is characteristic and brings out clearly the very unsatisfactory nature of our usual sources of information.

So much for the use of experiment in the fifth century B.C. The facts about scientific observation are similar. This time I shall take my example from Plato ; and, indeed, from a passage of Plato that might not seem very promising, a passage about Atlantis. There have been many theories and even futile controversies on this subject, but most people are now agreed in seeing in it a fairy-tale of the kind that we usually associate with the names of Jules Verne and H. G. Wells. Like the stories of these two writers, however, that of Plato is based on the scientific theories that were current at the time when it is supposed to have been told, that is to say about 420 B.C. It is clear that once the sphericity of the earth had been discovered by Pythagoras (doubtless from observation of lunar eclipses), it became impossible to reject the inference that our globe must be considerably larger than the supposed flat earth, and we find a formal statement of this conclusion in the Myth of Plato's *Phaedo*, which probably reproduces the views of the Pythagorean Philolaus. There we are told that the human beings who live between the Phasis and the Pillars of Heracles (or, as we should say now, in the basins of the Black Sea and of the Mediterranean) are comparable to ants or frogs living round a swamp, and that there are many other similar basins on the surface of the spherical earth. It was, in fact, easy to see that if the earth is a sphere, the curvature of its surface in the regions then known ought to be much greater than it is, unless one imagined beyond them a great stretch of *terra incognita*, and it was natural that they should at first imagine this as being occupied by a certain number of basins of the kind already known. But the theory adopted in Plato's *Timaeus* is slightly different. It is connected with the idea that there are several insular continents, and, in particular, that there was a very large one that had been submerged in the Atlantic in prehistoric times. It is not necessary, at the moment, to follow this part of the story any further. I only want to make it clear that all the accounts of this type took their origin from a new knowledge of the shape of the earth. The Greek scientific imagination could not accept the idea that the whole of the surface of the earth, outside the small part known to the Greeks, was uninhabited. Here is an example of the same spirit that led Anaximander, at an earlier date, to assert that there must be innumerable cosmic systems, each turning round its own particular centre, in the infinite ; a view that was revived later by Democritus and accepted by Epicurus. It is an example of scientific imagination, a thing which has also had its part to play in the history of discovery, but is not really connected with the subject that is now under discussion.

What is more interesting, from the point of view of our immediate object, is rather the means adopted to make it possible for Athens, at the time in question, to constitute a serious rival to Atlantis. It is clear that if the story has to show even the degree of probability that we demand of a fairy-tale, Attica must be represented as a populous and powerful country, and it must also be explained to us how it was that in historical times she was far from being fertile and certainly quite incapable of sustaining a population as large as that which is necessary for the story. At first sight this seems an even more fantastic and far-fetched idea than that of the submersion of a large continent in the Atlantic, and one cannot doubt that the scientific explanation provided would be quite inadequate as an explanation of the facts. But there is nothing remarkable about that. The science that is implied in fairy-tales is never adequate. All that is required is semblance of scientific explanation, and the only thing that is of interest from our point of view is to see how that semblance is obtained. As at the present day, the thing is done by starting from a point of view that is really scientific and exaggerating the possible consequences that may be supposed to flow from it. This

R

is how Jules Verne and H. G. Wells proceed, and Plato does exactly the same thing. What interests us, then, is not the fantastic use that is made of the scientific theories, it is the theories themselves. Now, if we read the beginning of Plato's *Critias* carefully, we observe that it gives evidence of a knowledge of geology and physiography that is very surprising for the time, and shows that the subject had been thoroughly studied by some one, not necessarily Plato himself. In fact, the account of the geological history of Attica given in the *Critias*, apart from the legendary tale based on it, leaves little to be desired as a description of the process of denudation and its economic results. As the *Critias* is little read at the present day, it may be worth while to sum up the theory expounded in it.

In the first place, then, Critias draws attention to the fact that if, as is required by the fairy-tale, prehistoric Athens had to maintain a large standing army, it was necessary that Attica should be fertile enough to permit of a large part of the population being permanently freed from the necessity of tilling the soil. Now, Attica was very far indeed from being fertile in historical times. Thucydides specially draws attention to the poverty of its soil, as explaining the fact that in ancient times it was relatively protected against invasion. Demosthenes tells us that Athens, more than any other state, was under the necessity of importing corn. Nevertheless, Critias says, even in more recent times, what remained of the soil could stand comparison with any other country, so far as fertility and capacity to provide pasturage went.

How can this be explained, and what does the phrase ' what remained of the soil ' mean ? First of all, we must notice, he says, that Attica extends into the sea like a promontory and that, therefore, she has a longer coast-line than the neighbouring states.

Moreover, the sea that surrounds her is very deep close
in to the shore.   But, in the course of the long period
with which we are dealing, there were, naturally, many
floods which swept away the soil from the high-lying
parts of the country, but this phenomenon did not, as
in many other countries, lead to the formation of any
alluvial plains or deltas worth talking about.   This is
owing to the depth of the adjacent sea.   The light
soil was simply washed away by the waters and sank
to the bottom.   The result was—exactly as in the
small islands of the Aegean—that what is left re-
sembles the skeleton of an emaciated body ; the good
productive earth has disappeared, leaving only the
skeleton of the country as it was in primitive times.
Where now there are nothing but barren limestone
rocks, there used to be rounded hills ; and where now
there is nothing but stony soil yielding a meagre
harvest, there used to be fertile fields.   Further, at
that period, the hills were well wooded, even those that
now can only maintain bees.   Moreover, the rain
instead of rushing away uselessly to the sea, in streams
enclosed in rocky channels, was absorbed into the soft
earth and filtered through it, so that there were springs
and streams in plenty, which also added to the fertility
of the soil.

   It would be interesting to know whose theory this
was, but it is obvious that at the present time it is impossible to have any certain knowledge on the subject.
There are certain data, however, supplied by Plato
himself, that allow one to formulate a provisional
hypothesis which may either be verified or else destroyed at any minute by new discoveries.   It seems
very probable that documents of importance for the
history of science may still turn up among the Egyptian
papyri.   We will point out, then, that Plato puts all
this into the mouth of a very old man called Critias.

It is surprising that all the historians and commentators have taken it as a matter of course that this Critias is Plato's well-known kinsman who made such a bad name for himself by the part he played in the revolution of the Thirty. At any rate, Plato has done all he can to show clearly that it refers to quite another Critias. In the first place, he emphasizes the great age of the Critias he brings into his dialogues, whilst the other, the rather undesirable person, died in 403 B.C., and did not live to old age. In fact, as I think I have shown elsewhere, the Critias who appears in the *Timaeus*, and gives his name to its sequel, is in reality the grandfather of his better-known namesake, and in consequence Plato's great-grandfather. If this is so, it follows that Plato, who is always very careful in matters of this kind, means us to understand that we are dealing with the science of the beginning of the fifth century B.C. The fact would be perfectly obvious to the public for whom he wrote, who knew all the facts concerning the Critias of the Thirty, and could not suspect Plato of publishing nonsense about the very illustrious family to which his mother belonged, by representing his cousin as a very old man several years before the oligarchical revolution of which he was the leader.

There is another slight indication that may help us. Aristotle speaks of a certain Critias who declared that the soul is the blood, because the blood is the seat of sensation, and the great commentator, Alexander of Aphrodisias, says that this Critias was not the member of the Thirty, but another, a namesake, whom he calls Critias the Sophist. Now we know that this theory, according to which thought and sensation depend on the blood, was precisely that of Empedocles, and we know that it was current at Athens at the beginning of the fifth century, for Aeschylus adopted it in his

tragedies.   We also know that Empedocles took part
in the Athenian colonization of Thurii in 444 B.C.   As
a matter of fact, we have no direct proof that he went
to Athens for this purpose, but it is very natural to
suppose that he was there at the time.   He was a
democratic leader, and it is exceedingly probable that
he sought refuge in Athens when he had to leave his
home, Agrigentum.   It is, therefore, quite possible
that he came across the elder Critias at this time ; but
it is no more than a possibility.   On one point, however, there is no doubt : it is certain that Empedocles
took an interest in geological questions.   It is true, of
course, that as a Sicilian he was more interested in
volcanic phenomena than in processes of the kind just
mentioned.

This comes out with sufficient clearness from the
fairly extensive fragments of his poem that have come
down to us.   In fact, he started the interest taken ' in
the things under the earth ' that seemed so shocking
to the pious Athenians of a later date.   But his system
required not only that he should explain how Fire
' tends to rise,' but also how Earth ' tends to sink.'
He considered the cosmic period in which we are
now living as being that in which the ' elements ' are
gradually separating themselves, a process destined to
end in Earth forming the centre, surrounded by Water,
Air, and Fire, in that order.   He cannot have failed to
be greatly interested in the process of denudation.
On the whole, I am inclined to think that the elder
Critias applied the principles he had learnt from
Empedocles to the phenomena observed by him in his
own country ; but, obviously, we have only circum-
stantial evidence to go upon.   The story, as it often
happens, stops short just when it is becoming interesting.   What I think quite certain is that these observations, and the theories based on them, belong to the

first half of the fifth century B.C., and it is easy to show that this does not involve any sort of anachronism.

We can even see that the knowledge of such things was pretty widely spread in the second half of the fifth century. No one would call Herodotus a scientist, and yet he has a perfectly correct notion of the formation of the delta of the Nile, and compares it with what has happened at the mouths of other rivers, the Achelous in particular, where, he tells us, alluvial deposits have already joined half the islands known as the Echinades to the mainland.

It will be remembered that Herodotus also took part in the Athenian colonization of Thurii. Thucydides also discusses the islands at the mouth of the Achelous, and goes into greater detail about them. He points out that they lie near together and are not ranged in a straight line, but in alternate rows, so that the stream of the Achelous, a broad, rapid, and muddy river, cannot find a direct channel to the sea. The islands bind the alluvial deposits to one another and prevent them from being dispersed. Thucydides adds that before long the islands will be united to the mainland. It is true that, by reason of the intervention of other causes, this prophecy has not been fulfilled ; but that is of little importance. The essential point is that the formation of the deposits in question was quite correctly understood at the time of the Peloponnesian War, and, above all, that this knowledge had been acquired by means of a careful comparison of examples taken from parts of the world far distant from each other.

But we can go still further back. Xenophanes, who spent most of his life in Sicily, at a still earlier date than that of Empedocles, asserted that the earth had once been mud and would become mud again. By way of proof, he cited the fact that fossils of all sorts of marine animals had been found in different parts of

the Greek world, and that shells had been found in
inland districts and on hills.   The imprint of a fish
and seaweed had been discovered in the quarries of
Syracuse, and at Malta the flat impressions of all sorts
of marine animals.   Xenophanes himself was not a
man of a scientific turn of mind, so far as we can judge
from what we can learn of his point of view, but he
seems to have been a disciple of Anaximander before
leaving Ionia, when it had fallen under the domination
of the Persians.   It is also clear that the observations
related by him are closely connected with the views of
Anaximander, for whom the origin of all life was to be
found in the sea.   In particular, Anaximander maintained that man must be descended from animals of
another species, and his reason for thinking this was
that while the young of other animals quickly learn to
find food for themselves, the young of man require a
long period of suckling.   If man had been originally
what he is now, he never could have survived.   For
him the human species was descended from fishes, and
we know that he found a confirmation of this view in
observations on certain viviparous sharks and dog-
fish.   Perhaps we are also entitled to believe that the
accounts of the discovery of the fossils go back to him
too.   In any case, they can hardly be later than the
year 500 B.C.

It will be noticed that most of these indications tend
to converge upon Empedocles, and there are others of
the same type.   In what is left to us of Empedocles
himself there are many traces of genuine scientific
observation, especially in biology, and Empedocles
was the founder of the Sicilian School of Medicine.
Doubtless the theories by which he is best known, that
of the four ' elements ' in particular, constitute pre-
mature generalizations, certain of which continued to
lead men into error in later ages.   The great advance

of his predecessors had been to rid themselves of the
'four elements,' but the theory of a single substance
had led to a result that was inacceptable, so he revived
the old view.   We must call to mind the highly un-
pleasant impression that is left on the reader by what
can only be described as the charlatanism of his religious poem.   From different points of view he is a
strange contradiction, but he is none the less interesting
as a human being.   Modern writers are apt to be a
little unjust to him for the reasons that have already
been pointed out, and I myself used to be very hard
on him.   But this only makes the study of his methods
more important than ever.   If it can be shown that
Empedocles made constant use of experiment and
observation, less difficulty will be found in believing
that other Greeks, who were much more true men of
science, did not neglect these methods of research.

HOW PLATONISM CAME TO ENGLAND

Read in the University of Leeds, January 10, 1924

In his discourse against Christianity, the Emperor Julian said:

> With a very few exceptions, you will not find that the men of western nations are disposed to the study of philosophy or geometry or anything of that sort, in spite of their long subjection to Roman rule. Those of them who are specially gifted acquire only the arts of debate and rhetoric ; they do not concern themselves with any other study. So great, it seems, is the force of nature.[1]

Now Julian was by way of being a Platonist, and he plainly means to say that he found western Europeans lacking in natural capacity for that philosophy and for the mathematical studies which are an essential part of it. He was thinking, no doubt, in the first instance, of the Gauls, whom he knew well, and it is true that rhetoric is, and always has been, an important element in French literature. Still it is curious that Julian should attribute incapacity for mathematics to the countrymen of Pascal and Descartes, to name no others. Something must have happened since the time of Julian to transform the Gallic genius, and it is very clear that he was wrong in ascribing its supposed limitations to ' nature ' ($\phi\acute{v}\sigma\iota\varsigma$). But Britain was in the same case as Gaul. Long before Julian, Juvenal tells us, in his exaggerated way, that ' eloquent Gaul has trained the pleaders of Britain and distant Thule

---

[1] Iulianus *contra Galilaeos,* 131 c. The passage may be conveniently read in its context in the Loeb Classical Library, Julian, vol. iii. p. 348.

talks of hiring a rhetorician ' (*Sat.*, xv. iii).   And yet
Britain was to produce Newton in later days, and all
English literature from Chaucer down to Wordsworth
and Shelley is inspired and informed by Platonism to
a degree quite unparalleled in any other country.
To-day I propose to say something of how that came
about.   I cannot, of course, exhaust the subject in a
single lecture, but Platonism in English literature
would indeed be a worthy theme for any one capable
of treating it.   It could only, of course, be attempted
by a scholar who knew Platonism ' from inside,' if I
may use the phrase, and that means by one who knew
Greek well.   It would then appear clearly how much
we should lose in the understanding of our national
literature if the knowledge of Greek were suffered to
die out among us.

It will, however, be necessary, before we come to the
influence of Platonism in England, to consider briefly
how it reached western Europe at all, and to do this
we must go back to the third century A.D., that is to
the century before the Emperor Julian.   From our
point of view, the most important fact, I think, is that
Plotinus, who revived Platonism after a long period of
neglect, founded his school at Rome, not at Alexandria,
or Athens, as might have been expected.   That was
the real starting-point of western European civilization.
It is true that the direct influence of Plotinus himself
on the West was not great.   He was not a Christian,
and, though he himself never even mentions Christianity, his disciple Porphyry, to whom we owe the
preservation of his teaching, was an ardent opponent
of the new religion, and the time was just passing away
when it was possible for any philosophy to flourish in
opposition to the Church.   Moreover, Plotinus and
Porphyry used their native language, Greek, as was
natural, and the knowledge of Greek was already be-

ginning to die out, even in Italy. The necessary re-
conciliation between Platonism and Christianity was
brought about in the next century by St. Augustine,
who, as he tells us in his *Confessions*, was converted
from the Manichaean heresy to Catholic Christianity
by reading certain 'Platonic books,' that is to say,
Latin versions of the teaching of Plotinus made by his
Roman followers. When Augustine set himself to
construct a Christian philosophy, it was on this foundation that he built, and so it came about that Platonism,
with certain important reservations and additions,
became, as it were, the official philosophy of the
Western Church throughout the earlier period of the
Middle Ages.

The ground was prepared, then, by St. Augustine,
and it was now possible for a Christian to be a Platonist.
It was not, however, till late in the fifth century A.D.
that an attempt was made to bring genuine Platonism
within the reach of the western part of the Roman
world, and that attempt was made by a young Roman
noble, Boethius, who resolved to translate the whole of
Plato and the whole of Aristotle into Latin with full
commentaries, and to accompany these with a series of
treatises in which the necessary mathematical basis of
Platonism was to be made clear. He also proposed
to show that Plato and Aristotle were substantially in
agreement on all important points. This great work
was never carried out. All Boethius managed to
accomplish was the translation of some of the logical
treatises of Aristotle ; for he was not permitted to live
much beyond his fortieth year. He had stood high
in the favour of the Gothic ruler of Italy, Theodoric,
but in A.D. 524 he was cruelly put to death on suspicion
of treasonable correspondence with the Emperor Justin
at Constantinople. Theodoric was getting old and
suspicious, and it is not probable that he ever really

understood what Boethius was trying to do, or that he would have approved it if he had.

But that was by no means the end, and it is certain that it was to his condemnation that Boethius owed most of his influence in later days ; for it was in prison before his death that he wrote his *Consolation of Philosophy*, the book that made his name precious to educated men for centuries, and which it is hardly an exaggeration to call the source of all that is best in the literature of western Europe. The idea of the book was suggested by a passage in Plato's *Phaedo* (82 e sqq.), and it represents Philosophy in person as appearing to Boethius in prison to console him and rebuke him for his despondency. The form of it is what is called *satura Menippea*, that is to say, each chapter is concluded by a short poem, and these are in a great variety of lyrical metres, which are handled with remarkable skill considering the lateness of their date. It was this book which fascinated all the best minds of the Middle Ages. Over 400 MSS. of it are known, and there are doubtless a good many more which have not been examined yet. I cannot doubt that a knowledge of it, in a translation at least, is absolutely necessary for all serious students of medieval and modern literature, and especially for all students of English literature.[1]

It is probable, indeed, that the *Consolation* did more for western Europe than ever the projected translations of Plato and Aristotle would have done. These, after all, would just have been translations, and even the best translations are apt to let all that is worth while in their originals evaporate, so that to read translations is rather like drinking champagne which has been

---

[1] Fortunately, that is easy now, since Boethius is included in the Loeb Classical Library. The ordinary student may be advised to omit the theological treatises at the beginning of the volume and go straight on to the *Consolatio*.

allowed to stand in glasses overnight. The translations of Aristotle into Latin which were made in the
thirteenth century created a cloud of misunderstanding which even the recovery and renewed study of the
originals has hardly dispelled yet. But the *Consolation*
is an original work which reveals a very attractive
personality, and it contains beyond a doubt the quint-
essence of Platonism, which it preserved for western
Europe during the period when Greek was practically
forgotten except in Ireland and Calabria.

That being so, it is not surprising that it is here we
find the earliest point of contact between English
literature and Platonism. King Alfred of Wessex had
visited Rome twice before he was ten years old, and it is
hardly surprising that he was inspired to follow in the
footsteps of Charlemagne, who had recently renewed
the Western Roman Empire in his own person.
Charles had to fight pagan Saxons, and Alfred had a
hard struggle with pagan Danes, but both of them felt
it to be their mission to revive the Graeco-Roman
civilization which had been almost lost, and that is how
they created England and France, the countries which
were destined to play the chief part in carrying on and
developing that civilization.

Now it fell out that, in pursuance of his plans, King
Alfred made a translation of the *Consolation* of Boethius,
and his biographer, Bishop Asser, wrote a commentary on the same work. On this I regret that I
cannot speak from first-hand knowledge, but it seems
evident that here we have the original source of the
Platonist tradition which was never altogether broken
in England for the next thousand years. From what
I can learn of Alfred's work, he seems to have taken
considerable liberties with his original. In particular,
the central figure of the book, Philosophy, is no longer,
as in Boethius, a *mulier reuerendi admodum vultus*, an

aged woman of grave face but unabated vigour, but an aged man. Alfred seems also to have added explanatory passages for the benefit of his English readers. For all that, there is no doubt that he conveyed to them the message of Platonism sufficiently well to create a lasting impression.

Of course the time came when it was necessary to do the work over again. The language of Alfred was no longer intelligible to the people, and though, as we shall see, the Platonic tradition still reached England from French and other sources, it was no longer accessible to them in their own tongue. That was remedied by no less a person than Geoffrey Chaucer, who once more gave his countrymen an English Boethius. That is readily accessible to us all (in the Globe edition of Chaucer, for instance), and is not very difficult to read. I note certain important features of it. In all essentials it is a good translation, but it was clearly the philosophic thought rather than the literary form of the original that Chaucer sought to convey. Otherwise it would be hard to explain the fact that he translated the verses of Boethius into prose, since Chaucer was himself a poet. The only hint we get of the form of the *Consolation* is that Chaucer has written *Prosa* and *Metrum* at the head of the prose and verse sections respectively. On the other hand, towards the end of the *Knight's Tale*, we have a very clear exposition of the central doctrine of Platonism, and that, of course, is in verse, though the original is mostly in the prose sections of Boethius. So far as I can judge, the Platonic passages of the *Knight's Tale* are taken straight from the original, and not from Chaucer's own prose translation, though I should not like to be positive about this. It is a point that would repay investigation. I feel pretty sure, too, that there is more Boethius in Chaucer than has yet been traced, though that is hardly more than an impression. In the interval between Lydgate and Spenser the tradition was mainly kept up in Scotland. The *Kingis Quhair*, usually attributed to James I., King of Scots,[1] begins with a description of the book of ' Boece,' and it is clear that the writer knew him at first-hand, since he speaks of ' his metre sweet ' and ' his fair Latin tongue.' After Spenser we are, of course, in an age of full-blown Platonism, marred in Elizabethan times by some exaggeration, and the rest of the story is too well known to require elucidation here. The only point I wish to make is that the Platonism of Boethius has been a constant factor in the evolution of English literature since the ninth century A.D., and that we cannot safely neglect it at any point.

I have considered this Boethian tradition first, because I believe that an original work like the *Consolation* must act more powerfully than any translation, even a translation of the great Athenian himself, can possibly do. It would, however, be a great mistake to suppose that western Europe was ever entirely cut off from a knowledge of Plato himself, so far at least as that could be gained from the peculiar word for word versions which were the rule in the Middle Ages. The *Timaeus* of Plato, for instance, or the greater part of it, had already been translated into Latin with a commentary by the fourth century A.D., and we shall come to that again. The sixth, seventh, and eighth centuries were almost a blank, both in the East and in the West, and it is these centuries which alone deserve the name of the ' Dark Ages.' Even then, some knowledge of Greek survived in two centres, Ireland and southern Italy. The influence of Ireland on Northumbria is well known, and I need not say more of it now, except to remind you of the name of Bede,

---

[1] Not, of course, the king who is called James I. in England.

and that it was his school which produced Alcuin, who made first York and then Paris the intellectual centre of western Europe. I wish rather to dwell on the relations of southern Italy and Sicily with England after the Norman Conquest, a subject which is less familiar, and on which I can, perhaps, throw a little new light.

Every one knows that the Norman Conquest of England took place in the year A.D. 1066, but it is often forgotten that the Normans conquered Sicily about the same time, and that there were intimate relations between the two islands which they ruled. The king of Sicily, who is known to history as William the Bad, was certainly a patron of learned Greeks, and we know that a certain Henry Aristippus—a pleasant combination of Greek and Norman names—brought a large number of Greek philosophical and scientific works from Constantinople to Sicily and translated them into Latin. Those that concern us here are the *Phaedo* and the *Meno* of Plato, and the preface to the translation tells us how he came to make his version. King William, he tells us, had commanded him to translate the works of St. Gregory Nazianzene, and Hugh, Archbishop of Palermo, requested him to make a Latin version of the *Lives of the Philosophers* by Diogenes Laertius, when a certain Englishman, whom he calls Roboratus, and whose real name was probably Robert, suggested that it would be better to do some dialogues of Plato. He set to work at once, and sent the *Phaedo* and the *Meno* to his patron who was hurrying back to England (*festinanti in Angliam*), and he makes suggestions for further work of the same kind which are a rather striking testimony to the interests of this Norman Englishman. He says that he is in a position to make versions of Euclid's *Optics*, Aristotle's *Analytics* and the book of Anaxagoras, which were at

Syracuse. What would we not give for the book of Anaxagoras now? It was still extant in the sixth century A.D., and there is no reason why a copy should not have been preserved in Sicily till the twelfth century.

At any rate, the versions of the *Phaedo* and the *Meno* arrived safely in England ; for several copies of it were made and are to be found in various libraries. The most interesting to us is the property of Corpus Christi College ; for it was written in 1423 and belonged to Humphrey, Duke of Gloucester, the brother of Henry v., whom we know from other sources to have been an ardent Platonist. It was for him that the earliest translation of the *Republic* was made by Decembrio, and the correspondence between the Duke and the translator still exists. It was, therefore, perfectly possible for an Englishman in the fourteenth and fifteenth centuries to have a considerable knowledge of certain important Platonic dialogues, though of course the translation is barbarous enough.

I have examined Henry Aristippus's version of the *Phaedo*, which has never been published, except for a few extracts, and I have found it possible to identify the manuscript which he used. It is one which is now at Vienna,[1] to which city it came from Florence, where it had belonged to a family, one of whose most distinguished members had been Grand Seneschal of Sicily. In the margin of the Corpus manuscript there is a long commentary which no one, so far as I know, has ever read. Who wrote it? It may have been Henry Aristippus, though that seems hardly probable, since his patron was in a hurry to get back to England. It looks as if it must have been written in England, and certainly not later than the beginning of the fifteenth century. It is high time that some one

---

[1] This is the MS. commonly known now as W (the first letter of *Wien*).

with a little leisure and good eyesight should try to
discover what this really means.

But after all, though it is interesting, and may even
prove important, to know that the *Phaedo* and the
Meno were accessible to Englishmen as early as the
latter half of the twelfth century (some time before the
works of Aristotle could be read even in a similarly
uncouth translation), that was not the main source of
English Platonism. Far more important was the
Platonism of France, the principal seat of which was
in the schools of Chartres. The philosophy taught
there was primarily based on the Latin version of the
Timaeus by Chalcidius, which was made in the fourth
century A.D. for Bishop Hosius of Cordova. This,
together with the *Consolation* and the mathematical
works of Boethius, gave the schoolmen of Chartres a
sufficient notion of the Pythagorean and Platonist
scientific tradition, and they were well able to make use
of it. They undoubtedly prepared the way for the
science of the Renaissance. Galileo, Kepler, and
Copernicus were all perfectly aware that they were
building on a Platonic foundation, and it was to Chartres
in the first place that we owe the preservation of that
tradition. The direct influence of the school of
Chartres on England was very great. John of
Salisbury, who was actually Bishop of Chartres when
he died, was acquainted with all the leading men of the
school, and it is from him that we learn most about
them. The University of Oxford, in particular, was
deeply affected by French Platonism, and it is to this
we owe the continuous tradition of mathematical
study in that place. The names of Grosseteste, Bishop
of Lincoln, and Roger Bacon deserve honourable
mention here. But great as this direct influence was,
the indirect influence of the schools of Chartres on
English literature was greater still. It so happened

that, just at this time, every nation in Europe was adopting the French literary tradition and abandoning its ruder native poetical forms. Here once more we come to Chaucer, whose *Parliament of Fowls* is specially instructive from this point of view. In particular, it was from Chartres that English poetry learnt to speak of Nature as a person, a way of thought and speech which can be traced from Chaucer to Wordsworth and beyond.

I cannot, of course, discuss this point fully here, as I am only trying to sketch the main outlines of a very important literary and philosophical development, with the hope that it may suggest to some of my hearers fruitful subjects for detailed study. Above all, I desire to make it plain that the twelfth century A.D. was not only the age which witnessed the birth of mature medieval art, especially in architecture, but that it was a time of boundless intellectual activity, above all in France. It was, however, starved of its proper intellectual nourishment by the extinction of Greek learning which followed the breach between the Eastern and Western Churches. The leading men of those days were quite aware of this. They knew very well that it was not safe to build upon translations as a foundation, and they made great efforts to remedy the defect in their knowledge. John of Salisbury tells us how he tried to learn Greek at Beneventum, and Grosseteste had a Greek vocabulary made for him by a Greek-speaking Sicilian, a vocabulary which still exists and is pathetically inadequate for its purpose. It is a serious historical mistake to suppose that the revival of Greek was an accident due to the fall of Constantinople in 1453. Men had been seeking to revive it before that, and a knowledge of Greek was fairly common in Italy quite early in the fifteenth century. We have seen that Humphrey, Duke of

Gloucester, got an Italian to translate the *Republic* of Plato for him into Latin. The revival of Greek was really due to the Councils of Florence and Ferrara, at which an attempt was made to adjust the differences between the Eastern and Western Churches, and the most interesting figure for us in them is the Greek Platonist Bessarion, afterwards Cardinal of the Roman Church, who made the original text of Plato accessible to western Europe. He left his manuscripts to the Library of St. Mark's at Venice, and all the early printed editions of Plato are derived in the main from these. All men could now read Plato for themselves if they would, and they have been free to do so ever since ; but it would be wrong to forget the men who did their best to anticipate the Revival of Letters in the twelfth century, and to whom English thought and English letters owe a special debt of gratitude.

ARISTOTLE

Annual Lecture on a Master-Mind.   Read to the British Academy,
July 2, 1924

THERE is hardly any philosopher but Aristotle of whom it is so true to say that he is hard to interpret just because he insists on discussing all the side issues of not very fundamental points, while what strike us as the real problems are dismissed in an oracular sentence. Nevertheless, one cannot help feeling that this is due, at least to some extent, to the curious way in which his teaching has been handed down to us. As we shall see, his whole career as an independent philosopher was exceptionally short.   What are now called the works of Aristotle are, in the main, his own personal manuscripts which he used as a foundation for his lectures.   It is not, therefore, surprising that those points of which he felt most sure should only be briefly indicated, while minor difficulties are discussed with great minuteness.   Moreover, it is of the first importance to notice that what we call the works of Aristotle were entirely unknown for more than two hundred years after his death, and were then recovered almost by accident.   On the other hand, the numerous works which he published during his lifetime, and by which alone he was known after his death, have almost entirely disappeared.   That is the problem with which I have been occupied for some years now, and indeed it has been obvious for some time that it was one which had to be solved before anything else could be done. I was not therefore surprised to find that it formed the subject of a new book by Professor Werner Jaeger of Berlin which only came into my hands in the present year.[1] The great merit of this work is that it abandons the untenable idea that the published works of Aristotle are all to be referred to his earlier life, while the unpublished lectures which we have belong to the time when he was at the head of the Lyceum at Athens. I venture to think, however, that Jaeger has not allowed sufficiently for the shortness of this Athenian period nor for the sudden way in which it was brought to an end. To me it seems rather that Aristotle's work was quite unfinished when he died in exile at the comparatively early age of sixty-two. I shall come back to that point later ; for the present I shall confine myself to what we know of the first two periods of his life. But first it will be necessary to consider carefully the evidence for the distinction I have drawn between the published works and the manuscripts of the lectures which were not recovered till the first century B.C.

I

Let us consider first the history of the works we still have. Strabo tells us that Aristotle's successor Theophrastus had left them to Neleus of Scepsis in the Troad, and that he bequeathed them to his successors, who were not philosophers, though they knew the value of the manuscripts very well. Indeed, they kept them locked up in a cellar to preserve them from the kings of Pergamus, who were searching for books in order to rival the collection at Alexandria. Ultimately they were sold to Apellicon of Teos for a large sum, and he edited them in a very imperfect manner. Soon after, in 87 B.C., Sulla took Athens and carried the library of Apellicon to Rome, where Tyrannio en-

---

[1] *Aristoteles, Grundlegung einer Geschichte seiner Entwicklung* (Berlin, 1923).

deavoured to produce a more correct edition. Ultimately, the manuscripts passed into the hands of
Andronicus of Rhodes, and were published by him
towards the end of the first century B.C.[1]

Now, there is not the slightest reason to doubt this
very definite statement. It will be noted that it does
not in the least suggest that the manuscripts in question
were unknown to Theophrastus. Indeed, it is distinctly implied that they were not, since we are told
that the lectures of Theophrastus himself formed part
of his bequest to Neleus of Scepsis. Moreover,
Strabo had exceptional opportunities of being well
informed on the point. He was a native of Pontus
and, on his mother's side, related to its kings ; he was
also a pupil of Tyrannio, no doubt at Rome, so he
could hardly have been ignorant of the discovery of
what we call the works of Aristotle. We cannot really
doubt, then, that these works were quite unknown
from the time of Theophrastus till the first century
B.C.[2]

This does not mean, of course, that no works of
Aristotle were known during that period, but only
that the treatises which make up our texts were never
intended for publication, and were not in fact published.
In one place,[3] Cicero speaks of ' the golden stream of
speech that Aristotle poured forth,' which certainly
does not strike us as a natural description of our Aristotle, especially if we remember that Cicero's literary
taste was distinctly more florid than ours. The truth
is rather that Aristotle published many works which,
of course, escaped the fate of the cellar at Scepsis, and

---

[1] Strabo, xiii. 608 ; Plutarch, *Sulla*, 26. 1.

[2] Zeller (*Eng. Trans.*, vol. i. pp. 147 sqq.) is very anxious to disprove this,
but he really only succeeds in showing that Theophrastus and Eudemus
knew the lectures of Aristotle, which is perfectly consistent with what Strabo
says.

[3] *Acad.*, ii. 38, 119.

it was of them that Cicero was speaking. No doubt he knew something of our Aristotle too ; for he was the patron of Tyrannio, but it is hardly probable that he had read much of him. When he speaks of Aristotle, he means chiefly the works Aristotle himself had published in his lifetime, and these have in large measure disappeared. Those, on the other hand, which were recovered from the cellar at Scepsis in Cicero's day were ultimately seen to give a truer view of Aristotle's philosophy in its developed form than the published works which had alone been hitherto known, and these have, therefore, failed to survive. Unfortunately, this has made it far more difficult for us to give an intelligible account of Aristotle's philosophical development, and that is what is of most interest to-day. It is the case, however, that very considerable portions of Aristotle's published works have only been identified in recent years, and this has made the problem a little easier.

The contrast between Plato and Aristotle in this respect is in many ways striking. We know now that the best known works of Plato were published when he was a young man and long before the foundation of the Academy, and it becomes more and more impossible to doubt that their chief purpose was to preserve the memory of the teaching of Socrates. The dialogues which he published after the foundation of the Academy are different in this respect, and, in particular, in the place assigned to Socrates, who more and more takes a secondary place until, in the *Laws*, he disappears altogether. It does not seem probable that Plato ever wrote his lectures ; for the Academy remained faithful to its founder's memory, and there is no reason to doubt that we still possess every word that Plato ever wrote. With Aristotle the case is very different. He too wrote a large number of works for the public, and it was by these alone he was known for several generations. He also gave lectures for over twenty years, and it is the manuscripts of these lectures that were discovered in the first century B.C.

The result has been, on the whole, unfortunate. Certainly, we may be glad that Aristotle found it necessary to write his lectures ; for otherwise we should have known as little of his most intimate convictions as we do of Plato's. The earliest commentators knew, of course, that the collection of treatises called the *Metaphysics* was by Aristotle, but were quite at a loss to account for the serious differences between that and the published works which had long been known. Indeed, before long the view was held that these published works were merely exercises in Platonic philosophy, and could not be regarded as evidence for the beliefs of Aristotle himself. On the other hand, the unpublished manuscripts which had been recovered from the cellar at Scepsis were the manuscripts from which Aristotle had lectured, and were therefore the only authority for his actual teaching. If we had only the lectures given by Plato in the Academy and the published works of Aristotle, we should still, no doubt, be able to see that Plato was a born writer, while Aristotle was not, but we should have a far more mathematical Plato and a considerably more popular Aristotle. As it is, we have only so much of Plato's philosophy as he thought it well to publish, while what we now have of Aristotle is almost entirely the lectures given in his school. Most of his published work has only a shadowy existence to-day and has to be reconstructed by inference. The only fairly complete specimen we possess is the *Constitution of Athens* discovered about a generation ago, which certainly belongs to Aristotle's later years, and must, in fact, have been written between 329/8 and 327/6

B.C.[1]   This shows that Aristotle continued to publish
all through his life, and the manuscripts discovered at
Scepsis are also of various dates and have not been
finally revised.   That, as has been said, is Professor
Jaeger's chief contribution to the subject.   It would
of course be impossible to discuss here in detail the
chronological arrangement which he adopts, though
I have no doubt that he is right in refusing to assign
all these works, as is generally done, to the last thirteen
years of Aristotle's life, when he was at the head of the
Lyceum at Athens.   According to him, they belong
largely to the intermediate period, shortly after Plato's
death, when Aristotle had left Athens, and are therefore
contemporary with, or even earlier than, a good many of
his published works.   It will therefore be best to go
through the three well-marked periods of Aristotle's
life, that of his membership of the Academy, that of his
absence in Asia Minor and Macedonia, and that of his
return to Athens, and to see, at least in broad outline,
how much of his work is to be referred to each of these.
This makes it necessary to consider what we know of
Aristotle's life.

II

In the first place, Aristotle was not an Athenian but
an Ionian.   It is, indeed, one of the most remarkable
facts about Greek philosophy that it was hardly
Athenian at all.   It began at Miletus in Ionia ; but,
from the time of Pythagoras, it had an independent
centre in the Ionian and Achaean cities of southern
Italy and Sicily.   It was not till the age of Pericles
that it was brought to Athens by Anaxagoras from the
east and by Parmenides and Zeno from the west, and

[1] See Jaeger, *op. cit.*, p. 350 n. 1.   He adopts Mr. Torr's date for reasons
which seem to be conclusive.

was there given a fresh start by Socrates, whose work
we know at first hand from Plato alone.   These two
are, no doubt, the greatest names in the history of
Greek philosophy, but we should never forget that
theirs are the only Athenian names of the first rank.
By the time Plato founded the Academy, the great days
of Athens were at an end, and he had already to look
abroad for the realization of his political views. When,
more than a generation later, Aristotle founded his
school in the Lyceum, he did so under Macedonian
patronage, and more because Athens was the natural
meeting-place for Ionians than for any other reason.
The number of born Athenians in the Academy had
been small, so far as we know, and in the Lyceum it
was smaller still.   Nevertheless, it was to Athens that
men came from all parts of the Greek world to study
philosophy, though they knew little, and cared little,
for Athenian politics.   Aristotle, who was the contemporary of Demosthenes, only mentions him twice
or thrice in his *Rhetoric*.   Indeed, now that Aristotle's
treatise on the Athenian Constitution, a work which
belongs to the last period of his life, has been recovered, we can see for ourselves how little he really
understood Athenian politics.

Aristotle was born at Stagirus (or, as it came to be
called, Stagira), on the east of the peninsula of Chal-
cidice, in 384/3 B.C.   His father, Nicomachus, was a
medical man and had been court physician to the king
of Macedon.   Aristotle's son, who was born in his
later years, was called after his grandfather in accordance with Greek custom, but that is practically all we
know about the family.   His father must have died
when Aristotle was quite young ; for the next thing we
hear about him is that his guardian, Proxenus, sent
him to study at Athens in 367/6 B.C. when he was
seventeen years old.   It was certainly not to study

medicine that he went there, but simply because it was the natural place for an Ionian youth of intellectual ambition to go. At that time the Platonic Academy was really the only centre of higher study in Greece. It is important to note that Eudoxus, the astronomer, seems to have come to Athens about the same time, and to have brought his pupils with him. From the *Nicomachean Ethics*, which was written long afterwards, we can see that Aristotle still looked up to Eudoxus with reverence. What is of even more importance is that, when Aristotle first joined the Academy, Plato was apparently not there. It was just about this time (368/7 B.C.) that Dionysius I., tyrant of Syracuse, died and that Plato, on the urgent recommendation of Dio, went to Syracuse to look after the education of Dionysius II. His second visit to Sicily took place in 361 B.C., and he did not return to Athens till the next year. Even then, he was not done with Syracuse. In 357 B.C. Dio returned to Sicily from exile and made himself master of Syracuse. Plato (who was seventy years old) did not accompany him, but several members of the Academy did, in particular his nephew Speusippus and Eudemus of Cyprus, and a period of troubles began. Callippus, who was also a member of the Academy, murdered Dio, and Plato wrote two long letters, which still exist,[1] to the friends and partisans of Dio, in which he defended himself and gave them advice. We can see from all this that, for the first ten years of Aristotle's membership, the personal influence of the head of the Academy on him must have been slight and intermittent, and even when he came back to Athens, Plato was chiefly occupied in writing the *Laws*, a work which was not published till after his death, and in delivering lectures which were largely mathematical. It is not easy to see how

[1] *Epp.*, vi. and vii.

Aristotle could follow him in this direction.   There is
no evidence that he was ever capable of appreciating
the strictly mathematical point of view.   Above all,
we know now that the Plato to whose school Aristotle
belonged for twenty years was no longer the Plato who
wrote the *Republic*.   That great work was probably
finished before he founded the Academy, and certainly
a good many years before Aristotle joined it.   Even
the *Parmenides* and the *Theaetetus* were, to all appearance, written before Aristotle came to Athens, and
there is a gap in Plato's literary work about this time.

Nevertheless, there can be no doubt at all that the
influence of Plato on Aristotle was very great indeed.
That follows at once from the fact that he remained a
member of the Academy until Plato's death, that is,
for a period of twenty years.   There is no doubt, in
particular, that he read all Plato's earlier writings and,
in particular, the *Phaedo*, which made a deep impression
upon him.   To him, of course, Socrates was little but
a name.   It is improbable that, in his time, any member
of the Academy remembered him or knew him otherwise than as he did, that is, as the chief figure in the
works of Plato's youth.   When Aristotle joined the
Academy, it was more than a generation since Socrates
had been put to death, and there were very few
Athenian members left.   The memory of a teacher
who wrote nothing is soon forgotten.   What is certain
is that Aristotle found in Plato's earlier works something new and, from his point of view, of the first
importance.   It would hardly be going too far to say
that during the first period of his membership of the
Academy, Aristotle was more of a Socratic than a
Platonist, or at least that he held views which were
certainly to be found in Plato's Socratic dialogues,
but which were hardly of first-rate importance in his
later teaching.

From this point of view it is extremely significant that one of his earliest works was the dialogue entitled *Eudemus*, which was substantially based on the *Phaedo*. The theme of this dialogue leaves little doubt as to its date. Eudemus of Cyprus (who must be carefully distinguished from Aristotle's disciple Eudemus of Rhodes) died before Syracuse in 354 B.C., when Aristotle was about thirty and had been a member of the Academy for some thirteen years. The theme of the dialogue was that the death of Eudemus was the true fulfilment of the dream that had promised him a safe return to his home within five years, a promise which was fulfilled by his death. The argument for the soul's immortality was clearly based on the *Phaedo*, and, in particular, on the doctrine that the soul was not an attunement (ἁρμονία) of the body (fr. 45 Rose). We can also see the influence of Plato's earlier works in the myth of Silenus, which was plainly composed on the model of the speech of Lachesis in the tenth book of the *Republic*. We may infer with certainty that, at the age of thirty, Aristotle was still a Platonist and, what is more, a Platonist of an early type.

Another, and a more important work which must be referred to much the same date, is the *Protrepticus*, which was an exhortation to the philosophic life addressed to a certain Themison of Cyprus. We know something of this work from what we can learn of the *Hortensius* of Cicero, which had so much influence on St. Augustine at a later date. It is here that we have the first instance of Bywater's work on the 'exoteric' treatises of Aristotle ; for he was able to restore large portions of the *Protrepticus* from the similarly entitled work of Iamblichus.[1] That is an extraordinary compilation. The greater part of it consists of extracts from Plato, but this is broken in the

---

[1] *J. Phil.*, ii. (1869), 55 sqq.

middle by a series of extracts from Aristotle, which Bywater was the first to identify as coming from the *Protrepticus*.

The most striking feature of the work was that it recommended in the strongest manner the contemplative life as the highest possible for those that are capable of it, and we shall see that this remained Aristotle's conviction throughout his life. He had no city, or none of any importance, and it was natural for an Ionian to take that view. Plato's attitude had been different. With Athenian politics he had little to do, but he had the foresight to see that the great struggle ahead was the preservation of the west for Greek civilization. With such ideas Aristotle had little sympathy, and the *Protrepticus* is chiefly interesting as showing how little he was influenced by them. In this work he upheld the claim of φρόνησις to be the leader of men, but it was still φρόνησις in the Platonic sense of the term, and not in that which he was to give it long afterwards himself.

III

In 348/7 B.C. Plato died, about eighty years old, and his nephew Speusippus succeeded him as head of the Academy. There was nothing now to keep Aristotle at Athens. He went to Asia Minor with Xenocrates, and the second period of his life begins. Once more we see a split between east and west which only the personality of Plato had been able to avert. There is no need to dwell upon the anecdotes about the succession to the Academy. Speusippus was an Athenian citizen, while Xenocrates and Aristotle were not, and it may well have seemed necessary at this time that the head of the Academy should be an Athenian who was legally capable of holding the property. At a later date, some way out of the difficulty must have been found, no doubt under Macedonian influence; for we find Xenocrates back at Athens as head of the Academy in 339, while Aristotle founded the Lyceum there in 335 B.C. For the present the interesting point is that the two leading men of Plato's school left Athens together for Asia Minor, where there was what may be fairly called a colony of the Academy under Coriscus and Erastus, who were settled at Assos and enjoyed the patronage of Hermias, tyrant of Atarneus, whom they had converted to Platonism. That is certainly significant, for it shows there was a real possibility of founding an Asiatic branch of the Academy in these regions. We know the circle of friends to whom Xenocrates and Aristotle went much better than we did, now that it is generally allowed that Plato's sixth epistle is genuine. The school had been founded by Coriscus and Erastus, who had been members of the Academy, and the epistle is addressed to them along with Hermias, whom Plato does not appear to know personally. Aristotle remained at Assos for three years, but, on the execution of Hermias by the Persians, he removed to Mitylene in Lesbos, where he married Pythia, the daughter of Hermias.

This raises one or two interesting points. In the first book of the *Metaphysics* Aristotle has occasion to criticize Plato's theory of Forms in a very curious way. He speaks of it throughout as a doctrine which ' we ' hold, even when he is criticizing it, and that can only mean that he still regarded himself as a member of the Academy. If so, the book must belong to the time when he was at Assos. The same thing seems to follow from the frequent references to Coriscus in certain works of Aristotle. They seem to imply that he was present at the lectures, and that is, of course, of the greatest importance in determining their date.

It may well be that Aristotle's call to superintend the education of Alexander in 342 B.C. was due to his intimacy with Hermias, who was certainly a Macedonian agent, as well as to his father's professional connexion with the Macedonian kings. Next to nothing is really known of Aristotle's work with Alexander. He says very little about him in his writings, and we do not really know how long they were together ; but it is clear at least that Aristotle never understood his distinguished pupil. By 335 B.C. he was back at Athens, where he opened his school under the protection of the Macedonian governor Antipater.

Now this means that Aristotle was away from Athens for about twelve years, from the age of thirty-seven to that of forty-nine, and we can hardly be wrong in holding that these were the most important years of his life. At first, no doubt, he only thought of continuing Plato's work, but it is evident that the change came soon. For twenty years he had been overshadowed by the personality of his master ; now it was high time for his native genius to show itself, if he had any. The Greeks were never in a hurry. Plato must have been forty when he founded the Academy, and the writings by which he is most familiar to us were all written before that, and had for their chief object to make Socrates known. Aristotle too was at first completely absorbed in his master, and there seems to be little doubt that it was Plato who started him on the lines he was to follow. It seems certain that, towards the end of his life, Plato had determined to direct the attention of his disciples to the study of animals and plants. That seems to follow from the fact that not only Aristotle, who had a natural

T

bent in that direction, but also Plato's nephew, Speusippus, had turned their attention to biology. The achievements of Speusippus in this may not have amounted to much, though he wrote a work entitled Ὅμοια, in which he made an attempt to found a classification of animals. The comic poets too made fun, in their own way, of the efforts of the Academy to establish a classification of animals and vegetables. But to Aristotle this new branch of inquiry seems to have come almost as a revelation. My colleague, Professor D'Arcy Thompson, has pointed out[1] that most of the species described by Aristotle belong to Asia Minor, and, in particular, to Lesbos, and, if that is so, it would settle the matter. On this point, it would appear that Professor Jaeger is wrong, and it may be noted that Coriscus appears not only in the logical treatises, but also in certain of the biological lectures.

In fact, if this is right, it is, I take it, the clue to the whole development of Aristotle. He was not a mathematician like Plato, but he found himself when Plato turned his attention to biology. Plato had never said anything of the doctrine of Forms (ἰδέαι, εἴδη) in any work that he wrote after the foundation of the Academy, except once in the *Timaeus*, where it is mentioned by a professed Pythagorean, but Aristotle, of course, knew all about it from the *Phaedo* and the *Republic*, where it is expounded by Socrates. Of course he also knew, so far as that was possible for him, the mathematical form in which the doctrine was expounded by Plato in his later years. To Aristotle, when once he had become interested in biology, the mathematical form in which Plato had presented the theory ceased to have any meaning, and here

---

[1] *On Aristotle as a Biologist* (Herbert Spencer Lecture, Clarendon Press, 1913).

once more we find Aristotle's Ionic nature asserting itself.

It is in the dialogue entitled *On Philosophy* that we find the first open breach with the Ideal Theory of Plato, and it was from this source alone that the Stoics and Epicureans of the next few generations knew what they knew about it. It was, in fact, a public announcement that Aristotle had a philosophy of his own to teach. From that point of view, it is, of course, a most serious loss, and we may be glad that it is gradually being repaired.[1] It is significant that the Platonic theory criticized is not that with which we are familiar in the *Phaedo* and the *Republic*, but that of what are called 'ideal numbers' (εἰδητικοὶ ἀριθμοί), a theory which we have to reconstruct as well as we can from what Aristotle tells us about it ; for it finds no place in Plato's published works. In this dialogue Aristotle spoke in person, and we possess a fragment of it (fr. 8 Rose), in which he said that he could not sympathize with the doctrine 'even if it is supposed that his opposition is due to a spirit of contentiousness.' That is a definite declaration enough. It is evident that this dialogue must be later than the first book of the *Metaphysics*, in which also the Platonic doctrine of Forms is criticized, but is spoken of throughout as a doctrine which 'we' hold. The only difference is that the dialogue *On Philosophy* was a public manifesto, while the criticism of the *Metaphysics* was intended for the school alone, and only saw the light long afterwards. It seems most natural to suppose that this breach with Platonism is connected with Aristotle's biological studies, though this is a point which I think Jaeger has missed. Yet surely it is here that we ought

---

[1] A comparison of Bywater's paper in *J. Phil.*, vii. 64, with the account of this dialogue given by Jaeger, pp. 125 sqq., will show how far this has proceeded.

to look for the origin of the divergence between Plato
and Aristotle.   Even to-day we can see that mathematicians have comparatively little difficulty in appreciating Platonism, while biologists are apt to be annoyed
by what strikes them as a certain unfairness to the
objects of their own study.   That was natural enough
until last century, and it was perfectly intelligible in
the fourth century B.C., but I should like to raise the
question whether it is quite so natural to-day.   I am
neither a biologist nor a mathematician, but I cannot
help wondering whether there is not, in the twentieth
century, a tendency for their opposite points of view
to come together.   In the fourth century B.C. this no
doubt seemed impossible, but I cannot help asking
whether, if Aristotle had known the modern theory of
evolution, he would have felt obliged to reject the
Platonic theory so decidedly as he does.   However
that may be, there can be no doubt of this, that it was
mainly Aristotle's passionate interest in biology that
led him to drop the theory of 'Ideas' altogether, though
it must never be forgotten that, even in his unpublished
lectures, he always speaks of Plato with reverence, even
when he feels obliged to differ from him.   In later
days, it was the Platonic Academy that commented
laboriously on his works, and it is to its members that
we owe most for the preservation and interpretation of
them.   It is possible, indeed, that the Neoplatonists
ignored too much the radical differences between the
two men ; but it is a fact that they devoted themselves
to the interpretation of Aristotle more than to that of
Plato.   They were at least dimly aware of the fact that
Aristotle was the only source of our knowledge of
Plato's later and more personal teaching.

    There can, however, be no doubt that Aristotle's
return to his Ionian predecessors had a wholly unfortunate effect on his general view of the world, and

this has had unfortunate results. The *Physics*, the *De Caelo*, and the *De Generatione et Corruptione* do not by any means represent such an advance on the Academy as his biological works do. In them everything depends upon the spherical earth being at rest in the centre of the universe while the starry heavens go round it once in twenty-four hours. There can be no doubt that the Academy had gone far beyond this, and that, under its influence, even the heliocentric theory had been evolved. It was just this that made Aristotle unacceptable to the great men of the Renaissance, and has stood in the way of a proper appreciation of him ever since. Aristotle in these matters was not Aristotle at his best, and his real greatness was as a biologist.

It would, however, take us too far to discuss these points in detail here, though I feel that I must say something more about what is often regarded as Aristotle's chief work, the *Metaphysics*. The very title of that work is of later date, and the word 'metaphysics' is never used by Aristotle himself. We have seen that Book I. was certainly composed when he was lecturing to his school at Assos, and that implies that Books II. and III. belong to the same period, when Aristotle still felt that he was a member of the Academy, though he had abandoned its principal doctrine, the theory of Forms. But at this point all connexion apparently ceases, and with Book IV. we come to a discussion of philosophical terminology, which appears to be an independent work, while the last two books contain a discussion, or rather two discussions, of the theory of ideal numbers held in the Academy, which does not appear to have any connexion with the rest of the work. Books V.-VII. seem to be of far later date than these ; for they deal with a more important subject and seem to embody views which Aristotle held later in life. Book x. is an entirely independent treatise, which appears to give an account of Aristotle's views on what he calls First Philosophy. The crux of the problem is certainly to be found here ; but un- happily it must remain a crux. We do not know in the least whether the *Metaphysics* was ever intended by its author to be regarded as a single work, no doubt to be revised, or whether it simply consists of those parts of his writings which did not appear to his editors to find a natural place elsewhere. We can only say that the title it bears has given rise to the later term ' meta- physics,' and that shows the importance of the matters it treats. But, as we have it, it is certainly not a coherent whole ; it consists of fragments of very different date, and it shows more than anything else that Aristotle's philosophy was never completed. It would be out of place to say more of it here.

I do, however, feel bound before concluding to say something about the *Ethics*. Every one knows that there are three works which bear this title in the Aristotelian *corpus*, the *Nicomachean Ethics*, the *Eude- mian Ethics*, and the *Magna Moralia*. The last of these may be left out of account for the present, but the two first present a very real problem. During the nine- teenth century most editors (including myself) ac- quiesced in the view that the *Nicomachean Ethics* was Aristotle's, while the *Eudemian Ethics* was ascribed to Eudemus, but of late this has been questioned, and it has, in my opinion, been finally disproved by Jaeger. According to him there are three well-marked stages in Aristotle's moral philosophy, represented by (1) the *Protrepticus*, which was published and represents the advanced Platonic period, (2) the *Eudemian Ethics*, which belongs to the intermediate stage, and (3) the *Nicomachean Ethics*, which is one of Aristotle's latest works. This, he holds, is clear from the agreement

of the *Eudemian Ethics* with the *Protrepticus*, especially
as that work can now be supplemented from Iamblichus.
Even apart from that, the reference (*B*. 1, 1218^b, 34)
to ἐξωτερικοὶ λόγοι proves that the work is genuinely
Aristotelian.   That it was written during his residence
in Asia Minor seems to follow from the appearance in
it of Coriscus (1220^a, 19, and 1240^b, 25).

That the *Eudemian Ethics* comes between the *Protrepticus* and the *Nicomachean Ethics* appears, Jaeger
holds, from many things, above all, perhaps, from the
way in which the ' three lives,' the theoretic, the
practical, and the apolaustic, are shown to be derived
from wisdom (φρόνησις), goodness (ἀρετή), and
pleasure (ἡδονή) quite in the Platonic manner.   It is
obvious that this could find no place in the *Nicomachean Ethics*, where the old Platonic use of φρόνησις
as equivalent to σοφία is given up and replaced by a
distinction between speculative σοφία and practical
φρόνησις.   It is to be observed, however, that the
Nicomachean Ethics takes a much higher view of σοφία
or intellectual wisdom than the other.   It is not, in
fact, an adequate account of the matter to say, as Jaeger
does (p. 250), that the theoretic life is only brought in
at the end of the *Nicomachean Ethics* without ethical
goodness being made dependent upon it.   That is
true, no doubt, but it is very far from being the whole
truth.   It is quite in accordance with the philosophical
method which Aristotle had learnt from Plato to keep
the main purpose of a discussion to the end ; and,
when the contemplative life is discussed in the
Nicomachean Ethics, that is done with an ardour and
intensity which cannot be paralleled in any other
part of the work.   That, too, I take it, is why
φρόνησις or ' practical wisdom ' is given only a
secondary importance in the sixth book.   The whole
treatise is intended to lead up to the assertion of

the unique pre-eminence of speculative wisdom or σοφία.

In fact, if the last few pages of the *Nicomachean Ethics* are genuine—and no one has suggested that they are not—we find that the ultimate good for man is just the exercise of the theoretic or contemplative ' part ' of the soul. The degradation of φρόνησις or practical wisdom in Book VI. seems intended to exalt the position of σοφία or theoretical wisdom, and its activity θεωρία, even higher than before. If, then, the *Nicomachean Ethics* belongs to the last years of Aristotle's life, as Jaeger holds it does, we shall be driven to conclude that, at the time of his death, Aristotle was on the point of teaching a system in which everything was to be subordinated to the theoretic or contemplative life. I would suggest that the same idea may be used to interpret the account of νοῦς in the third book of the *De Anima*. That has led to endless controversy, but I venture to think that the apparent discrepancy between this and the earlier books is due to the same cause. The apparent degradation of our psychical faculties which impresses us in the first two books of the *De Anima* is like the apparent degradation of φρόνησις in the sixth book of the *Ethics*, and is meant to prepare the way for the exaltation of Mind (νοῦς), just as the lower position assigned to practical wisdom (φρόνησις) in the other case is intended to prepare the way for the exaltation of theoretical wisdom (σοφία). It is very certainly characteristic of Greek philosophical writings to keep the main point till the end or near it ; and, if we argue from the neglect of certain ideas in the earlier portion of such works, we are very apt to go wrong. On the other hand, if we read on to the end and then look back, we shall often find things which have appeared difficult to understand at first appear in a new light.

Only we must remember all the time that, in trying to understand these works of Aristotle, we are not dealing with published works, but with lectures. If we remember that, we shall not be at all clear that Jaeger is right in saying that, for the average Greek of that time, the method of these works was strange and repellent (p. 360). Though the average Athenian might no doubt find them so, we must always remember that Aristotle was not an Athenian, and that his hearers were even less so. We have only to glance at the Ionic scientific literature of a century earlier, such as the treatise of Hippocrates, Περὶ ἀέρων ὑδάτων τόπων, to feel that he is carrying on the traditional Ionic scientific style and the traditional Ionic attitude to the world. I cannot feel that Jaeger is right in saying (p. 360) that there was anything fundamentally new in Aristotle's attitude to such things. He seems more nearly right in saying (p. 434) that Aristotle had also the world-horizon of the Ionian, of which no Athenian ever dreamt, though I should certainly except Plato, who was an Athenian, and yet combined an even wider sympathy than Aristotle's with an interest in practical matters which Aristotle showed himself incapable of feeling. Here, too, Aristotle is a typical Ionian, though he had lived for twenty years under the influence of an Athenian of pan-Hellenic sympathies.

IV

Nowhere does this appear more clearly than at the end of his life. He had been the tutor of Alexander the Great, but he seldom mentions him. He does not seem to have been conscious of the fact that his position at Athens during the last thirteen years of his life depended on Antipater. And yet, when Antipater

left Athens and Alexander died (323 B.C.), he had to
leave Athens at once, and went to Chalcis in Euboea,
where he too died soon afterwards in his sixty-third
year. It is worthy of notice that Plato had been head
of the Academy till he was eighty, while Socrates was
just over seventy when he was put to death at the
height of his powers. The Greeks of this time lived
to great ages, and there can be no doubt at all that
Aristotle's comparatively early death has deprived us
of that final revision of his system which he would
certainly have undertaken, and of which, as has been
indicated, some traces can be discovered even now.
Most of the best of what we have belongs to the time
when he was not at Athens, and the last thirteen years
of his life represent an incomplete period which was
brought to an end by political events with which he had
nothing to do, and in which, surprising as it may seem,
he took no interest. I venture to think that what is
most wanted is a study of his thought in these last
years, for which, as I have tried to show, there are
really certain data which Professor Jaeger has ignored.
According to him, it would seem that Aristotle spent
his last years in anticipating the learning and science of
Alexandria, and in some respects that is certainly
true. I feel convinced, however, that it is not the
whole truth, or even the most important part of it. I
believe, on the contrary, that it is still possible to
ascertain more than has yet been found out as to the
chronological order of his works. That has been
successfully done in the case of Plato, and, though it
may be more difficult in that of Aristotle, I have little
doubt that it could be done here too. Then, I believe,
we should see that the latest stage of Aristotle's philosophy was rather different from what it appears to be in
the valuable work which Professor Jaeger has already
given us. No doubt he is the first writer who has

attempted to follow up his development, but there is still, I think, something to be done if we could only determine what were his latest writings.   It is certain at least that the man who wrote the last pages of the *Nicomachean Ethics* had still something more to say when his work was prematurely interrupted.

Printed in Great Britain
by T. and A. CONSTABLE LTD.
at the University Press
Edinburgh